The Historical Jesus Quest

'Tis a pity, cried my father ... that truth, brother Toby, should shut herself up in such impregnable fastnesses, and be so obstinate as not to surrender herself sometimes upon the closest siege.'

Laurence Sterne, *Tristram Shandy*

THE HISTORICAL JESUS QUEST

Landmarks in the Search for the Jesus of History

Edited by

Gregory W. Dawes

Westminster John Knox Press
Louisville, Kentucky

PUBLISHING

Cover design by PAZ Design Group
Cover illustration by Georges Rouault courtesy Scala/Art Resource, NY

This edition published in 2000 by
Westminster John Knox Press
Louisville, Kentucky

This book is printed on acid-free paper that meets the American National Standards Institute Z39.48 standard. ∞

PRINTED IN THE UNITED STATES OF AMERICA

00 01 02 03 04 05 06 07 08 09 — 10 9 8 7 6 5 4 3 2 1

Library of Congress Cataloging-in-Publication Data is on file at the Library of Congress, Washington, D.C.

ISBN 0-664-22262-5

Contents

Acknowledgments

The editor would like to thank the following publishers and individuals for permission to reprint the material found in this anthology.

E.J. Brill (Leiden):
Benedictus Spinoza, *Tractatus theologico-politicus*, transl. Samuel Shirley (Leiden: E.J. Brill, 1989), pp.140-60.

Rhena Schweitzer Miller:
Albert Schweitzer, *The Mystery of the Kingdom of God: The Secret of Jesus' Messiahship and Passion* transl. Walter Lowrie (London: A. & C. Black, 1925), pp.84-92, 253-73.

Albert Schweitzer, *My Life and Thought: An Autobiography* transl. C.T. Campion (London: George Allen & Unwin, 1933), pp.65-75.

James Clarke & Co. Ltd (Cambridge):
William Wrede, *The Messianic Secret* transl. J.C.G. Greig; Library of Theological Translations (1901; London: James Clarke & Co., 1971), pp.129-45, 211-30.

T. & T. Clark (Edinburgh):
Karl Barth, *Church Dogmatics, vol. 1:2 The Doctrine of the Word of God* transl. G.T. Thomson and Harold Knight (Edinburgh: T. & T. Clark, 1956), pp.492-95.

Ernst Troeltsch, 'Historical and Dogmatic Method in Theology' (1898) in *Religion in History: Ernst Troeltsch—Essays translated by James Luther Adams and Walter F. Bense* (Edinburgh: T. & T. Clark, 1991), pp.11-32.

Augsburg Fortress Publishers (Minneapolis, MN):
Martin Kähler, *The So-Called Historical Jesus and the Historic, Biblical Christ* (1896) transl. by Carl E. Braaten; Seminar Editions (Philadelphia, PA: Fortress, 1964), pp.46-71.

Reimarus: Fragments ed. Charles H. Talbert; transl. by Ralph S. Fraser; Lives of Jesus Series (Philadelphia PA, Fortress Press, 1970), pp.62-76, 122-134, 243-54.

David Friedrich Strauss, *The Life of Jesus Critically Examined* 4th ed. (1840), transl. Mary Ann Evans / George Eliot (Ramsey, NJ: Sigler Press, 1994), pp.41-44, 87-92, 777-781.

Johannes Weiss, *Jesus' Proclamation of the Kingdom of God* (1892) transl. Richard H. Hiers and David L. Holland; Lives of Jesus Series (Philadelphia, PA: Fortress, 1971), pp.79-81, 101-104, 129-36.

Philip Hefner:
Albrecht Ritschl, 'Instruction in the Christian Religion' in *Albrecht Ritschl: Three Essays* transl. by Philip Hefner (Philadelphia, PA: Fortress, 1972), pp.222-32.

SCM Press Ltd (London):
Rudolf Bultmann, 'Liberal Theology and the Latest Theological Movement' (1924) in *Faith and Understanding* ed. Robert W. Funk; transl. by Louise Pettibone Smith; The Library of Philosophy and Theology (London: SCM, 1969), pp.28-52.

Ernst Käsemann, 'The Problem of the Historical Jesus' (1953) in *Essays on New Testament Themes* transl. by W.J. Montague; Studies in Biblical Theology 41 (London: SCM, 1964), pp.15-47.

Preface

The preparation of this volume grew out of the experience of teaching a graduate-level course on the subject of the historical Jesus. The aim of the course was to introduce students to the history of this famous debate, and the first thing I became aware of was a gap in the existing literature. While books and articles on the historical Jesus continue to multiply, little attention is paid to the work of the great pioneers, those scholars who first raised the question of what the historian (rather than the theologian) might have to say about Jesus. The contemporary reader approaching the topic for the first time could be forgiven for thinking that the discussion began ten or twenty years ago. Even when students become aware of the work done in the eighteenth or nineteenth centuries, there is little opportunity for any first-hand contact. Students may be familiar with the names of Hermann Samuel Reimarus, Johannes Weiss, and Albert Schweitzer (to name only three). They may even be able to offer a potted history of their achievements, drawn from their textbooks. But it is unlikely they will have read any of their work.

Yet the importance of these earliest studies can hardly be overestimated. It was in the eighteenth and nineteenth centuries that practically all our current questions about Jesus were first posed. Moreover, the answers given during this hundred or so years of discussion continue to shape our current debates. The old adage that those who are ignorant of history are condemned to repeat it is, of course, an over-simplification. The contexts within which biblical scholarship is done continue to change, and the answers given in our own age will certainly be different from those given then. Nonetheless, there is much we can learn from both the insights of our predecessors and the blind alleys down which they allowed themselves to be led.

An anthology of this sort is, of necessity, an exercise in exclusion, and the reader could rightly protest that many important authors are not represented. My only plea is that some selection had to be made. Perhaps more seriously, in compiling such a work one runs the risk of viewing the past only through the perspective of our current concerns and of reading these authors in isolation from the world in which they wrote. For this reason the student should be warned that this anthology is not a guide to the intellectual world of the eighteenth or nineteenth centuries (even if my introductory comments make some attempt to put each reading in its context). In compiling this anthology I have had only one aim in mind: that of allowing students easy access to a few of the figures whose influence has proved to be enduring.

If there is a *leitmotif* running through these selections, it is the idea of the 'kingdom of God'. Given that this theme was central to the teaching of Jesus, what did these words refer to, and how are we to understand them today? Here, as in many other respects, the work of Hermann Samuel Reimarus was prophetic, as he attempted in a bold but rather simplistic way to understand what the 'kingdom of God' would have meant to Jesus' contemporaries. By way of contrast, the extract from the work of Albrecht Ritschl offers an insight into how the teaching of Jesus was understood by one of the greatest liberal theologians of the nineteenth century. The debate on this issue really begins in earnest with the publication of the work of Ritschl's son-in-law Johannes Weiss, and is brought to a certain climax with the 'consistent eschatology' of Albert Schweitzer. Schweitzer takes issue with the scepticism of William Wrede, arguing that the Gospel's depiction of Jesus is quite intelligible if seen against the apocalyptic worldview of late second temple Judaism. However, this intelligibility is bought at a price. For Schweitzer's Jesus seems to belong so thoroughly to his own time and place that it seemed the chasm between his context and ours can no longer be bridged.

Alongside these discussions a second theme can be discerned. For while the historians continued to discuss the shape of Jesus' life and ministry, the theologians debated what religious significance their findings might have. What impact would the 'historical criticism' of the Bible have on Christian faith? What did it mean for the study of theology? Therefore interspersed with

extracts from the work of the exegetes, the student will find a
number of philosophical and theological discussions. The pio-
neering work in this regard is that of Benedict Spinoza, who was
the first to outline the programme for a thoroughly historical
study of the Bible and to argue for its significance. However, the
theologian who applied the historical method most consistently
to his work was Ernst Troeltsch, and it is therefore with these
two thinkers that our anthology begins. Between the time of
Spinoza and that of Troeltsch, David Friedrich Strauss had both
deepened the scepticism with which the Gospel accounts were
regarded and attempted to redeem their religious significance
with the help of the category of 'myth'. The theological issues
came to a head with the work of the 'dialectical theologians' of
the early twentieth century, represented here by Rudolf Bultmann and Karl Barth, whose protests were anticipated in the
work of Martin Kähler. For different reasons all three thinkers
cast doubt upon the significance of historical research for faith.
Coupled with the 'thoroughgoing eschatology' of Schweitzer,
their criticisms effectively put an end to the quest until it was
cautiously re-opened in 1953 by Bultmann's student Ernst
Käsemann. It is with Käsemann's work (generally thought of as
inaugurating the 'New Quest') that the present collection ends.

The general pattern of the book owes something to the
schematisation of the history of this discussion found in the
summary article written by Dr Tom Wright (1992) in volume
three of the *Anchor Bible Dictionary*. I have grouped the readings
into an introduction, which sets out some of the key issues, and
eight chapters, which span the years between the time of Reimarus and that of Käsemann. My own contribution has been to
write a brief introduction to each extract, which is indented to
distinguish it from the work being anthologized. These intro-
ductions offer a brief biographical sketch, before attempting to
set the reading in the context of the historical Jesus quest as a
whole. To help the student grapple with the original, the intro-
ductions also contain a summary of the author's central argument, and (in some cases) a summary of the larger work from
which the extract has been taken. In the case of foreign-
language phrases which are not in common English use I have
taken the liberty of adding a translation. David Friedrich

Strauss's citations from the work of Origen (ca. 185–254 CE) offered particular difficulties. Here I have not only offered a translation, but I have occasionally corrected the Greek found in the English edition of his work and made one comment about the possible origin of a quotation. All these translations and alterations are found in square brackets. Finally, I have occasionally added scriptural references to make the argument clearer. These, too, along with any earlier editorial additions, are enclosed in square brackets to distinguish them from the original text. In the case of the reading from Spinoza, I have turned his supplementary notes (printed separately in Samuel Shirley's translation) into footnotes. Finally, I have corrected the text of William Wrede's book in several places in light of the list of *errata* which accompanied its publication.

I am grateful to the publishers of the works cited for permission to reproduce the extracts found here. Full bibliographical details are to be found in the acknowledgements which precede this preface. The format of each chapter does not allow for extensive references, but for biographical information I have relied on the editors of these works, as well as the relevant articles in the *Lexikon für Theologie und Kirche* (1957-68) and the *Theologische Realenzyklopädie* (1977–). In the case of two of our thinkers, Rudolf Bultmann and Karl Barth, I have been able to draw upon their published autobiographical reflections (Bultmann, 1956; Barth, 1966). Further information came from the biographies of Benedict Spinoza by Margaret Gullan-Whur (1998), of David Friedrich Strauss by Horton Harris (1973), of Ernst Troeltsch by Hans-Georg Drescher (1991), of Albert Schweitzer by James Brabazon (1975), and of Karl Barth by Eberhard Busch (1975). The articles collected in the *Historical Handbook of Major Biblical Interpreters* (1998), edited by Donald McKim, were never far from hand. The reader may note the substantial overlap between my selection of authors and that of *The Bible in Modern Culture* by Roy Harrisville and Walter Sundberg (1995). The overlap is coincidental, but encouraging, since it suggests that these are indeed some of the most important figures to be studied. I am grateful to Professor Alistair Fox of the Division of Humanities at the University of Otago for granting both a short period of study leave and a research grant to enable the completion of this work. My research assistant and graduate student Ms Donna Hendry put in many hours of work, electronically scanning the readings and making comprehensible once again texts which passage through a computer had rendered meaningless. Finally, my thanks are due to Dr David Orton for honouring this work by including it among the first books to be published by Deo Publishing.

Works Cited

Barth, Karl (1966). *How I Have Changed My Mind*. Richmond, VA: John Knox Press.

Brabazon, James (1975). *Albert Schweitzer: A Biography*. New York, NY: G. P. Putnam's Sons.

Bultmann, Rudolf (1956). 'Autobiographical Reflections' (*Lebenslauf*). In *Existence and Faith: Shorter Writings of Rudolf Bultmann*. Translated by Schubert M. Ogden. London: Hodder and Stoughton, 1961. Pp.283-88.

Busch, Eberhard (1975). *Karl Barth: His Life from Letters and Autobiographical Texts*. Translated by John Bowden. London: SCM, 1976.

Drescher, Hans-Georg (1991). *Ernst Troeltsch: His Life and Work*. Translated by John Bowden. London: SCM, 1992.

Gullan-Whur, Margaret (1998). *Within Reason: A Life of Spinoza*. London: Jonathan Cape.

Harris, Horton (1973). *David Friedrich Strauss and His Theology*. Monograph Supplements to the Scottish Journal of Theology. Cambridge: Cambridge University Press.

Harrisville, Roy A. and Walter Sundberg (1995). *The Bible in Modern Culture: Theology and Historical-Critical Method from Spinoza to Käsemann*. Grand Rapids, MI: Eerdmans.

Historical Handbook of Major Biblical Interpreters (1998). Edited by Donald K. McKim. Downers Grove, IL: InterVarsity.

Lexikon für Theologie und Kirche (1957-68). Edited by Josef Hofer and Karl Rahner. 2nd edition. Freiburg im Breisgau: Herder.

Theologische Realenzyklopädie (1977–). Edited by Gerhard Krause and Gerhard Muller. Berlin: W. de Gruyter.

Wright, N. T. (1992). 'Jesus, Quest for the Historical'. In *Anchor Bible Dictionary* vol 3. Edited by David Noel Freedman. New York, NY: Doubleday. Pp.796-802.

Introduction
The Divorce between History and Faith

Benedict Spinoza and Ernst Troeltsch

The question of the historical Jesus is such a familiar one today that it is difficult for us to realise how recent a question it is. For more than 1600 years the idea of asking such a question never arose. More precisely, in the minds of the Christian interpreters of the Bible there was no difference between the Jesus of history and the Jesus of the Church's proclamation. Insofar as the Christian scriptures spoke of the incarnation of God at a particular point in human affairs, the accuracy of their reports was taken for granted. Beginning in about the seventeenth century a fateful change began to occur, a change which would result in a divorce (or at least an uneasy separation) between the claims of faith and those of history. The following readings are intended to offer some insight into that change. For this separation to occur, at least two things had to happen. The taken-for-granted authority of the Bible needed to be undermined, and a sense of historical distance needed to be developed. The authors whose work is reproduced in this introductory chapter illustrate both processes at work.

Benedict Spinoza (1632–77)

The first of our authors, Benedict Spinoza, was neither a biblical scholar nor an historian, but first and foremost a philosopher. Neither was he a Christian, having been born into a Jewish family of Portuguese origin. His grandfather had fled the Inquisition in Portugal and moved to France, having outwardly professed Catholicism in order to escape persecution. Along with many other so-called 'marranos', Spinoza's father had then taken refuge in the relatively tolerant atmosphere of the Netherlands, where he became a prosperous merchant. Baruch Spinoza, as he was then known, received a thorough education under the guidance of his Jewish teachers, including the erudite Rabbi Manasseh ben Israel (1604-57), the spiritual head of the community in Amsterdam. After some years working in his father's import business, which brought him into contact with the wider Dutch society, in 1856 Spinoza began to retire from business affairs and devote himself to scholarship.

The same year marked his break with the Jewish community, from which he was publicly excommunicated, apparently for a lack of respect for Jewish religious authority. It was at this time that he ceased to use his Hebrew name Baruch in favour of its Latin equivalent, Benedict, and for the rest of his life he associated with groups of free-thinking Christians. At times he uses remarkably Christian language—when he discusses the Bible, it is evidently the Christian canon he has in mind—but he seems to have never formally identified himself with any branch of the Christian faith. Spinoza developed an interest in the developing science of optics, and learned the art of lens-grinding. In 1663 published the only work to appear under his name during his lifetime, entitled *Descartes' Principles of Philosophy*. In 1670 his *Tractatus theologico-politicus* ('Theological and political discussion') was published, but anonymously to protect its author. (In fact, its authorship soon became widely known.) In 1673 Spinoza refused the offer of a chair in philosophy at the University of Heidelberg because of the religious conditions attached. He died, after a long period of illness, at the age of only forty-four.

The following extract comes from Spinoza's *Tractatus theologico-politicus*. The work is an extended plea for freedom of conscience within a commonwealth free from domination by any particular religious party. In order to establish this freedom of thought, Spinoza must deal with the religious authority recognized by all Christians, namely the authority of the Bible. The *Tractatus* is made up of some twenty chapters. The earliest chapters deal with prophecy, the place of Israel in God's plan, the law of God, the biblical narrative and belief in miracles. The extract reproduced here is chapter seven of the work, which outlines Spinoza's recommendations for the interpretation of the

Bible. The chapters which follow this discussion represent a (somewhat haphazard) application of Spinoza's historical method of biblical interpretation to some particular issues, particularly regarding the dating of the biblical writings. In later chapters Spinoza goes on to distinguish faith from philosophy, thus liberating reason from theology. The final chapters are dedicated to a discussion of the constitution of commonwealth in which 'every man may think as he please, and say as he thinks'.

There are a number of remarkable features about Spinoza's proposal for a new method of biblical interpretation. Worth noting first of all is his expressed abhorrence for religious controversy. It is to be remembered that Spinoza is writing in the aftermath of the wars of religion which had wracked Europe between 1618 and 1648, and his pleas for religious freedom should be read in this context. More important (for our purposes) is Spinoza's method of biblical interpretation, which he outlines early in the chapter. This has three stages. The first is an examination of the language of the Bible, particularly Hebrew (in which Spinoza himself was trained). The second is a systematic classification of the topics dealt with within the biblical writings, distinguishing particularly between those whose meaning is clear and those which are obscure or which contradict other biblical passages. The third stage is a historical study of each book, which would endeavour to identify its authorship, the context within which it was written, as well as the history of its transmission. The pattern of this third stage in particular will be familiar to any student of the present day who has ever taken an introductory course in biblical studies.

However, perhaps the most remarkable feature of this discussion, and the one which is most indicative of the new spirit of Spinoza's age, is his insistence that the biblical interpreter is interested in discovering only 'the meaning' of the biblical texts, not their truth. It is this which most clearly marks the beginning of the fateful separation between history and faith. Spinoza's argument here is that if the literal meaning of the text is in conformity with what the Bible says elsewhere, it is to be accepted, no matter how contrary this meaning might seem to 'the natural light of reason'. It is for this reason that Spinoza conducts an extended attack on the interpretative methods of the great Jewish scholar Moses Maimonides (1135–1204), who—along with his Christian contemporaries—took for granted the divinely guaranteed accuracy of the Bible. For this reason Maimonides was prepared to reinterpret the biblical writings (using the variety of hermeneutical tools Judaism had developed) until the 'discovered' meaning conformed with what was already believed to be true. Spinoza's reply is that one should simply endeavour to discover what the biblical authors intended, even if we must judge them to have been mistaken. He maintains that this is not fatal to faith, since faith is primarily a matter of right conduct, and with regard to moral matters there is little that is controversial in the biblical writings. Disagreements with reason occur in those passages in which the biblical authors deal with matters of philosophical speculation, where 'their narratives conform especially to the prejudices of their age'. But these matters are to be distinguished from matters of faith.

Leaving aside Spinoza's view of faith, what is critical here is his distinction between meaning and truth. Although Spinoza says nothing about 'the historical Jesus', the discussion of which would have to wait until the following century, this distinction marks a new stage in the history of both the Jewish and the Christian interpretation of the Bible. It would have been unthinkable to rabbinic, patristic and medieval interpreters, or those of the Reformation. It represents a first step towards the undermining of the authority of the biblical picture of the world. It was now only a matter of time before the biblical depiction of Jesus would be identified with the meaning of the text, and the historical Jesus with its truth. Although the implications of this distinction would not become clear for another hundred years, the movement of thought which would give rise to the historical Jesus quest was underway.

Tractatus Theologico-Politicus

Of the Interpretation of Scripture

On every side we hear men saying that the Bible is the Word of God, teaching mankind true blessedness, or the path to salvation. But the facts are quite at variance with their words, for people in general seem to make no attempt whatsoever to live according to the Bible's teachings. We see that nearly all men parade their own ideas as God's Word, their chief aim being to compel others to think as they do, while using religion as a pretext. We see, I say, that the chief concern of theologians on the whole has been to extort from Holy Scripture their own arbitrarily invented ideas, for which they claim divine authority. In no other field do they display less scruple and greater temerity than in the interpretation of Scripture, the mind of the Holy Spirit, and if while so doing they feel any misgivings, their fear is not that they may be mistaken in their understanding of the Holy Spirit and may stray from the path of salvation, but that others may convict them of error, thus annihilating their personal prestige and bringing them into contempt.

Now if men were really sincere in what they profess with regard to Holy Scripture, they would conduct themselves quite differently; they would not be racked by so much quarrelling and such bitter feuding, and they would not be gripped by this blind and passionate desire to interpret Scripture and to introduce innovations in religion. On the contrary, they would never venture to accept as Scriptural doctrine what was not most clearly taught by Scripture itself. And finally, those sacrilegious persons who have had the hardihood to alter Scripture in several places would have been horrified at the enormity of the crime and would have stayed their impious hands. But ambition and iniquity have reached such a pitch that religion takes the form not so much of obedience to the teachings of the Holy Spirit as of defending what men have invented. Indeed, religion is manifested not in charity but in spreading contention among men and in fostering the bitterest hatred, under the false guise of zeal in God's cause and a burning enthusiasm. To these evils is added superstition, which teaches men to despise reason and Nature, and to admire and venerate only that which is opposed to both. It is therefore not surprising that, to make Scripture appear more wonderful and awe-inspiring, they endeavour to explicate it in such a way that it seems diametrically opposed both to reason and to Nature. So they imagine that the most profound mysteries lie hidden in the Bible, and they exhaust themselves in unravelling these absurdities while ignoring other things of value. They ascribe to the Holy Spirit whatever their wild fancies have invented, and devote their utmost strength and enthusiasm to defending it. For human nature is so constituted that what men conceive by pure intellect, they defend only by intellect and reason, whereas the beliefs that spring from the emotions are emotionally defended.

In order to escape from this scene of confusion, to free our minds from the prejudices of theologians and to avoid the hasty acceptance of human fabrications as divine teachings, we must discuss the true method of Scriptural interpretation and examine it in depth; for unless we understand this we cannot know with any certainty what the Bible or the Holy Spirit intends to teach. Now to put it briefly, I hold that the method of interpreting Scripture is no different from the method of interpreting Nature, and is in fact in complete accord with it. For the method of interpreting Nature consists essentially in composing a detailed study of Nature from which, as being the source of our assured data, we can deduce the definitions of the things of Nature. Now in exactly the same way the task of Scriptural interpretation requires us to make a straightforward study of Scripture, and from this, as the source of our fixed data and principles, to deduce by logical inference the meaning of the authors of Scripture. In this way—that is, by allowing no other principles or data for the interpretation of Scripture and study of its contents except those that can be gathered only from Scripture itself and from a historical study of Scripture—steady progress can be made without any danger of error, and one can deal with matters that surpass our understanding with no less confidence than those matters which are known to us by the natural light of reason.

But to establish clearly that this is not merely a sure way, but the only way open to us, and that it accords with the method of interpreting Nature, it should be observed that Scripture frequently treats of matters that cannot be deduced from principles known by the natural light; for it is chiefly made up of historical narratives and revelation. Now an important feature of the historical narratives is the appearance of miracles; that is, as we showed in the previous chapter, stories of unusual occurrences in Nature, adapted to the beliefs and judgment of the historians who recorded them. The revelations, too, were adapted to the beliefs of the prophets, as we showed in chapter 2; and these do, indeed, surpass human understanding. Therefore knowledge of all these things—that is, of almost all the contents of Scripture—must be sought from Scripture alone, just as knowledge of Nature must be sought from Nature itself.

As for the moral doctrines that are also contained in the Bible, although these themselves can be demonstrated from accepted axioms, it cannot be proved from such axioms that Scripture teaches these doctrines: this can be established only from Scripture itself. Indeed, if we want to testify, without any prejudgment, to the divinity of Scripture, it must be made evident to us from Scripture alone that it teaches true moral doctrine; for it is on this basis alone that its divinity can be proved. We have shown that the chief characteristic which established the certainty of the prophets was that their minds were directed to what was right and good; hence this must be made evident to us, too, before we can have faith in them. We have already shown that miracles can never give proof of God's divinity, apart from the fact that they could be wrought even by a false prophet. Therefore the divinity of Scripture must be established solely from the fact that it teaches true virtue. Now this can be established only from Scripture. If this could not be done, our acceptance of Scripture and our witness to its divinity would argue great prejudice on our part. Therefore all knowledge of Scripture must be sought from Scripture alone.

Finally, Scripture does not provide us with definitions of the things of which it speaks, any more than Nature does. Therefore, just as definitions of the things of Nature must be inferred from the various operations of Nature, in the same way definitions must be elicited from the various Biblical narratives as they touch on a particular subject. This, then, is the universal rule for the interpretation of Scripture, to ascribe no teaching to Scripture that is not clearly established from studying it closely. What kind of study this should be, and what are the chief topics it should include, must now be explained.

1. It should inform us of the nature and properties of the language in which the Bible was written and which its authors were accustomed to speak. Thus we should be able to investigate, from established linguistic usage, all the possible meanings of any passage. And since all the writers of both the Old and the New Testament were Hebrews, a study of the Hebrew language must undoubtedly be a prime requisite not only for an understanding of the books of the Old Testament, which were written in that language, but also for the New Testament. For although the latter books were published in other languages, their idiom is Hebraic.

2. The pronouncements made in each book should be assembled and listed under headings, so that we can thus have at hand all the texts that treat of the same subject. Next, we should note all those that are ambiguous or obscure, or that appear to contradict one another. Now here I term a passage obscure or clear according to the degree of difficulty with which the meaning can be elicited from the context, and not according to the degree of difficulty with which its truth can be perceived by reason. For the point at issue is merely the meaning of the texts, not their truth. I would go further: in seeking the meaning of Scripture we should take every precaution against the undue influence, not only of our own prejudices, but of our faculty of reason in so far as that is based on the principles of natural cognition. In order to avoid confusion between true meaning and truth of fact, the former must be sought simply from linguistic usage, or from a process of reasoning that looks to no other basis than Scripture.

For further clarification, I shall give an example to illustrate all that I have here said. The sayings of Moses, 'God is fire', and 'God is jealous', are perfectly clear as long as we attend only to the meanings of the words; and so, in spite of their obscurity from the perspective of truth and reason, I classify these sayings as clear. Indeed, even though their literal meaning is opposed to the natural light of reason, this literal meaning must nevertheless be retained unless it is in clear opposition to the basic principles derived from the study of Scripture. On the other hand, if these statements in their literal interpretation were found to be in contradiction with the basic principles derived from Scripture, they would have to be interpreted differently (that is, metaphorically) even if they were in complete agreement with reason. Therefore the question as to whether Moses did or did not believe that God is fire must in no wise be decided by the rationality or irrationality of the belief, but solely from other pronouncements of Moses. In this particular case, since there are several other instances where Moses clearly tells us that God has no resemblance to visible things in heaven or on the earth or in the water, we must hence conclude that either this statement or all those others must be explained metaphorically. Now since one should depart as little as possible from the literal meaning, we should first enquire whether this single pronounce-ment, 'God is fire', admits of any other than a literal meaning; that is, whether the word 'fire' can mean anything other than ordinary natural fire. If the word 'fire' is not found from linguistic usage to have any other meaning, then neither should this statement be interpreted in any other way, however much it is opposed to reason, and all other passages should be made to conform with it, however much they accord with reason. If this, too, should prove impossible on the basis of linguistic usage, then these passages would have to be regarded as irreconcilable, and we should there-fore suspend judgment regarding them. However, since the word 'fire' is also used in the sense of anger or jealousy (Job ch.31 v.12), Moses' pronouncements are easily reconciled, and we can properly conclude that these two statements, 'God is fire' and 'God is jeal-ous' are one and the same statement.

Again, as Moses clearly teaches that God is jealous and nowhere tells us that God is without passions or emotions, we must evidently conclude that Moses believed this, or at least that he intended to teach this, however strongly we may be convinced that this opinion is contrary to reason. For, as we have shown, it is not permissible for us to manipulate Scripture's meaning to accord with our rea-son's dictates and our preconceived opinions; all knowledge of the Bible is to be sought from the Bible alone.

3. Finally, our historical study should set forth the circumstances relevant to all the extant books of the prophets, giving the life, character and pursuits of the author of every book, detailing who

he was, on what occasion and at what time and for whom and in what language he wrote. Again, it should relate what happened to each book, how it was first received, into whose hands it fell, how many variant versions there were, by whose decision it was received into the canon, and, finally, how all the books, now universally regarded as sacred, were united into a single whole. All these details, I repeat, should be available from an historical study of Scripture; for in order to know which pronouncements were set forth as laws and which as moral teaching, it is important to be acquainted with the life, character and interests of the author. Furthermore, as we have a better understanding of a person's character and temperament, so we can more easily explain his words. Again, to avoid confusing teachings of eternal significance with those which are of only temporary significance or directed only to the benefit of a few, it is also important to know on what occasion, at what period, and for what nation or age all these teachings were written down. Finally, it is important to know the other details we have listed so that, in addition to the authenticity of each book, we may also discover whether or not it may have been contaminated by spurious insertions, whether errors have crept in, and whether these have been corrected by experienced and trustworthy scholars. All this information is needed by us so that we may accept only what is certain and incontrovertible, and not be led by blind impetuosity to take for granted whatever is set before us.

Now when we possess this historical account of Scripture and are firmly resolved not to assert as the indubitable doctrine of the prophets anything that does not follow from this study or cannot be most clearly inferred from it, it will then be time to embark on the task of investigating the meaning of the prophets and the Holy Spirit. But for this task, too, we need a method and order similar to that which we employ in interpreting Nature from the facts presented before us. Now in examining natural phenomena we first of all try to discover those features that are most universal and common to the whole of Nature, to wit, motion-and-rest and the rules and laws governing them which Nature always observes and through which she constantly acts; and then we advance gradually from these to other less universal features. In just the same way we must first seek from our study of Scripture that which is most universal and forms the basis and foundation of all Scripture; in short, that which is commended in Scripture by all the prophets as doctrine eternal and most profitable for all mankind. For example, that God exists, one alone and omnipotent, who alone should be worshipped, who cares for all, who loves above all others those who worship him and love their neighbours as themselves. These and similar doctrines, I repeat, are taught everywhere in Scripture so clearly and explicitly that no one has ever been in any doubt as to its meaning on these points. But what God is, in what way he sees and provides for all things and similar matters, Scripture does not teach formally, and as eternal doctrine. On the contrary, we have clearly shown that the prophets themselves were not in agreement on these matters, and therefore on topics of this kind we should make no assertion that claims to be the doctrine of the Holy Spirit, even though the natural light of reason may be quite decisive on that point.

Having acquired a proper understanding of this universal doctrine of Scripture, we must then proceed to other matters which are of less universal import but affect our ordinary daily life, and which flow from the universal doctrine like rivulets from their source. Such are all the specific external actions of true virtue which need a particular occasion for their exercise. If there be found in Scripture anything ambiguous or obscure regarding such matters, it must be explained and decided on the basis of the universal doctrine of Scripture. If any passages are found to be in contradiction with one another, we should consider on what occasion, at what time, and for whom they were written. For example, when Christ says, 'Blessed are they that mourn, for they shall be comforted', we do not know from this text what kind of mourners are meant. But as Christ thereafter teaches that we should take thought for nothing save only the kingdom of God and his righteousness, which he commends as the highest good (Matth. ch.6 v.33), it follows that by mourners he means only those who mourn for man's disregard of the kingdom of God and His righteousness; for only this can be the cause of mourning for those who love nothing but the kingdom of God, or justice, and utterly despise whatever else fortune has to offer.

So, too, when Christ says, 'But if a man strike you on the right cheek, turn to him the left also' and the words that follow, if he were laying this command on judges in the role of lawgiver, this precept would have violated the law of Moses. But he expressly warns against this (Matth. ch.5 v. 17). Therefore we should consider who said this, to whom, and at what time. This was said by Christ, who was not ordaining laws as a lawgiver, but was expounding his teachings as a teacher, because (as we have already shown) he was intent on improving men's minds rather than their external actions. Further, he spoke these words to men suffering under oppression, living in a corrupt commonwealth where justice was utterly disregarded, a commonwealth whose ruin he saw to be imminent. Now we see that this very same teaching, which Christ here expounds when the ruin of the city was imminent, was also given by Jeremiah in similar circumstances at the first destruction of the city (Lamentations ch.3. 30). Thus it was only at the time of oppression that the prophets taught this doctrine which was nowhere set forth as law; whereas Moses (who did not write at a time of oppression, but—please note—was concerned to found a good commonwealth), although he likewise condemned revenge and hatred against one's neighbour, yet demanded an eye for an eye. Therefore it clearly follows simply on Scriptural grounds that this teaching of Christ and Jeremiah concerning the toleration of injury and total submission to the wicked applies only in situations where justice is disregarded and at times of oppression, but not in a good commonwealth. Indeed, in a good commonwealth where justice is upheld, everyone who wants to be accounted as just has the duty to go before a judge and demand justice for wrongdoing (Lev. ch.5 v.1), not out of revenge (Lev. ch.19 v.17, 18), but with the purpose of upholding justice and the laws of his country, and to prevent the wicked from rejoicing in their wickedness. All this is plainly in accord with natural reason. I could produce many more similar examples, but I think this is sufficient to explain my meaning and the usefulness of this method, which is my only object at present.

Now up to this point we have confined our investigation to those Scriptural pronouncements which are concerned with moral conduct, and which can be the more easily elucidated because on such subjects there has never been any real difference of opinion among the writers of the Bible. But other Biblical passages which belong only to the field of philosophical speculation do not yield so easily to investigation. The approach is more difficult, for the prophets differed among themselves in matters of philosophical speculation (as we have already shown) and their narratives conform especially to the prejudices of their particular age. So we are debarred from deducing and explaining the meaning of one prophet from some clearer passage in another, unless it is most plainly established that they were of one and the same mind. I shall therefore briefly explain how in such cases we should elicit the meaning of the prophets from the study of Scripture. Here, again, we must begin from considerations of a most general kind, first of all seeking to establish from the clearest Scriptural pronouncements what is prophecy or revelation and what is its essential nature; then what is a miracle, and so on with other subjects of a most general nature. Thereafter we must move on to the beliefs of individual prophets, and from there finally to the meaning of each particular revelation or prophecy, narrative, and miracle. We have already pointed out with many apposite examples what great caution we should exercise in these matters to avoid confusing the minds of the prophets and historians with the mind of the Holy Spirit and with factual truth, and so I do not think it necessary to say any more on this subject. But with regard to the meaning of revelation, it should be observed that this method only teaches us how to discover what the prophets really saw or heard, and not what they intended to signify or represent by the symbols in question. The latter we can only guess at, not infer with certainty from the basis of Scripture.

We have thus set out our plan for interpreting Scripture, at the same time demonstrating that this is the only sure road to the discovery of its true meaning. I do indeed admit that those are better informed (if there are any) who are in possession of a sure tradition or true explanation transmitted from the prophets themselves, as the Pharisees claim, or those who have a pontiff whose interpretation of Scripture is infallible, as the Roman Catholics boast. However, as we cannot be sure either of the tradition in question or of the authority of the pontiff, we cannot base any certain conclusion on them. The latter is denied by the earliest Christians, the former by the most ancient sects of the Jews; and if, furthermore, we examine the succession of years (to mention nothing else) through which this tradition is traced right back to Moses, which the Pharisees have accepted from their Rabbis, we shall find that it is incorrect, as I shall prove elsewhere. Therefore such a tradition should be regarded with the utmost suspicion; and although our method requires us to accept as uncorrupted a certain tradition of the Jews—namely, the meaning of the words of the Hebrew language, which we have accepted from them—we can be quite sure of the one while doubting the other. For while it may occasionally have been in someone's interest to alter the meaning of some passage, it could never have been to anyone's interest to change the meaning of a word. Indeed, this is very difficult to accomplish, for whoever would try to change the meaning of a word would also have to explain all the writers who wrote in that language and used that word in its accepted meaning, in each case taking account of the character and intention of the writer; or else he would have to falsify the text, a task requiring much circumspection. Then again, a language is preserved by the learned and unlearned alike, whereas books and the meaning of their contents are preserved only by the learned. Therefore we can readily conceive that the learned may have altered or corrupted the meaning of some passage in a rare book which they had in their possession, but not the meaning of words. Besides which, if anyone should wish to change the customary meaning of a word, he would find it difficult to maintain consistency thereafter both in his writing and in his speaking.

For these and other reasons we may readily assume that it could never have entered anyone's mind to corrupt a language, whereas there may frequently have been an intention to corrupt the meaning of a writer by altering what he wrote or by giving it a wrong interpretation. Therefore, since our method (based on the principle that knowledge of Scripture must be sought only from Scripture) is the only true method, if there is anything that it cannot achieve for us in our pursuit of an entire understanding of Scripture, we must regard this as quite unattainable.

At this point I have to discuss any difficulties and shortcomings in our method which may stand in the way of our acquiring a complete and assured knowledge of the Holy Bible. The first important difficulty in our method is this, that it demands a thorough knowledge of the Hebrew language. Where is this now to be obtained? The men of old who used the Hebrew language have left to posterity no information concerning the basic principles and study of this language. At any rate, we possess nothing at all from them, neither dictionary nor grammar nor textbook on rhetoric. The Hebrew nation has lost all its arts and embellishments (little wonder, in view of the disasters and persecutions it has suffered) and has retained only a few remnants of its language and of its books, few in number. Nearly all the words for fruits, birds, fishes have perished with the passage of time, together with numerous other words. Then again, the meanings of many nouns and verbs occurring in the Bible are either completely unknown or subject to dispute. We are deprived not only of these, but more especially of the knowledge of Hebrew phraseology. The idiom and modes of speech peculiar to the Hebrew nation have almost all been consigned to oblivion by the ravages of time. So we cannot always discover to our satisfaction all the possible meanings which a particular passage can yield from linguistic usage; and there are many passages where the sense is very obscure and quite incomprehensible although the component words have a clearly established meaning.

Besides our inability to present a complete account of the Hebrew language, there is the further problem presented by the composition and nature of that language. This gives rise to so many ambiguities as to render it impossible to devise a method[1] that can teach us with certainty how to discover the true meaning of all Scriptural passages; for apart from the sources of ambiguity that are common to all languages, there are others peculiar to Hebrew which give rise to many ambiguities. These I think it worth listing here.

First, ambiguity and obscurity in the Bible are often caused by the fact that letters involving the same organ of speech are substituted one for another. The Hebrews divide all the letters of the alphabet into five classes in accordance with the five oral instruments employed in their pronunciation, namely, the lips, the tongue, the teeth, the palate and the throat. For example, א, ח, ע, ה, Aleph, Ghet, Hgain, He, are called gutturals, and are used one in place of another without any distinction apparent to us. For instance, אל, el, which means 'to', is often used for על, hgal, which means 'above', and vice-versa. As a result, any parts of a text may often be rendered ambiguous or appear to be meaningless utterances.

---

[1] That is, impossible for us who are not used to this language and lack a systematic account of its phraseology.

A second ambiguity arises from the multiple meanings of conjunctions and adverbs. For example, ו vau, serves indiscriminately to join and to separate, and can mean 'and', 'but', 'because', 'however' and 'then'. כ, ki, has seven or eight meanings:—'because', 'although', 'if', 'when', 'just as', 'that', 'a burning', and so on. This is the case with almost all particles.

Thirdly—and the source of many ambiguities—verbs in the Indicative mood lack the Present, the Past Imperfect, the Pluperfect, the Future Perfect, and other tenses in common use in other languages. In the Imperative and Infinitive Moods verbs lack all the tenses except the Present, and in the Subjunctive there are no tenses at all. And although all the tenses and moods thus lacking could have been supplied, with ease and even with great elegance, by definite rules deduced from the fundamental principles of language, the writers of old showed complete disregard for such rules, and indiscriminately used Future for Present and Past, and contrariwise Past for Future, and furthermore used Indicative for Imperative and Subjunctive, to the great detriment of clarity.

Besides these three sources of ambiguity in Hebrew there remain two more to be noted, both of which are of far greater importance. First, the Hebrews do not have letters for vowels. Secondly, it was not their custom to punctuate their texts, nor to give them force or emphasis; and although vowels and punctuation thus lacking are usually supplied by points or accents, these cannot satisfy us, having been devised and instituted by men of a later age whose authority should carry no weight with us. The ancient writers did not employ points (that is, vowels and accents), as is abundantly testified; men of later ages added both of these in accordance with their own interpretation of the Bible. Therefore the accents and points that we now have are merely contemporary interpretations, and deserve no more credibility and authority than other commentaries. Those who fail to realise this do not understand the justification of the author of the Epistle to the Hebrews (ch.11 v.21) in giving an interpretation of the text of Genesis ch.47 v.31 very different from that of the pointed Hebrew text—as if the Apostle ought to have been taught the meaning of Scripture by those who inserted points! In my opinion it is the latter who should be regarded as at fault. To make this clear to all, and to show how different interpretations arise simply from the absence of vowels, I shall here set down both interpretations.

Those who inserted the points interpreted the passage as follows:—'and Israel bent over (or, changing ע Hgain into א Aleph, a letter of the same organ, towards) the head of the bed'. The author of the Epistle reads, 'and Israel bent over the head of his staff', reading 'mate' for 'mita', the only difference being in the vowels. Now since in this part of the story there is only a question of Jacob's age, and not of his illness which is mentioned in the next chapter, it seems more probable that the historian intended to say that Jacob bent over the head of his staff (which men of advanced age employ to support themselves), not of the bed; and this is especially so because this interpretation does not require the substitution of one letter for another. Now my purpose in giving this example is not only to harmonise the passage in the Epistle to the Hebrews with the text of Genesis, but also to show how little confidence is to be placed in modern points and accents. Thus he who would interpret Scripture without any prejudice is in duty bound to hold these in doubt and to examine them afresh.

To return to our theme, such being the structure and nature of the Hebrew language, it is quite understandable that such a number of ambiguities must arise that no method can be devised for deciding them all. For we have no grounds for expecting that this can be completely achieved from a comparison of different passages, which we have shown to be the only way to elicit the true meaning from the many senses which a particular passage can yield with linguistic justification. It is only by chance that a comparison of passages can throw light on any particular passage, since no prophets wrote with the deliberate purpose of explaining another's words, or his own. And furthermore, we can draw no conclusion as to the meaning of one prophet or apostle from the meaning of another except in matters of moral conduct, as we have already convincingly demonstrated; no such conclusions can be drawn when they are dealing with philosophical questions, or are narrating miracles or history. I could bring further examples to prove this point, that there are many inexplicable passages in Scripture; but I prefer to leave this subject for the present, and I shall proceed to a consideration of the points that still remain: the further difficulties we encounter in this true method of Scriptural interpretation, or in what way it falls short.

One further difficulty consequent upon this method is this, that it requires an account of the history of all the Biblical books, and this for the most part we cannot provide. As I shall make clear at some length at a later stage, we either have no knowledge at all or but doubtful knowledge of the authors—or if you prefer the expression, the writers—of many of the books. Again, we do not even know on what occasion or at what time these books of unknown authorship were written. Furthermore, we do not know into whose hands all these books fell, or in whose copies so many different readings were found, nor yet again whether there were not many other versions in other hands. When I touched on this topic I did make a brief reference to the importance of knowing all these details, but there I deliberately passed over certain considerations which must now be taken up.

If we read a book relating events which are incredible or incomprehensible, or which is written in a very obscure style, and if we do not know the author or the time or the occasion of its composition, it will be vain for us to try to achieve a greater understanding of its true meaning. Deprived of all these facts we cannot possibly know what was, or could have been, the author's intention. But if we are fully informed of these facts, we are in a position to form an opinion free from all danger of mistaken assumptions; that is to say, we ascribe to the author, or to him for whom he wrote, no more and no less than his just meaning, concentrating our attention on what the author could have had in mind, or what the time and the occasion demanded. I imagine that everyone is agreed on this; for it often happens that we read in different books stories that are much alike, and form very different judgments of them according to our opinions of the writers. I remember once having read a book about a man named Orlando Furioso who used to ride a winged monster in the sky, fly over any regions he chose and single-handed slay huge numbers of men and giants, together with other similar fantastic happenings which are quite incomprehensible in respect to our intellect. Now I had read a similar story in Ovid about Perseus, and another story in the books of Judges and Kings about Samson, who single-handed and unarmed slew thousands of men, and of Elijah, who flew through the air and finally went to heaven in a chariot and horses of fire. These stories, I repeat, are obviously similar, yet we form a very different judgment of each. The first writer was concerned only to amuse, the second had a political motive, the third a religious motive, and it is nothing else but our opinion of the writers that brings us to make these judgments. It is therefore evident that in the case of obscure or incomprehensible writings, it is essential for us to have some knowledge of the authors if we seek to interpret their writings. And for the same reasons, to choose the correct reading out of the various readings of unclear narratives, we have to know in whose manuscript these different readings are found, and whether there were ever some other versions supported by men of greater authority.

In the case of certain books of the Bible, our method of interpretation involves the further difficulty that we do not possess them in the language in which they were first written. The Gospel according to Matthew and undoubtedly the Epistle to the Hebrews were written in Hebrew, it is commonly held, but are not extant in that form. There is some doubt as to the language in which the Book of Job was written. Ibn Ezra, in his commentaries, asserts that it was translated into Hebrew from another language, and that this is the reason for its obscurity. I say nothing of the apocryphal books, since their authority is of a very different kind.

Such then, is a full account of the difficulties involved in this method of interpreting Scripture from its own history, such as we possess. These difficulties, which I undertook to recount, I consider so grave that I have no hesitation in affirming that in many instances we either do not know the true meaning of Scripture or we can do no more than make conjecture. But on the other hand I must again emphasise, with regard to all these difficulties, that they can prevent us from grasping the meaning of the prophets only in matters beyond normal comprehension, which can merely be imagined; it is not true of matters open to intellectual perception, whereof we can readily form a clear conception.[2] For things which

---

[2] By things comprehensible I mean not only those which can be logically proved but also those which we are wont to accept with moral certainty and to hear without surprise, although they can by no means be proved. Anyone can comprehend Euclid's propositions before they are proved. Similarly, I call comprehensible those narratives, whether of future or past events, that do not exceed human belief, and likewise laws, institutions and customs, although they cannot be proved with mathematical certainty. But mysterious symbols, and narratives that exceed all human belief, I call incomprehensible. Yet even among these there are many that yield to examination by our method, so that we can perceive the author's meaning.

of their own nature are readily apprehended can never be so ob-
scurely worded that they are not easily understood; as the proverb
says, 'a word to the wise is enough'. Euclid, whose writings are
concerned only with things exceedingly simple and perfectly
intelligible, is easily made clear by anyone in any language; for in
order to grasp his thought and to be assured of his true meaning
there is no need to have a thorough knowledge of the language in
which he wrote. A superficial and rudimentary knowledge is
enough.

Nor need we enquire into the author's life, pursuits and character, the language in which he wrote, and for whom and when,
nor what happened to his book, nor its different readings, nor how
it came to be accepted and by what council. And what we here say
of Euclid can be said of all who have written of matters which of
their very nature are capable of intellectual apprehension.

Thus we can conclude that, with the help of such an historical
study of Scripture as is available to us, we can readily grasp the
meaning of its moral doctrines and be certain of their true sense.
For the teachings of true piety are expressed in quite ordinary
language, and being directed to the generality of people they are
therefore straightforward and easy to understand. And since true
salvation and blessedness consist in true contentment of mind and
we find our true peace only in what we clearly understand, it most
evidently follows that we can understand the meaning of Scripture
with confidence in matters relating to salvation and necessary to
blessedness. Therefore we have no reason to be unduly anxious
concerning the other contents of Scripture; for since for the most
part they are beyond the grasp of reason and intellect, they belong
to the sphere of the curious rather than the profitable.

I consider that I have now displayed the true method of Scriptural interpretation and have sufficiently set forth my opinion on
this matter. Furthermore, I have no doubt that it is now obvious to
all that this method demands no other light than the natural light
of reason. For the nature and virtue of that light consists essentially
in this, that by a process of logical deduction that which is hidden
is inferred and concluded from what is known, or given as known.
This is exactly what our method requires. And although we grant
that our method does not suffice to explain with certainty everything that is found in the Bible, this is the consequence not of the

defectiveness of the method but of the fact that the path which it tells us is the true and correct one has never been pursued nor trodden by men, and so with the passage of time has become exceedingly difficult and almost impassable. This I imagine is quite clear from the very difficulties I have recounted.

It now remains for me to examine the views of those who disagree with me. The first to be considered is held by those who maintain that the natural light of reason does not have the power to interpret Scripture, and that a supernatural light is absolutely essential for this task. What they mean by this light that is beyond the natural light I leave them to explain. For my own part, I can only surmise that they wish to admit, using rather obscure terminology, that they too are for the most part in doubt as to the true meaning of Scripture; for if we consider their explanations, we find that they contain nothing of the supernatural—indeed, nothing but the merest conjectures. Let them be compared, if you please, with the explanations of those who frankly admit that they possess no other light but the natural light. They will be found to be remarkably similar; that is to say, their explanations are human, the fruit of long thought, and elaborately devised. As to their assertions that the natural light is insufficient for this task, that is plainly false, for two reasons. In the first place, we have already proved that the difficulty of interpreting Scripture arises not from the lack of power of the natural light, but from the negligence (not to say malice) of those who failed to compile a historical study of Scripture while that was still possible. Secondly, everyone will admit, I imagine, that this supernatural light is a divine gift granted only to the faithful. Now the prophets and the apostles preached not only to the faithful, but especially to unbelievers and the impious. So their audiences must have been capable of understanding the meaning of the prophets and the apostles; otherwise these latter would have appeared to be preaching to children and babies, not to men endowed with reason. Moses, too, would have ordained his laws in vain if they could have been understood only by the faithful, who stand in no need of law. Therefore those who look to a supernatural light to understand the meaning of the prophets and the apostles are sadly in need of the natural light; and so I can hardly think that such men possess a divine supernatural gift.

Maimonides took a quite different view; for he held that every passage of Scripture admits of various—and even contrary—meanings, and that we cannot be certain of the true meaning of any passage unless we know that, as we interpret it, there is nothing in that passage that is not in agreement with reason, or is contrary to reason. If in its literal sense it is found to be contrary to reason, then however clear the passage may appear, he maintains that it must be interpreted in a different way. This view he sets out most clearly in chapter 25 of part 2 of his book 'More Nebuchim' [*Guide of the Perplexed*], where he says: 'Know that it is not the Scriptural texts concerning the creation of the world that withholds me from saying that the world has existed from eternity. The texts that teach that the world was created are not more numerous than those that teach that God is corporeal. There are ways, not barred to us, nor even difficult of access, by which we can explain those texts that deal with the question of the world's creation. Our explanation could have followed the same lines as when we denied corporeality of God; and perhaps this might have been much easier to achieve, and we might have explained the texts and established the eternity of the world more plausibly than when we explained Scripture in a way that removed the notion of corporeality from God, blessed be He. Yet there are two reasons that prevent me from so doing and from believing that the world is eternal. First, there is clear proof that God is not corporeal, and it is necessary to explain all those passages whose literal meaning is contrary to that proof; for it is certain that they must then have an explanation other than the literal. But the eternity of the world has not been proved; so it is not necessary to do violence to the Scriptural texts and explain them away merely because of a plausible opinion, when we might incline to a contrary opinion with some degree of reason. Secondly, the belief that God is incorporeal is not contrary to the basic tenets of the Law, whereas the belief that the world is eternal, in the way that Aristotle held, destroys the very foundations of the Law.'

Such are the words of Maimonides, and they clearly confirm what we said above. For if he had been convinced on rational grounds that the world is eternal, he would not have hesitated to distort and explain away Scripture until it appeared to teach the same doctrine. Indeed, he would have been quite convinced that Scripture, in spite of its plain denials at every point, intended to teach this same doctrine of the eternity of the world. So he cannot be sure of the true meaning of Scripture, however clearly stated, as long as he can doubt the truth of what it says, or as long as he is not convinced of it. For as long as we are not convinced of the truth of a statement, we cannot know whether it is in conformity with reason or contrary to it, and consequently neither can we know whether the literal meaning is true or false.

If this view were correct, I would unreservedly concede that we need a light other than the natural light to interpret Scripture; for nearly all the contents of Scripture are such as cannot be deduced from principles known by the natural light, as we have already shown. Thus the natural light does not enable us to reach any decision as to their truth, nor therefore as to the true sense and meaning of Scripture. For this purpose we should necessarily need another kind of light. Then again, if this view were correct, it would follow that the common people, for the most part knowing nothing of logical reasoning or without leisure for it, would have to rely solely on the authority and testimony of philosophers for their understanding of Scripture, and would therefore have to assume that philosophers are infallible in their interpretation of Scripture. This would indeed be a novel form of ecclesiastical authority, with very strange priests or pontiffs, more likely to excite men's ridicule than veneration. And although our own method demands a knowledge of Hebrew, for which study the common people can likewise have no leisure, it is not open to the same sort of objection. The common people of the Jews and Gentiles for whom the prophets and apostles once preached and wrote, understood the language of the prophets and apostles and thereby they also comprehended the meaning of the prophets, but without understanding the rational justification of the prophets' message. Yet, according to Maimonides, this understanding was also necessary if they were to grasp the meaning of the prophets. There is nothing, then, in our method that requires the common people to abide by the testimony of biblical commentators, for I can point to a people who were familiar with the language of the prophets and apostles. But Maimonides cannot point to a people capable of understanding the causes of things, which would be a necessary basis for understanding the meaning of the prophets. And as to the common people of our own time, we have already shown that whatsoever is necessary for salvation, even though its rational justification be not understood, can be readily grasped in any language, because it is couched in ordinary and familiar terms; and it is this understanding, not the testimony of biblical commentators, that gains acceptance with the common people. And as for the rest of Scripture, the common people are on the same footing as the learned.

But let us return to the view put forward by Maimonides, and examine it more closely. In the first place, he assumes that the prophets were in agreement on all matters, and that they were outstanding philosophers and theologians; for he holds that they based their conclusions on scientific truth. But in chapter 2 we have shown that this is not so. Then again, he assumes that the meaning of Scripture cannot be established from Scripture itself. For scientific truth is not established from Scripture itself, which does not engage in demonstrations and does not validate its teaching by appealing to definitions and first causes. And therefore, according to Maimonides, neither can Scripture's true meaning be established from itself, and should not be sought from it. But it is evident from this chapter that this point, too, is false. We have demonstrated both by reasoning and by examples that the meaning of Scripture is established from Scripture alone, and should be sought only from Scripture even when it is speaking of matters known by the natural light of reason. Finally, he assumes that it is legitimate for us to explain away and distort the words of Scripture to accord with our preconceived opinions, to deny its literal meaning and change it into something else even when it is perfectly plain and absolutely clear. Such licence, apart from being diametrically opposed to the proofs advanced in this chapter and elsewhere, must strike everyone as excessive and rash.

However, granting him this considerable degree of liberty, what in the end can it effect? Assuredly, nothing whatsoever. Those things that are not subject to proof and which make up the greater part of Scripture cannot yield to an enquiry of this sort, nor be explained or interpreted according to this rule; whereas by pursuing our method we can explain many things of this kind and investigate them with confidence, as we have already shown both by reason and by concrete example. And in the case of things that are by their nature comprehensible, their meaning can easily be elicited merely from their context, as we have also shown. Thus this method of Maimonides is plainly of no value. Furthermore, he clearly deprives the common people of any confidence they can have in the meaning of Scripture derived from simply perusing it; and yet this confidence is available to all by pursuing a different method. Therefore we can dismiss Maimonides' view as harmful, unprofitable and absurd.

As to the tradition of the Pharisees, we have already declared that it lacks consistency, while the authority of the Popes of Rome stands in need of clearer evidence. This is my only reason for impugning the latter, for if they could prove it from Scripture itself with the same degree of certainty as did the Jewish High Priests of long ago, I should not be influenced by the fact that among the Popes there have been found heretics and impious men. Among the Hebrew High Priests, too, in the past were found heretics and impious men, who gained the priesthood by underhand means; and yet by Scriptural sanction they possessed the supreme power to interpret the Law. See Deut. ch.17 v.11, 12 and ch.33 v.10, and Malachi ch.2 v.8. But since the Popes can produce no such evidence, their authority remains highly suspect. The example of the Jewish High Priest ought not to deceive one into thinking that the Catholic religion also stands in need of a high priest; for it should be noted that the laws of Moses, being his country's civil laws, necessarily stood in need of some public authority to uphold them. If every man were free to interpret the civil laws as he chose, no state could survive; by that very fact it would be instantly dissolved, and public right would become private right.

Now with religion the case is quite different. Since it consists in honesty and sincerity of heart rather than in outward actions, it does not pertain to the sphere of public law and authority. Honesty and sincerity of heart is not imposed on man by legal command or by the state's authority. It is an absolute fact that nobody can be constrained to a state of blessedness by force or law; to this end one needs godly and brotherly exhortation, a good upbringing, and most of all, a judgment that is independent and free.

Therefore, as the sovereign right to free opinion belongs to every man even in matters of religion, and it is inconceivable that any man can surrender this right, there also belongs to every man the sovereign right and supreme authority to judge freely with regard to religion, and consequently to explain it and interpret it for himself. The supreme authority to interpret laws and the supreme judgment on affairs of state is vested in magistrates for this reason only, that these belong to the sphere of public right. Thus for the same reason the supreme authority to explain religion and to make judgment concerning it is vested in each individual, because it belongs to the sphere of individual right.

It is, then, far from true that the authority of the Hebrew High Priest in interpreting his country's laws enables us to infer the Pope's authority to interpret religion; on the contrary, a more obvious inference is that the interpretation of religion is vested above all in each individual. And this again affords further proof that our method of Scriptural interpretation is the best. For since the supreme authority for the interpretation of Scripture is vested in each individual, the rule that governs interpretation must be nothing other than the natural light that is common to all, and not any supernatural right, nor any external authority. Nor must this rule be so difficult as not to be available to any but skilled philosophers; it must be suited to the natural and universal ability and capacity of mankind. We have shown that our rule answers to this description; for we have seen that such difficulties as are now to be found in it have arisen from the negligence of men, and are not inherent in our method.

Ernst Troeltsch (1865-1923)

If the questioning of the authority of the biblical writings was the first condition for the emergence of the historical Jesus question, the development of a sense of history was the second. While the modern sense of history can be traced to the Renaissance, it was in the nineteenth century that the discipline of historiography received its present form. Our second author stands at the end of the nineteenth century and the beginning of the twentieth. Therefore, while Spinoza represents the earliest stages of the development of historical criticism, Troeltsch represents an age in which Spinoza's method has become securely established. He is therefore well placed to describe these changes and their significance for Christian faith.

Like Spinoza, Ernst Troeltsch is not a biblical scholar, but is remembered as an historian, philosopher and theologian. He was born near Augsburg and brought up in that city. After initial university studies in Erlangen and Berlin, the young Troeltsch travelled to Göttingen, to attend classes under the great Albrecht Ritschl (1822-89). However his association with Ritschl's theology was to be short-lived. Already during his first period as a university teacher, also in Göttingen, Troeltsch began to move in a new direction, characterized by a rediscovery of the significance of history. Along with biblical scholars such as William Wrede (1859-1906), Johannes Weiss (1863-1914) and his old friend Wilhelm Bousset (1865-1920), Troeltsch became one of the founders of what was soon known as the 'history of religions school' (*die religionsgeschichtliche Schule*). This loose association of scholars insisted on treating Christianity as one religion among others and understanding it as (among other things) a product of the religious world of its time. Troeltsch's later work, in Bonn, Heidelberg, and Berlin, was influenced by the work of the great founder of modern sociology, Max Weber (1864-1920), with whom Troeltsch formed a close friendship; for a time they even occupied apartments in the same house. His work on early Christianity made Troeltsch an important figure, not only as a historian, but also as one of the first sociologists of religion.

The essay which follows was written in 1898, as a response to an attack on Troeltsch's work by Friedrich Niebergall (1866-

1932), a disciple of Julius Kaftan (1848-1926), with whom Troeltsch had also been engaged in a controversy. Niebergall's criticisms of Troeltsch had centred on what he had seen as Troeltsch's historical relativism, which hindered the historian from making the kind of absolute claims which Christianity had traditionally made for itself. Troeltsch's reply deals briefly with Niebergall's arguments, which he sees as reflecting those of Kaftan, but it quickly becomes a general statement of the difference between what Troeltsch describes as a 'dogmatic' and a 'historical' approach to theology. The resulting essay has become something of a minor classic, a concise summary of what a thorough-going historical criticism of the Bible would involve.

Troeltsch summarized historical method under three headings: criticism, analogy, and correlation. The principle of 'criticism' means that the documentary witnesses to the past must not be taken at face value, but carefully examined, to assess the accuracy of the picture they give. Since no witnesses to the past are to be accepted as absolutely authoritative, it follows that our picture of the past can only ever be a matter of probability, the result of a critical, but fallible, sifting of the evidence. The second principle is that of 'analogy', which states that in reconstructing the past the historian can do nothing other than assume that the past was like the present. The behaviour of historical actors can be understood only by reference to the behaviour of people today, and the distortions from which our knowledge suffers today can help us to recognize similar distortions in the documents before us. Therefore our judgements of probability about the past must be based on analogous experiences in our own time. The third principle is that of 'correlation', and may be taken as the leading idea of the 'history of religions school'. It is the idea that all phenomena of the past must be understood as the products of a particular context: no phenomenon (not even that of early Christianity) stands in isolation, but is influenced and conditioned by the totality of events out of which it emerges.

It would be difficult to find a better statement of the assumptions underlying the distinction between the Jesus of the historian and the Christ of historic Christianity. For traditional

Christianity's assertion of the authority of the apostolic witness flies in the face of the principle of criticism, while its assertion that Jesus is a figure without parallel leaves little room for the principles of analogy and correlation. Until very recent times, Christians did not normally regard their religion as simply one religion among others, any more than the New Testament writers thought of their faith as a joint product of the Jewish and Greco-Roman religious worlds. At first sight, therefore, historical criticism might appear to be not so much a theological method as the end of theology. Yet for Troeltsch it was not so. Against Niebergall he argues that his method can avoid relativism, that even at the end of this process the theologian can discern, in the religious development of humanity, the gradual unfolding of a divine revelation. For at the high point of this process of religious development, in the history of Israel and the life of Jesus, the religious spirit of humanity broke through its bondage to the natural world, to produce a spiritual faith in which all previous religious developments are recapitulated. Although the most the historian can say about this faith is that it is the highest product of the human religious spirit to date, it is impossible for us to imagine anything higher.

Allied to such a confident view of the religious value of history, the historical method could indeed produce theologically constructive results. Would that confidence view of history survive the intellectual and political developments of the early twentieth century? At the time Troeltsch penned these words, the answer to that question lay well in the future.

Historical and Dogmatic Method in Theology

In compliance with the kind request of Professor Niebergall and the wishes of the editorial board, I am taking the liberty of adding a few remarks to the essay of this theologian. They are intended to shed additional light on the controversy, and not only to clarify those of my views which he has attacked but also to defend my total position in the philosophy of religion and theology against his strictures. Since Niebergall is essentially espousing the ideas of his teacher, Julius Kaftan, the following remarks also represent my final word in my exchange with that distinguished Berlin theologian and member of the High Consistory.[1] I shall let this be my final word because further discussion would be of little avail in view of the fact that the opposition between us is one of principle.

I have deliberately spoken of my 'theological method'. For our primary concern here involves methodology rather than apologetics or any particular point of dogma. Apparently Niebergall, because of his presuppositions, has not quite perceived this point; for he takes the authoritarian concept of revelation for granted and regards anything beyond Christianity as merely 'natural decor'. He and others who share his view do not regard theology as such as problematical; they see only minor problems that can be patched over, and consequently they assume the same attitude on the part of everyone else. Admittedly, such an attitude has its merits and even a certain practical importance, since it reflects a common need. But it is also possible to take an entirely different approach, starting from basic principles, and my labors have more and more led me to this approach. I have not borrowed 'grounds against our supernaturalism' from any scholar in order then to meet them by my 'view of the history of religion as a continuing revelation'.

For some two hundred years these grounds have been readily available. It was not necessary for me to borrow them. Nor was my starting point the competing claims of various revelations or some 'pantheistic' concept of evolution. Such vistas are fairly obvious and have been treated often enough—however superficially—in theological apologetics. Instead, I have explicitly called attention to the much deeper ground where the disintegration of the Christian world of ideas actually originates. Though related to these other matters, this ground is still relatively independent and in any case absolutely decisive. I am referring to *the historical method as such*, to the problem of 'Christianity and history', which is to be understood not as the defense of Christianity against particular results of histori-

---

[1] See my essays 'Die Selbständigkeit der Religion' ['The Independence of Religion'] and 'Geschichte und Metaphysik' ['History and Metaphysics'] in *Zeitschrift für Theologie und Kirche*; as well as Kaftan's essay 'Die Selbständigkeit des Christentums' ['The Independence of Christianity'], by which he means its supernatural revelation and redemptive power.

cal criticism but rather as the effect of modern historical methodology on the interpretation of Christianity itself. Once applied to the scientific study of the Bible and church history, the historical method acts as a leaven, transforming everything and ultimately exploding the very form of earlier theological methods. I have clearly indicated that this was the starting point of my labors and I have developed in detail the consequences of this position.

Significantly, my efforts in this direction have made no impression whatever upon Niebergall. He proceeds as though no difficulty at all existed in this connection, and as though, with the admission that the historical context played a conditioning role, all difficulties were solved and the old dogmatic method substantially saved. He is astonishingly insensitive to the consequences flowing from the historical method. In comparison, the older apologists of the eighteenth century and the few rigid supernaturalists of the present may well be found to have attained a deeper insight.

Yet Niebergall's stance is a common one, perhaps more characteristic of contemporary theology than any other. Only particular problems raised by historical criticism are considered; one by one, they are then either rejected or designated as harmless, as the case may be. When Christianity is treated systematically, the historical-critical approach is abandoned. By focusing only on various needs, postulates, claims, theories of knowledge, or other intangible generalities, contemporary theologians attempt to validate the old authoritarian concept of revelation; and with the help of this concept they weave together a tolerable dogmatic system. Exegetes and historians are left to see for themselves how they may authenticate these purely dogmatic postulates in relation to their research. Historians, for their part, generally prefer to confine themselves to the conditioning role of the historical context and leave the theoretical questions to the dogmatists. In this sort of theology one is constantly being shuttled back and forth between the two groups.

In contrast to the foregoing, I wish most emphatically to call attention to what is signified by the historical method, the historical mode of thought, and the historical sense. I am not thinking here of the earlier historiography, which limited its criticism to particular fragments of history, providing information about interesting foreign lands or accumulating archival material. What I have in mind is the genuine historical scholarship of the present, which

involves a definite approach to the whole sphere of culture, constitutes a method of representing the past and the present, and
therefore implies some extraordinary consequences. Here we are
concerned principally with three essential aspects: the habituation
on principle to historical criticism; the importance of analogy; and
the mutual interrelation of all historical developments.

The first of these three items indicates that in the realm of history there are only judgements of probability, varying from the
highest to the lowest degree, and that consequently an estimate
must be made of the degree of probability attaching to any tradition. Accordingly, our overall attitude to the enormous body of
material our civilization derives from memory and tradition is
fundamentally changed, even when our attitude toward the particular contents of this material has not yet undergone any correction. But the latter, too, is subjected by historical criticism to
analysis, correction, and transformation in a thousand ways, with
the final result being never more than probably correct.

It is obvious that the application of historical criticism to religious tradition must result in a profound change in one's inward
attitude to it and in one's understanding of it. Indeed, such a
change has actually taken place. But the operation of historical
criticism in this area signifies above all the definitive inclusion of
the religious tradition with all traditions that require preliminary
critical treatment. If the manner of operation of various traditions
is thus shown to be in principle the same, the traditional objects
and events (which must first be ascertained critically) will hardly fail
to show a corresponding similarity.

The second basic postulate of the historical method is that the
instrumentality that makes historical criticism possible is the em-
ployment of analogy. Analogous occurrences that we observe both
without and within ourselves furnish us with the key to historical
criticism. The illusions, distortions, deceptions, myths, and parti-
sanships we see with our own eyes enable us to recognize similar
features in the materials of tradition. Agreement with normal,
customary, or at least frequently attested happenings and conditions
as we have experienced them is the criterion of probability for all
events that historical criticism can recognize as having actually or
possibly happened. The observation of analogies between similar
events in the past provides the possibility of imputing probability

to them and of interpreting what is unknown about the one by reference to what is known about the other.

But this omnipotence of analogy implies the similarity (in principle) of all historical events—which does not, of course, mean identity. While leaving all possible room for differences, however, the analogical method always presupposes a common core of similarity that makes the differences comprehensible and empathy possible. Hence, the acceptance of historical criticism entails recognition of the significance of this analogical approach for the investigation of the history of Christianity. Biblical criticism itself is based on analogies to the ways of tradition in which other vestiges of antiquity have come down to us. Similarly, the conditions assumed by historical criticism were in numberless cases ascertainable only through the seeking out of analogies. Jewish and Christian history are thus made analogous to all other history. Actually, fewer and fewer historical 'facts' are regarded as exempt from the exigencies of the analogical principle; many would content themselves with placing Jesus' moral character and the resurrection in this category.

We have already seen that the importance of analogy as a method leveling all historical phenomena rests on the assumption of a basic consistency of the human spirit and its historical manifestations. The consequence of this position is the third basic concept of history, namely, the interaction of all phenomena in the history of civilization. This concept implies that there can be no change at one point without some preceding and consequent change elsewhere, so that all historical happening is knit together in a permanent relationship of correlation, inevitably forming a current in which everything is interconnected and each single event is related to all others. Now, the principles of historical explanation and understanding are implicit in this position. At every point there do indeed emerge unique and autonomous historical forces that, by virtue of our capacity for empathy, we perceive to be related to our common humanity. At the same time, however, these unique forces also stand in a current and context comprehending the totality of events, where we see everything conditioned by everything else so that there is no point within history which is beyond this correlative involvement and mutual influence.

There is no need for us to demonstrate that this approach constitutes the foundation of all principles of historical explanation.

The historian's craft combines the art of intuiting the original import of the sources with the discovery of correlative and mutually determinative changes. The historian's ultimate problems arise from the attempt to understand the nature and basis of the whole historical context and to arrive at value judgements regarding its various forms.

The scholarly investigation of the Bible has accordingly become involved with the general political, social, and intellectual history of antiquity, and the investigation and evaluation of Christianity has at last been placed within the framework of the history of religion and culture. The exigencies of their own research have gradually compelled the scholars to elucidate the beginnings of the religion of Israel by analogies from the religions of other Semitic peoples and to relate the profound and original transformation of the religion of Yahweh to the general conditions prevailing in Western Asia, especially to its great catastrophes and its general intellectual horizon. Judaism had to be interpreted by reference to the conditions of the Exile and its institutional reorganization, and its profoundly altered conceptual framework had to be explained in terms of ideas absorbed during the Exile. The rise of Christianity had to be related to the disintegration of Judaism, to the political movements and the apocalyptic ideas of the time; and the establishment of the Christian church had to be studied in the light of the interaction of primitive Christianity with the surrounding world of the Roman empire. Indeed, no comprehensive view can any longer fail to see in the mighty movement of Christianity the culmination of antiquity. Major developments in the Near East and the West prepared the way for this culmination. Very different lines of development finally converged in it.

Now, all these necessities were entailed by the historical method itself, which, once admitted at any one point, necessarily draws everything into its train and weaves together all events into one great web of correlated effects and changes. It is not at all necessary here to adopt the distinctly Hegelian notion of Strauss that the Idea does not like to pour all its fullness into a single individual. No general philosophical theory is required to arrive at this result. The historical method itself, by its use of criticism, analogy, and correlation, produces with irresistible necessity a web of mutually interacting activities of the human spirit, which are never independent and absolute but always interrelated and therefore understandable only within the context of the most comprehensive whole.

In its origin, of course, this method was not independent of general theories. No method is. But the decisive test is the usefulness and fruitfulness of a method, its perfection through application, and its contribution to the achievement of continuity and understanding. No one can deny that wherever the historical method has been applied it has produced surprisingly illuminating results, and that confidence in its ability to illuminate previously obscure areas has been consistently vindicated. Such success is its sole—but wholly sufficient—validation.

Give the historical method an inch and it will take a mile. From a strictly orthodox standpoint, therefore, it seems to bear a certain similarity to the devil. Like the modern natural sciences, it represents a complete revolution in our patterns of thought vis-à-vis antiquity and the Middle Ages. As these sciences imply a new attitude toward nature, so history implies a new attitude toward the human spirit and its productions in the realm of ideas. Everywhere the older absolutistic or dogmatic approach, which regarded particular conditions and ideas as simply 'given' and therefore absolutized them into unchangeable norms, is being supplanted by the historical approach, which regards even those matters that are alleged to be most obviously 'given' and those powers that control the largest number of people as having been produced by the flow of history. Jurisprudence, ethics, sociology, political theory, and aesthetics have been affected to their very depths by the historical approach and have been aligned with historical viewpoints and methods. Whether this historicizing of our entire thinking should be regarded as a boon is not the question here. On this point, Nietzsche's brilliant essay, 'On the Use and Abuse of History', contains observations worth heeding. In any case, we are no longer able to think without this method or contrary to it. All our investigations regarding the nature and goals of the human spirit must be based on it. Goethe's words still apply:

> Those who will not account
> to themselves for the past thirty centuries
> may continue to live
> in the dark, day-by-day, grossly ignorant.

Thus, the historical method has also penetrated theology, first subtly and piecemeal with all sorts of limitations and reservations, then ever more energetically and comprehensively, with the result that here also it accomplished what it had done everywhere else, namely, a transformation in principle of our entire mode of thought and our whole attitude toward the subject. To be sure, at first only particular results entered the general consciousness, and with them an uncomfortable insecurity. But subconsciously, the fundamental significance of the historical method is all-pervasive, driven by the logic of an inner necessity. The success of the method in the solution of particular problems urges its extension to the whole field, to the way the subject itself is approached. Here again, direction is not given by some theory or system but by the exigencies of the objects of historical investigation, which seem to come alive and are rendered comprehensible as soon as they are approached with the historical method. Those who expressed objections or reservations about it were compelled to retreat step by step until they were reduced to invoking, as a defence, the uncertainties engendered by deficiencies in the sources and the tradition.

The particular views that resulted from the historical treatment of Jewish and Christian religious traditions are not, however, the most decisive aspect of the development, their intrinsic importance notwithstanding. What is crucial are the consequences of the method as such, which in the nature of the case are two. In the first place, historical criticism brings a measure of uncertainty to every single fact and shows that certainty attaches only to its effects upon the present; the historical link between original fact and present influence must remain at least partly obscure. But this is to loosen the connection between religious faith and all particular facts. To be sure, the connection is not broken, but its character is changed. Now it becomes impossible to base religious faith on any single fact: faith and fact are linked by large and broad connections; their relationship is mediate, not direct.

In the second place, these connections between faith and fact are themselves not isolated and unconditioned but are most closely correlated with a much larger historical context; they arise out of this context, they share its substance, and they must be understood in relation to it. It does not follow, however, that the originality of the particular historical fact is thereby denied. What does follow is that its originality is analogous to others emerging from the common context and is neither more nor less mysterious than these. The creative significance of the personages who dominate the great life-complexes need not be denied. But the personages of Judaeo-Christian history are neither more nor less irrational than those of Greek and Persian history.

One implication of the historical method is extremely important. It follows from the univocity and the total interconnection of historical events that their evaluation and judgement no less than their explanation and description must begin with the total context. Although numerous theologians seek to persuade us that the proper starting point is the isolated claim and judgement of the Christian community, no just estimate of Christianity can be formed except by reference to the total context—even as the self-judgement of the Greeks or the Romans cannot be allowed to determine our estimate of their permanent contribution to the human spirit.

Obviously, this is how the historical method works. It relativizes everything, not in the sense that it eliminates every standard of judgement and necessarily ends in a nihilistic skepticism, but rather in the sense that every historical structure and moment can be understood only in relation to others and ultimately to the total context, and that standards of values cannot be derived from isolated events but only from an overview of the historical totality. This relativism and respect for the historical totality belong together, as indeed they are always conjoined in the practical application of the method. This spirit of historical investigation has gradually permeated every facet of historical theology; Christianity, too, must be regarded as an entity to be explained and evaluated in relation to the total context of which it forms a part. Indeed, only the investigations carried out in this spirit have produced authentic historical knowledge; all the animadversions against the historical method have represented only checks upon it or corrections of particular results, but no viable alternative. For these reasons the old dogmatic method has become untenable for anyone who has become historically sensitive. This fact, and it alone, is the starting point of all theories like the one I am proposing. Once employed, the inner logic of the method drives us forward; and all the counter-measures essayed by the theologians to neutralize its effects or to confine them to some limited area have failed, despite eager efforts to demonstrate their validity.

Indeed, no one is in a position to see these consequences more clearly than the biblical scholar, particularly in the concrete work of his speciality. Even someone who is unable to accept any of our theories is bound to be aware, after the discussions of the idea of the kingdom of God or of Jesus' messianic consciousness, that it is impossible to arrive at some supra-historical core with a method that necessarily raised such problems as these and, precisely through them, has advanced our historical understanding. Conversely, one need only survey the enormously complicated apparatus that [Theodor] Zahn [1838-1933] has constructed for the purpose of annulling the results of the historical method to become aware that nothing has been accomplished in behalf of his approach; he has merely matched results with results, rather than method with method. Moreover, it will be apparent that his tortuous deductions can scarcely provide a basis for the old naively secure relationship to tradition that was the presupposition of the old dogmatic method.

If this is the situation, only one consequence appears possible. The historical method must be consistently applied. This implies not only recognition of the relative uncertainty of all historical knowledge (and consequently the awareness that the connection of religious belief with particular historical events is only mediate and relative) and the resolute subjection of the Judaeo-Christian tradition to all the consequences of a purely historical method (without fearing or seeking to bypass the results). Most importantly, it implies that Christianity should be seen in its involvement with general history. The scholarly investigation and evaluation of Christianity must begin with the general context of universal history. Now, to apply the historical method to theology with utter, uncompromising consistency means to base theology on the historical method, which is oriented to universal history; and since our concern is with Christianity as both religion and ethic, the method will have to be that of the history of religion [*religions-geschichtliche Methode*]. This idea of a theology based upon the history of religion, which was envisaged from the very beginning of historical criticism (first by the Deists and then in various forms by Lessing, Kant, Herder, Schleiermacher, DeWette, and Hegel, and finally by Baur and Lagarde), I have sought to sketch in my previous works, attempting to give it the form required since the elimination of the rationalistic concept of religion-in-general and of the Hegelian dialectic of the Absolute.

I cannot now enter again into the details. That task will have to wait for a more comprehensive work. I only desire to stress that, although many of these specific studies are important, what is decisive for me is the method. I have no doubt that even a presentation of the Christian life-world based on the method of the history of religion will fail to convince the atheist and the religious skeptic. This is not, however, my concern, which is limited to attempting to satisfy the intellectual need for consistency and uniformity of view and approach. Nor do I doubt that this method—only the details of which are my own—will attract but few followers at first, either on the right or on the left; nor does this fact concern me. What is of primary importance is that the scholar should attain a firm conviction by means of the exposition. I have the greatest confidence, however, that the implication of the historical method will necessarily lead through the present confusion and derangement of biblical studies to its full and resolute application. Only then will the worst of our fears (regarding apologetics) be lifted from our hearts, and we shall be able to behold with greater detachment and freedom the glory of God in history.

The need for a consistency that makes possible such detachment and freedom is bound to lead an increasing number of theologians, or at least people who are intellectually concerned about religion, in the direction indicated. The simple result will be, as I have already written, the following:

> All human religion is rooted in religious intuition or divine revelation, which in specifically religious personalities achieves the power to establish new communities; the faithful subsequently enter into this experience, though with diminished originality. The belief in God contained in this intuition (which is concealed in nature religion at the beginning of religious history, when the religious consciousness takes naturalistic forms) decisively breaks through these limits in the religion of Yahweh—notwithstanding many comparable beginnings elsewhere—and in the preaching of Jesus, which, emerging out of the religion of Yahweh, undergoes an infinitely rich development that was impossible to predict at the outset. But in this development the concern was always with life oriented to faith in the living God and with the interpretation of the particular situation in the light of this faith.

This new method in theology would not be adequately characterized, however, unless I contrasted it with the old method, consistently and authentically interpreted. This comparison is especially necessary in view of the remarks of Niebergall and the theologians close to him, who have claimed this method as their own even though they were not very clear about its essential nature. If the new method is to be termed the history-of-religion method, since its subjects all tradition to criticism first and, where a question of principle is involved, always starts from the total historical reality in order to derive its standards of value from this totality, the older one is to be termed the dogmatic method. It starts from a firm point of origin completely beyond the relativity of historical scholarship and thence arrives at absolutely certain positions that, at best, may subsequently be related to the insights and opinions governing the rest of human life. By its principles this method is absolutely opposed to the historical one. Its essence is that it possesses an authority that, by definition, is separate from the total context of history, not analogous to other happenings, and therefore not subject to historical criticism and the uncertainty attaching to its results. The dogmatic method seeks to commit persons to certain particular facts of history, especially insofar as these attest the authority and destroy all historical analogy to it. The dogmatic method can bring about such a commitment because its facts are not those of ordinary history and hence can be neither established nor demolished by historical criticism; they are safeguarded, rather, by a miraculous transmission and sealed by an inward testimony in the heart.

The dogmatic method accordingly lacks the main features of the method of secular historical scholarship, namely, criticism, analogy, and correlation. Indeed, it combats these features most energetically and admits them, at best, only in regard to the most immaterial details. It cannot abide historical criticism, not because it is narrow-minded but because it cannot suffer the uncertainty of results that is connected with such criticism, and because its facts possess a character that contradicts every critical presupposition—indeed, the very possibility of criticism. The dogmatic method cannot admit analogies or make use of them because it would then have to surrender its own innermost nature, which consists in the denial of any analogical similarity between Christianity and other forms of religious development. It cannot submerge itself in the total historical context because its monopoly on dogmatic truth can be recognized only in its antithesis to this context, in the assertion that its own constitutive causality is 'wholly other'.

To be sure, the dogmatic method also claims to be based upon 'history'. But this is not the ordinary, secular history reconstructed by critical historiography. It is rather a history of salvation [*Heilsgeschichte*], a nexus of saving facts which, as such, are knowable and provable only for the believer. These facts have precisely the opposite characteristics of the facts that secular, critical historians can regard, on the basis of their criteria, as having actually taken place.

When dogmatic apologetics stresses the 'historical' character of Christianity in order to appeal to the secular appreciation of historical and social forces (which generally prevails among us, as over against purely individual efforts and discoveries), this is pure obscurantism. Such apologetics has already caused enough confusion in theology. Today all kinds of things are labeled as 'historical' and as 'facts' which are nothing of the kind, and which ought not to be so labeled, since they are miraculous in nature and can only be apprehended by faith. The miracles of the Judaeo-Christian tradition are often assigned a label that sounds general and obscures their difference from the secular world. This camouflage is dropped only when the discussion has safely passed to the sphere of theology. Even Niebergall has followed this approach quite freely. Yet, it is apparent that genuine dogmatics is poorly served by such a 'historical' force that ultimately is merely fortuitous. It has need, rather, of a history that, by concentrating the necessary absolute truth at one point, sets itself apart from ordinary history, which relativizes all truths by showing their mutual interdependence. To safeguard its own uniqueness, the dogmatic method requires an open rupture with this kind of history: otherwise it would become subject to all of its conditions, the mutual limitations of its phenomena, and the continuing possibility of change.

In all these matters the traditional dogmatic method operates quite consistently and correctly. It claims an authority that is dogmatic rather than historical, intrinsic rather than based on comparison, immutable rather than sharing the conditions of historical existence. It does not seek historical greatness, based on actual strength and influence or on philosophical reflection, but rather a foundation for dogmatic truths, characterized as supernatural by special marks and thus essentially non-historical. Consequently, everything depends on the evident demonstration of this supernatural character that establishes dogma even as it vitiates history. Whether greater emphasis be placed on the internal or the external manifestations or supernaturalism, ultimately, its internal manifestation in the operations of grace always serves to prove the credibility of the external manifestation, which alone vitiates historicity. The miraculous is truly decisive, and, since a miracle confined to the psychological sphere is not sufficiently different from the life of the soul as we encounter it universally in history, such a delicate miracle only becomes useful when solid 'physical' miracles can be deduced from it. Ultimately, everything depends on this external manifestation of supernaturalism. It would be better honestly to take one's stand on it rather than to talk of a 'history' that is not history at all but rather its opposite.

Only this proof by miracle provides the dogmatic method with a firm foundation and a methodological principle. It will be recalled that the historical method issued from the metaphysical assumption that all things, including the activities of the human mind, are totally interconnected; that it achieved autonomy through elaboration; and that it then had yet again to formulate general theories regarding the essence of history and the principles by which it formed its historical judgements. Similarly, the dogmatic method possesses a general metaphysical principle that was originally only rather implicitly present but which became clearly and precisely explicit in the course of its elaboration. Only the proof for the supernatural character of its authority or for the miraculous provides the decisive metaphysical foundation for the dogmatic method, without which it could be regarded as a knife lacking both handle and blade. The division of the domain of history into one area devoid of miracles and subject to the normal working of historical criticism and another area permeated by miracles and accessible to study only through methods based on inner experiences and the humble subjection of reason is the primary theoretical basis of the dogmatic method. The construction of such a concept of history and the establishment of a separate methodology for the history of dogma or the history of salvation, with special conditions independent of ordinary history, is the basic presupposition of the dogmatic method in theology. Consequently, the theological investigations of recent centuries are replete with this special methodology geared to the history of salvation, which vitiates and distorts the methodology of secular history in various ways, and with distinctive Christian theories of knowledge supposedly based either on the principle of ecclesiastical obedience or on regeneration and inner experience. Only fatigue caused by such fruitless apologetics can excuse the astonishing habit of contemporary dogmatists who believe that they are able to pluck fruit without having a tree or who, after cutting a small, dry twig from an old trunk, expect fruit to grow from this twig. But ultimately the essence of the problem is not exhausted by this great distinction between two realms of history and between two opposite methods corresponding to these realms. For the duality of the realms of history must be derived from a necessary ground both in the nature of God and in human nature. In the final analysis the duality of history is related to a duality in the divine nature. This duality is therefore regarded and maintained by the dogmatic method as the foundational and primary support of its concepts. God is not part of the nexus of interrelated forces continually affecting one another, nor is God involved in every vital movement only as the purposive will that produces the motion of the total system. God is also capable, rather, of extraordinary activities (as compared to regular modes of operation) which break through and abrogate the ordinary operation of the system. Everything depends on this concept of God.

No less fundamental, however, is the concept of humanity necessitating such a distinctive mode of divine operation, that is, the concept of a hereditary sinfulness due to a fall from the regular, normal, and uniform cosmic order and the concept of a salvation that requires a restoration of this order by extraordinary means. These dualistic concepts of the human and the divine are indispensable presuppositions of the dogmatic method with its dualism of two historical methods—one critical and relativistic, operative in secular history; and the other absolute and apodictically certain, appropriate to the history of salvation. Here, too, weariness with the labors of apologetics has induced many modern theologians to neglect or abandon these theories. In particular, the remarkable discovery of the irrelevance of metaphysics to theology has led to a renunciation of the proof of this dualism, even though the dualism itself necessarily continued to be recognized as valid. As though a non-metaphysical theology were not bound to eliminate this dualism and its consequences! The result would be that theology would turn into the phenomenological and historical study of religion, in which the truth-content of the religious phenomenon must first be ascertained; while a new, more cautious, and more limited metaphysics would emerge, characterized by abandonment of the miracle-dualism and based on moral certitude or sensitivity [*Gefühl*].

For the young theologian beginning to study, nothing is more astounding than the contradiction between the alleged indifference of such fundamental concepts as God, the primal state, original sin, and miracles, on the one hand, and the working assumption of their entire validity (except for some accommodating concessions regarding the influence of the pre-modern worldview), on the other. One can become accustomed to anything and make a virtue out of every necessity; but with any sense for clarity, consistency, and intellectual precision, one can hardly resign oneself to such a virtue with equanimity. For this reason most young theologians will ultimately return to the old metaphysical bases of the dogmatic method; from all their studies they will only retain the impression that the proof of these bases is a matter of no particular importance. The dogmatic method is thus pushed forward by an inner necessity towards the type of theology suggested above, just as the historical method necessarily leads to a theology that is fundamentally based on the history of religion.

It is not my intention to develop in detail the scope of the dogmatic method, but only to sketch it in its essence and to contrast it with the historical method. One might term the old method 'Catholic' because it was created by Catholic theologians and received its classic formulation from them; and one might term the new method 'Protestant' because in the last analysis it grew out of the Protestant criticism of the Catholic doctrine of authority. Yet, on the one hand, the old method is so deeply imbedded in the inclinations of human nature to dogmatism and is so necessary a product of historically unsophisticated periods that it would not make sense to term this method specifically Catholic; for it is also employed in Jewish and Muslim theology. On the other hand,

Protestant historical criticism was only partial and apologetic in intent; Protestantism arose in an era that was by no means historical in its outlook. It was not until the Enlightenment that an essentially historical outlook emerged; the allegedly unhistorical outlook of the Enlightenment belongs to the realm of legend. To be sure, the Enlightenment began by critically emancipating itself from the recognized authorities and thus its first task was to put everything on one level. But its leveling efforts immediately led to a new task, the task of differentiation and graduation, which required that all the phenomena dealt with be first transformed into purely historical ones. In this transitional stage the Enlightenment made supernatural dogmatism, in part, rational; and where this was not possible, it worked out a new worldview based on history. The latter, of course, had to weave together historical data and materials of general validity, and is entitled to be termed 'historical' only a posteriori. At this very point the difference between the two methods becomes plain.

Thus, the only appropriate terms are the *dogmatic* and the *historical* method. Each has its own foundation and problems; each is consistent within itself. My concern, however, is not to detail the particular problems of each, but only, because of their respective consistencies, to insist on their incompatibility. With this insistence, the main objective of this paper is attained. I only wish to add a few remarks concerning my position in this methodological controversy. These comments will serve to defend my position against some objections of Niebergall and, incidentally, to illuminate the distorted manner in which he himself espouses the dogmatic method.

His first objection to my method is on the score of its difficulty and the subjective conditions of its implementation. It goes without saying that the production of a scale of values among the great cultural types [*Geistestypen*] of history depends on subjective judgements and can never be fully conclusive. I have always stressed this point explicitly. Nevertheless, I am convinced that, given a sharp and penetrating analysis of the nature of these types, people who are seriously concerned about ethical and religious matters—neither frivolous nor trying to be merely clever but really in earnest about finding meaning in life—may arrive at a relative degree of consensus. This conviction is based on a belief that is both religious and ethical, namely, that ultimately the essential uniformity of human nature provides a foundation for consensus in recognizing supreme standards of value and that, because of this foundation, the consensus will prevail. As for Niebergall's strictures concerning the difficulties of implementing my approach, I can say only that no amount of emphasis upon the difficulties in a method that is inherently possible can justify the adoption of a method that is inherently impossible. It only challenges us to greater devotion to the task.

Niebergall also criticizes me for connecting the scale of values I have constructed with a metaphysics of history that makes it possible to deduce values, in a logically progressive and increasingly profound sequence, from the nature of the human spirit or rather from its transcendent ground as it operates in the spirit. I am unable here to consider in detail his remarks about intellectualism and practical reason, which are completely incomprehensible to me in their present form. I only note that no one who considers history to be pure chaos will undertake to derive a scale of values from it by the exercise of reason. For the deduction of such a scale of values it is indispensable to believe in reason as operative in history and as progressively revealing itself. This belief, too, is primarily of ethical and religious origin; but it is a belief that is confirmed, in my judgement, by the deepening of personal life which is constantly taking place in history.

The third objection adduced by Niebergall is the danger of self-deception to which one is exposed in such a production of a scale of values. I do not intend to inquire whether the danger resulting from the application of the historical approach is greater than that arising from the special apologetic conditions of the dogmatic method, geared as it is to the history of salvation, whose practitioners feel no obligation to warn against such a hazard. The point I would emphasize, rather, is that I do not regard the danger as wholly insuperable. Actually, one does not always endeavor to demonstrate a preconceived thesis with all the devices of cunning, yet with the greatest possible appearance of impartiality, as many theologians believe who are absolutely unable to think otherwise. In such an intricately complex and extremely individualistic culture as our own, it is often difficult to know where to take one's stand; and it is actually possible, without any preconceived preference for Christianity, to desire to orient oneself through a comparative survey. If as a consequence one reaches the judgement that Christianity is the highest ethical and religious force, this result need not at all have been antecedently present—not even where there was a relative appreciation for Christianity from the outset, such as any serious person naturally would feel. The ultimate avowal of Christianity as the supreme religious force of history, which is the outcome for me, is something quite different from a relative and preliminary appreciation that is connected, moreover, with a serious intent not necessarily to commit oneself to this initial and immediate judgement.

Finally, Niebergall attacks me for inconsistency inasmuch as I, while ostensibly oriented to historical relativism, yet emerge at the end with the recognition of the 'absoluteness' of Christianity, a conclusion that in his judgement is quite impossible for me. It must be admitted that Niebergall has here pointed correctly to vacillations not only in my mode of expression but also in my way of thinking as they appear in various essays spread over several years. It would have been possible for him to observe that I have actually tended to draw the consequences of the historical method ever more strictly and that I have finally come to characterize the term 'absoluteness' as only a rationalized and disguised vestige of the dogmatic method. I believe, in fact, that the term is not terribly important—but only because its opposite, the much-maligned 'relativism', is not so important to me as it would appear to be from the dogmatic point of view. Indeed, I would say that it is the essence of my view that it thoroughly combats historical relativism, which is the consequence of the historical method only within an atheistic or a religiously skeptical framework. Moreover, my view seeks to overcome this relativism through the conception of history as a disclosure of the divine reason.

It is here that we see the undeniable merits of the Hegelian doctrine, which needs only to be freed of its metaphysics of the absolute, its dialectic of opposites, and its specifically logical conception of religion. The point is that history is not a chaos but issues from unitary forces and aspires towards a unitary goal. For the believer in religion and ethics, history is an orderly sequence in which the essential truth and profundity of the human spirit rise from its transcendent ground—not without struggle and error, but with the necessary consistency of a development that has had a

normal beginning. The contrasts are rather superficial and incidental. In essence, the differences among the great historical structures
are not very great, and the actual ideas and values in the world are
infinitely rarer than is supposed, although their manifestations and
ramifications are innumerable. With the great idealists, I believe
that in this apparent chaos the divine depth of the human spirit
reveals itself from different directions, and that the belief in God,
provided only that it is actually belief in God and not self-seeking
magic, is at its core identical in all its forms. Moreover, I hold that
this belief in God, by the internal consistency of the divine force
that empowers it, continues to increase in energy and depth to the
degree permitted by the original tie of the human spirit to nature.

Only at one point was this limitation broken through. This
point, however, was located at the center of great contemporary
and subsequent religious developments, namely, in the religion of
the prophets of Israel and in the person of Jesus. Here a God distinct from nature produced a personality superior to nature with
eternally transcendent goals and the willpower to change the world.
Here a religious power manifests itself, which to anyone sensitive
enough to catch its echo in one's own soul, seems to be the conclusion of all previous religious movements and the starting point
of a new phase in the history of religion, in which nothing has yet
emerged. Indeed, even for us today it is unthinkable that something
higher should emerge, no matter how many new forms and combi-
nations this purely inward and personal belief in God may yet
enter. Clearly, this position constitutes neither dogmatic absolutism
nor the confrontation of historical scholarship by Christianity, nor
the exemption of Christianity from the flux, the conditioning, and
the mutability of history. But it provides a stopping point that is
attainable through a historical mode of thought geared to the
philosophy of history, and that is adequate for the religious person.
More we do not need, and more we cannot achieve. Here we find
the religious support for our life and thought that has constituted
the dynamic center of our European civilization, and which remains a vital power capable of further development.

It is true that the relationship of this European religion to the
religions of the Orient is still a great and dark question for the
future. But insofar as we recognize in the transcendence of nature,
which constitutes the faith of the prophets, and in the active and

lively love of God and humanity which constitutes the faith of Jesus, the decisive and elevating forces of religion, we can persevere in our traditional faith and leave further developments to the future. In this connection also, Niebergall has measured me by needs that are taken for granted by him. He has not put himself into a religious mood that really finds its rest and support in such thoughts. To his opinion that the reader of my work has to ride through a very cold land and then pass through a dark tunnel before emerging into the smiling fields of home, I might reply that the distant land is not so cold, the tunnel not so dark, nor the ultimate point of arrival so inviting as he supposes.

For my part, I have considerable misgivings about the position of Niebergall. Here again I shall forgo consideration of the epistemological explanations with which he supports his position and the formulation of which he regards as constituting the major part of difference from my own work. These matters are not crucial for the problem as a whole. For if the question to be decided is whether the scale of values in the spiritual life is to be derived from a philosophy of history or from an authoritarian judgement based on supernatural considerations, then it is quite pointless to stress factors of sentiment and will, which naturally enter into every value judgement. One can never base authoritarian supernaturalism on the practical character of all values, since this same practical character applies also to non-Christian and non-religious values. Rather, we are dealing exclusively with the basis of the authority that the dogmatic method requires as its starting point.

In this regard there is no doubt that Niebergall agrees with the intentions of the traditional dogmatic method. He desires the doctrine of a supernaturalistic authority: not a 'historical absolute but one that is dogmatic and apologetic', an 'absolute apart from and opposed to the history of religion'; that is, apart from and opposed to the views of historical criticism in general. He wants a 'realm lying beyond the history of religion'; that is, a realm lying quite beyond secular history. He is concerned with 'absoluteness as an immediate derivation from God' in contrast to the merely mediate derivation from God of ordinary history and the history of non-Christian religions, which is based on a 'merely natural endowment'. He conceives of the absolute as a 'faith that absolute values have been supernaturally revealed at one point in history';

that is, values having an absoluteness that is primarily authenticated by their supernatural mode of revelation. Despite all Niebergall's talk about his respect for history and the practical motivation of all faith, one must not permit oneself to be deceived: what he wants is outside of and contrary to history. He wants a history of a higher order, which has different presuppositions from ordinary history and events that are distinguishable by criteria not provided by ordinary history. When he speaks of the 'autonomy of Christianity', 'practical motivation', or 'historical character', such terms are euphemisms for the miraculous, which theologians of his type prefer not to call by its correct name.

The intentions of Niebergall are never fulfilled, however. His mode of thought falls far short of what he aspires to achieve, namely, a 'pure and bright supernaturalism'. One hears next to nothing from Niebergall concerning a consistent foundation for supernaturalism in the concept of God, the primal state, the Fall, and redemption. His work contains only pitiful vestiges of any other demonstration of supernaturalism actually derived from history, that is, from the miraculous character of sacred history. He intends to establish the biblical revelation as his starting point, a priori authentic and normative for his approach to history. This intention, which he emphatically proclaims, is constantly being crossed, however, by the contrary procedure of starting from general history and searching it for the possible disclosure of absolute values corresponding to human need. He acts as though he knew nothing of Christianity and were seeking, as a universal human postulate, for some absolute, redemptive revelation. From this stance he discovers the historical 'fact' of Christianity and rejoices to find it satisfying all his requirements. The historical mode of thought has here produced a deep impression after all. What should have been the starting point of the dogmatist now appears as the contingent result of a search of history. The result has been that, instead of being deduced from the concept of God and Adam's fall, theology is being authenticated by reference to human needs. Everything now depends on the legitimacy of these needs and the fact of their satisfaction, which is no more automatically guaranteed for these needs than for any others.

I do not wish to expatiate further upon these needs—the need (ostensibly demonstrated by Kant) of theoretical doubt for supernatural revelation, or the need of morality for authority, for a guarantee of victory, and for the atonement of sins. All these needs may be legitimate, but it cannot be denied that these needs themselves are in the first instance purely historical forms which do not lead beyond history. Of greater importance is the question why the satisfaction of these needs should be regarded as taking place in Christianity in an absolute manner. Here again the emphasis is not placed upon an inner necessity that enables Christianity alone to satisfy these needs, but recourse is taken—with an apparent objectivity that is very popular in contemporary theology—to the purely factual 'claim' of Christianity. Here we meet the same dialectical comedy as before. One comes upon the 'historical fact' of a tremendous claim and appears completely surprised by this fact, as though it were something astounding and overwhelming. The claim of Christianity is made into its essence, and the erstwhile theology of miracle now becomes a theology of claim. Christianity claims to be absolute truth and redemption. Without recognition of this claim Christianity is unattainable. But the assertion of claims, of course, no more proves their validity than the existence of needs guarantees their satisfaction—all the less so as various religions advance competing claims that require decision on the basis of some kind of criterion. In all of these expositions a dread of the real roots of the dogmatic method and a superficial accommodation to purely historical arguments are the only operative factors. Actually existing needs and claims are said to form the basis of the theory. But needs and claims are themselves products of history. They are to be understood in their historical context, to be illuminated, and possibly to be corrected, as have a hundred other needs and claims. By no means do needs and claims indicate some higher reality removed from historical relativity and criticism.

Thus everything depends on whether these needs are satisfied not merely by a claim but by a higher reality. In the last analysis Niebergall's views necessarily affirm this position. But how feeble and cautious is his assertion of a higher supernatural reality and causality as opposed to secular history! He stresses 'supernaturalism' and 'immediacy' as appropriate to revelation, in order to support a distinctive causality that would give special status to Christianity as the means-oriented natural causality would not. But even this emphasis is expressed only in the most general terms. To be absolute, 'Christianity must be based upon a special revelation that must somehow be made comprehensible as revelation'. This 'somehow' is typical of contemporary theology, which in its refinement disdains the concerns of the older apologetics and disposes of them 'somehow'. If one seeks clues to this 'somehow' in Niebergall, only one attempt at more precise definition will be found, along with the crude manipulation of some famous models. The personality of Jesus must be such as to break through the ordinary historical causality. But even in this context Niebergall speaks primarily of the mysterious and underivable essence of the personality, as though the same observations were not true of every personality.

> Here in the ground of the soul there remains a gap in the causal nexus which is the greater, the more unique and developed is the personality. It is this gap that provides full scope for the operation of a higher power. We believe that the revelation that we religiously apprehend and revere sets in at this point, which resists all analysis. ... Starting with Jesus, the reservoir of revelation fed both from heaven and by terrestrial streams, we proceed upwards along the course of these tributaries.

And at another point he says, 'We resolve to attribute beneficent powers that come to our assistance in deepest need to the intervention of God, because we know of no earthly source from which they could have been derived.'

What should one say to such remarks? Should one admire the modesty of a theology that has come to the point of finding its foundation ultimately in a gap? Or should one stress the uncertainty with which even this gap is asserted, in view of the fact that no clear distinction is made between the gaps in the causal nexus which characterize the personal life of ordinary human beings and the particular gap within the personality of Jesus, which is the only one that concerns us at this point? I think that one can only say that such a doctrine of authority and revelation has been deeply affected by the spirit of historical criticism, analogy, and relativity. Indeed, it has been almost destroyed. All that remain are some pathetic and quite general claims. In this respect, the older dogmatic doctrine was better and more understandable.

This judgement is made entirely from a scholarly perspective and refers only to the consistency of the ideas. Practically, such an enervation and edentulation of the old authoritarian doctrine may be a very good thing. In practical life, it is impossible to get along without such mediating positions; and in church affairs, the mediating groups may constitute a very desirable transitional form. In closing these observations, we may stress that *sub specie aeternitatis* ['in the light of eternity'] all the differences we have noted may be quite unimportant. Consequently, they need not excessively disunite us in our earthly pilgrimage.

1

The Gospels as Fraud

Hermann Samuel Reimarus (1694–1768)

The works of Benedict Spinoza and Ernest Troeltsch illustrate the conditions which had to be fulfilled before the
question of the historical Jesus could be raised. The taken-
for-granted authority of the Bible needed to be called into
question, and a sense of historical distance with its associated
methods of criticism needed to be developed. Spinoza's
Tractatus was a first attempt to develop a critical method of
biblical study, while Troeltsch's essay looked back on these
new developments from a later perspective and summed up
their significance for faith. For the first major attempt to offer
a portrait of the historical Jesus we must return to a writer
who lived about a century after Spinoza, namely Hermann
Samuel Reimarus.

There is little in the course of Reimarus's life which
might have led his contemporaries to expect that he would
eventually produce a work of radical biblical criticism. As a
young man Reimarus was educated at a preparatory school,
where his father was an instructor, in his native city of Hamburg. After attending the *Gymnasium* (academic high school)
Reimarus left Hamburg in 1714 to attend the University of
Jena, where he studied classical philology, philosophy, and
theology. From 1716 to 1723 he studied and taught philosophy in Wittenberg, taking time off in 1720-21 to tour Eng-
land and Holland, and to do research at Oxford and Leiden.
From 1723 to 1727 he held the post of rector of a high
school at Wismar, before taking up a position as a teacher of

Hebrew and Oriental languages, once again at the Hamburg *Gymnasium*, where he worked for the next forty years. Other than the *Fragments* (see below) his many writings include *The Principal Truths of Natural Religion* (1754) and *The Doctrine of Reason* (1766). While these located his thought firmly within the German Enlightenment tradition, they seemed to lend rational support to 'revealed religion'. It was only after Reimarus's death that the extent of his alienation from traditional Christianity would become clear.

The work for which Reimarus is best known was entitled *Apology or Defence of the Rational Worshippers of God*. Reimarus refrained from publishing it during his lifetime on account of its controversial character. After Reimarus's death, the philosopher Gotthold Ephraim Lessing (1729-81) took upon himself the task of offering fragments of the work to the public, which he did between 1774 and 1778. In order to protect the reputation of Reimarus, Lessing claimed simply to have found these fragments in the Duke of Brunswick's library at Wolfenbüttel, where he was employed as librarian, and so they first saw the light of day under the title *Fragments of the Wolfenbüttel Unknown*. Lessing continued to maintain his silence regarding their authorship, and it was some forty years before the identity of the author of these fragments would be publicly confirmed. The *Fragments* cover a wide range of topics, but it is the last two which are of particular significance. These are entitled 'On the Resurrection Story', published in 1777, and 'On the Intention of Jesus and His Disciples', published in 1778. It is these fragments, restored to their original order by Charles Talbert, to which the following extracts belong.

Reimarus identifies the core of Jesus' teaching as his message of repentance in preparation for the coming of the Kingdom of God. He maintains that Jesus' moral teaching was a simple one and was opposed to the external and legalistic religion of the Pharisees. He argues that the phrase 'the Kingdom of God' is to be understood according to the conventional understanding of the Jews of Jesus' time, since neither John the Baptist nor Jesus indicated that it was to be understood differently. That understanding was of a temporal kingdom under the rule of God's Messiah. Jesus himself had claimed the Messianic dignity and had waited in vain for a popular uprising to put him on the throne. This expectation was shared by the disciples throughout Jesus' ministry. It was only after the crucifixion and the crushing of their hopes that they reformulated their teaching and began to speak of Jesus as a suffering saviour who died for the sins of the world and was raised to life by God. The resurrection narratives are clearly unreliable as historical sources, and the story of the resurrection can only be regarded as a deliberate act of fraud, brought about by the disciples so as to ensure that they could maintain their positions of power and privilege.

It is not difficult to imagine the horror with which these claims were greeted by Christians of the eighteenth century. Even at a greater remove we may judge Reimarus's work to be more polemical than scholarly. Yet whatever the weaknesses of Reimarus's depiction of the historical Jesus, he succeeds in identifying some of the key issues which will dominate the later discussion. In particular, it is to his credit to have grasped the proclamation of repentance and the kingdom of God as the core of Jesus' teaching and to have attempted an interpretation of this phrase within the context of the Jewish religious world of Jesus' age. Similarly, Reimarus was correct to suggest that the Gospels have been rewritten in the light of later Christian beliefs. Even if later scholars were quick to distance themselves from some of Reimarus's conclusions, they would all be obliged to grapple with his questions.

From the *Wolfenbüttel Fragments* **VI** and **VII**[1]

Reprinted from *Reimarus: Fragments*, edited by Charles H. Talbert, copyright ©1990 Fortress Press. Used by permission of Augsburg Fortress.

[1] Footnotes found here are those given by Paul Rilla, the editor of Lessing's Collected Works (*Gotthold Ephraim Lessing: Gesammelte Werke* [Berlin: Aufbau Verlag, 1956], vols. 7-8), as selected by Charles Talbert in the 1970 Fortress Press edition from which this text is taken. The biblical references were supplied by Rilla and in some cases corrected by Talbert, and the translations in square brackets are Talbert's.

Reimarus begins his discussion of 'The Intention of Jesus and His Disciples' by offering a brief description of the Judaism of Jesus' day, which links this section to the discussion of the Old Testament (Fragment V). Reimarus is very critical of what he sees as the 'hypocrisy and sanctimoniousness' of the Pharisees, and this sets the scene for the description of Jesus' own teaching which follows. The material of Part I comes from Fragment VII.

Part I

§ 2

Now when Jesus began to teach he undertook primarily to castigate and reform the trifling matters and the misuse committed by the Pharisees and to preach a better righteousness than theirs. From a reading of the New Testament it can be obvious to everyone that a great portion of Jesus' sayings is directed against the distorted sanctimoniousness of the scribes and Pharisees in outward ceremonies. Nevertheless, he admitted the correctness of their view concerning immortality and salvation, and not only defended this opinion against the Sadducees, but impressed it diligently upon the people. He introduces Abraham and Lazarus into his parables, representing them as living in abundant joy in the realm of glory [Abraham: Matt. 8:11; Luke 13:28. Lazarus: Luke 16:23, 25]; he urges the people not to fear those who can merely destroy the body and not the soul. Rather, they should fear God, who can plunge both body and soul into hell; he speaks urgently of the kingdom of heaven and the last judgment that God shall preside over, etc. Consequently, his teaching had a considerable advantage not only over that of the Pharisees, but also over that of the Old Testament, where such essential principles of religion were not even considered and where there is mention only of earthly promises and rewards, all hope for man ending abruptly with his death. Thus Paul correctly says of him that he did away with death and in its place brought to light life and immortality through the gospel [2 Tim. 1:10]. For it was not the law that made perfect, but the introduction of a better hope, by means of which we approach God. Augustine says, *jam Christi beneficio etiam idiotis notam creditamque animae immortalitatem vitamque post mortem futuram.* ['It is Christ's merit that he also taught the ignorant about the immortality of the soul and life after death so that they believed in it.'] Thus it seems to be chiefly to the Christian doctrine that we must ascribe the fact that the Sadducees and their followers from that time on almost completely lost ground among the Jews. I shall add to this advantage of Jesus' teaching the further fact that Jesus also invites the heathen into the kingdom of God and, unlike Moses, does not command that they be despised and eradicated with fire and sword. 'Go', he says, 'and teach all heathen, preach the Gospel to all creatures' [Matt. 28:19, combined with Mark 16:15]. Indeed, he does not entirely exclude from this hope even those heathen who remain firmly rooted in their imperfect understanding; he says that it shall go easier with Tyre and Sidon at the last judgment than with many of the Jews [Matt. 11:22; Luke 10:14].

§ 3

Hence, just as there can be no doubt that Jesus in his teaching referred man to the true great goal of religion, namely, eternal salvation, we are concerned now with just this one question: What sort of purpose did Jesus himself see in his teaching and deeds? Jesus left us nothing in writing; everything that we know of his teaching and deeds is contained in the writings of his disciples. Especially where his teaching is concerned, not only the evangelists among his disciples, but the apostles as well undertook to present their master's teaching. However, I find great cause to separate completely what the apostles say in their own writings from that which Jesus himself actually said and taught, for the apostles were themselves teachers and consequently present their own views; indeed, they never claim that Jesus himself said and taught in his lifetime all the things that they have written. On the other hand, the four evangelists represent themselves only as historians who have reported the most important things that Jesus said as well as did. If now we wish to know what Jesus' teaching actually was, what he said and preached, that is a *res facti*—a matter of something that actually occurred; hence this is to be derived from the reports of the historians.

Now since there are four of them and since they all agree on the sum total of Jesus' teaching, the integrity of their reports is not to be doubted, nor should it be thought that they might have forgotten or suppressed any important point or essential portion of Jesus' teaching. Thus it is not to be assumed that Jesus intended or strove for anything in his teaching other than what may be taken from his own words as they are found in the four evangelists. Everyone will grant, then, that in my investigation of the intention of Jesus' teaching I have sufficient reason to limit myself exclusively to the reports of the four evangelists who offer the proper and true record. I shall not bring in those things that the apostles taught or intended on their own, since the latter are not historians of their master's teaching but present themselves as teachers. Later, when once we have discovered the actual teaching and intention of Jesus from the four documents of the historians, we shall be able to judge reliably whether the apostles expressed the same teaching and intention as their master.

§ 4

Jesus' discourses in the four evangelists can not only be read through quickly, but we also immediately find the entire content and intention of his teaching expressed and summarized in his own words: 'Repent, and believe in the gospel' [Mark 1:15]. Or, in another place, 'Repent, for the kingdom of heaven is at hand' [Matt. 4:17]. And in another place he says, 'I have come to call sinners to repentance', [Mark 2:17; Matt. 9:13; Luke, 5:32]. Further, 'I must preach the good news of the kingdom of God ... for I was sent for this purpose' [Luke 4:43]. And it is this very thing that impelled John, Jesus' forerunner, to prepare the way for him, 'Repent, for the kingdom of heaven is at hand' [Matt. 3:2]. Both these things, the kingdom of heaven and repentance, are so connected that the kingdom is the goal, while repentance is the means or preparation for this kingdom. By the kingdom that was at hand, announced to the Jews by the gospel or 'joyful news', we understand (to use the Jewish expression) the kingdom of the Christ or Messiah for which the Jews had so long waited and hoped. The matter is self-evident: Since Jesus had come as the Messiah and since John specifically proclaimed this, it is expressed in the figure of speech actually used among the Jews of that day so that, when they heard of the kingdom of heaven that was to come, they understood nothing other than the kingdom of the Messiah. Since Jesus and John do not explain this term in any other way they wanted to have it understood in the familiar and customary meaning. Thus when it is said that the kingdom of heaven is near at hand, that means the Messiah will soon reveal himself and establish his kingdom. When it says believe in the gospel, that is another way of saying, believe in the joyful news of the imminent coming of the Messiah and his kingdom. The people were thus to prepare and make themselves ready through repentance for this now imminent kingdom of the Messiah, that is, by a change in thinking and spirit, in that they leave off wickedness and the tendency to commit it and with all their hearts turn to good and godliness. This demand was not only reasonable in all ages, but also was considered necessary among the Jews for the advent of the Messiah, just as they indeed believe to this present day that it is particularly the lack of repentance and betterment that delays the Messiah's advent, so that if they once were to do the proper penance the Messiah would come immediately. The person who reads and reflects upon all Jesus' words will find that their content applies collectively to these two things: either he describes the kingdom of heaven and commands his disciples to proclaim it, or he shows how men must undergo a sincere repentance and not cling to the sanctimonious nature of the Pharisees.

§ 5

I shall first discuss in somewhat more detail the repentance which Christ preached; here I shall be aided by the memories of my readers, who have heard the New Testament diligently from their youth on. That is, each one will remember how all of Jesus' teaching was concerned with meekness, gentleness, mercy, peaceableness, reconciliation, generosity, the willingness to serve, uprightness, true love and faith in God, prayer, renunciation of all hatred, even of one's enemies, the avoidance of evil desires and vain speech, denial of the self, and especially directed

toward an inwardly active character. Further, it will be recalled
how Jesus declared all outward ceremonies to be a little thing
compared with the great commandments of love of God and of
one's neighbor, without which all other commandments are
useless and how he rebukes and castigates the hypocritical sanctimoniousness of the Pharisees, which they boastfully sought
after in outward trifles while ignoring love and the betterment of
their own hearts. One need but examine the beautiful Sermon
on the Mount [Matt. 5-7], that most explicit of all Jesus'
speeches, and he will be thoroughly convinced that Jesus' sole
intention is man's repentance, conversion, and betterment, insofar as these consist of a true inner and upright love of God, of
one's neighbor, and of all that is good. Accordingly, when he
elsewhere explains the moral law better than had ever been
done, or castigates the hypocrisy of the Pharisees, or defends his
own neglect of the ceremonies of the law, it shows the most
intimate connection with his main teaching. He demonstrates
how up until now the law 'You shall not kill, you shall not
commit adultery, you shall not bear false witness' had been interpreted falsely and narrowly only in respect to gross outward
vices, and in part had even been misused to justify many wicked
deeds. Or he shows how unjustly the right of retaliation had
been used as a pretence for hatred and revenge taken upon one's
enemy; or how hypocritically alms had been bestowed when the
giving of them was loudly trumpeted about. He shows also how
hypocritically prayer had been offered on street corners, or fast-
ing, if one deliberately distorted his demeanor and features. He
squeezes open the festering sores of the Pharisees: they made
their phylacteries and fringes[2] splendidly wide and large, uttered
long prayers, carefully avoided touching unclean things, vigorously washed face and hands, even paid tithes on mint and dill,
and whitewashed the graves of the prophets. Since, however,

---

[2] Cf. Matt. 23:5. 'Phylacteries' contained the strips of parchment on which
Bible verses were written. During prayer these were enclosed in parchment
capsules and were attached by leather straps to the forehead and left arm to
remind the wearer of his duty in fulfilling the law both through his mind and
his heart. Later these were looked upon as a defense against demonic powers
and were worn as amulets. 'Fringes' evidently are the tassels worn by the Jews
on the four corners of their outmost garment. According to Num. 15:38-39
they were to be a reminder of God's commandments. [Rilla]

they were full of spiritual pride, they were ambitious for titles and ranks, foreclosed widows' mortgages, swore falsely and heedlessly, were given to theft and gluttony, and had no scruples against killing the prophets and denying with vain pretence the love owed their parents. Of all this Jesus rightly says that it is straining out gnats while swallowing camels, that is, being careful in minutiae while ignoring the greatest commandments of meekness, love, and mercy—indeed, even annulling God's commandments with subtle and twisted human interpretations and embellishments. Often the Pharisees themselves give Jesus an opportunity to demonstrate the great advantage of moral duties over outward ceremonies. If he is called to account because his disciples do not wash themselves before eating bread, he shows how man is contaminated not only by what goes into his mouth, but also by what comes from his heart: murder, adultery, whoremongering, deceit, guile, and the like [Matt. 15:2; 11:17-19]. If people express amazement that he dines with publicans and sinners, he admonishes them to learn that God has more joy in mercy and the repentance of sinners than in sacrifices. If he is attacked for healing the sick on the Sabbath, or for his disciples' plucking ears of grain on the Sabbath and thus performing a type of manual labor (reaping, specifically), he instructs them that the Sabbath was decreed for man's sake and hence must yield to the law of necessity and love and not prevent man's doing good to his neighbor [Mark 3:2; 2:24, 25, 27; Matt. 12:10, 11, 12].

§ 6

Thus the goal of Jesus' sermons and teachings was a proper, active character, a changing of the mind, a sincere love of God and of one's neighbor, humility, gentleness, denial of the self, and the suppression of all evil desires. These are not great mysteries or tenets of the faith that he explains, proves, and preaches; they are nothing other than moral teachings and duties intended to improve man inwardly and with all his heart, whereby Jesus naturally takes for granted a general knowledge of man's soul, of God and his perfections, salvation after this life, etc. But he does not explain these things anew, much less present them in a learned and extravagant way. To the same extent that he wished to see the law fulfilled and not done away with in respect to his own person, he shows others how the whole law and the prophets hang on these two commandments [Matt. 22:37-40; Mark 12:29-31; Luke 10:27]: that one love God with all his heart, and his neighbor as himself, and that consequently the repentance and improvement of man is contained in this essence of the whole Old Testament. Jesus calls this to the attention of the people when they come to him and ask what they must do to be saved: 'Do that, and you shall live.' He says that salvation depends simply upon one's doing the will of his heavenly father, and he recognizes as brothers all who do such. Even if on that day men would say, 'Lord, Lord! did we not prophesy in your name ... and do many mighty works in your name?' Jesus will still say, 'Depart from me, you evildoers' [Matt. 7:22, 23]. Unlike these are the sheep that he will place on his right hand and the blessed who shall inherit the kingdom, those who have fed the hungry, given drink to the thirsty, lodging to the stranger, clothing to the naked, and who have visited those in prison [Matt. 25:32ff.]. When now he sends his disciples out into all the world to teach he immediately explains what this teaching is to consist of: 'Teach them to observe all that I have commanded you' [Matt. 28:20]. The criterion that he also applies to false prophets is not whether they entertain this or that mistaken opinion, or have a false system, or are heterodox and heretical or cause others to be so, but 'by their works you shall know them'. In his view the false prophets are those who go about in sheep's clothing but who are like ravenous wolves beneath; that is, their sole intent, beneath the guise of love and innocence, is nothing more than to cause harm to other men; further, those who produce such fruits as does a rotten tree, or who fail to do the will of the heavenly father, are evildoers [Matt 7:15-23].

§ 7

I cannot avoid revealing a common error of Christians who imagine because of the confusion of the teaching of the apostles with Jesus' teaching that the latter's purpose in his role of teacher was to reveal certain articles of faith and mysteries that were in part new and unknown, thus establishing a new system of religion, while on the other hand doing away with the Jewish religion in regard to its special customs, such as sacrifices, circumcision, purification, the Sabbath, and other Levitical ceremonies. I am aware, of course, that the apostles, especially Paul, worked at this and that later teachers in part forged more and more mysteries and articles of faith and in part also abandoned the Jewish ceremonies more and more, until eventually Moses' laws were completely done away with and an entirely different religion had been introduced. But I cannot find the least trace of either of these things in all the teachings, sermons, and conversations of Jesus. He urged nothing more than purely moral duties, a true love of God and of one's neighbor; on these points he based the whole content of the law and the prophets and commanded that the hope of gaining his kingdom and salvation be constructed on them. Moreover, he was born a Jew and intended to remain one; he testifies that he has not come to abolish the law, but to fulfill it. He simply points out that the most essential thing in the law does not depend upon external things. The further remarks that he makes about the immortality and salvation of the soul, the resurrection of the body to face judgment, the kingdom of heaven and the Christ or Messiah who was promised in Moses and the prophets, were both familiar to the Jews and in accord with the Jewish religion of that day, and were especially aimed at his intention of establishing such a kingdom of heaven among them as their Messiah, thus bringing about the blessed condition, both in religion and in external things, for which they had long since been given cause to hope. In order that this may be more clearly understood I shall show in more detail two aspects of Jesus' teaching: (1) that he proposed no new mysteries or articles of faith, and (2) that he had no intention of doing away with the Levitical ceremonial law.

§ 8

Now, as far as the first is concerned, that Jesus taught no new mysteries or articles of faith or undertook to teach them, I can refer to a considerable extent to what has already been said, from which there is sufficient evidence that Jesus considered the goal of all his work as a teacher to be repentance and the preaching of an upright, active character. But it is also remarkable that when Jesus demands faith of a person he always specifies certain precepts that one should believe in and accept as true. Of course, it would be an absurd and blind faith that would refer to specific precepts with which believers themselves were unfamiliar. They would be required to believe and would not know themselves what they were to believe. The faith that Jesus demands is simply trust in him; thus in most passages of his discourses he refers to his miraculous power: 'Do you believe that I am able to do this?' [Matt. 9:28]. 'O woman, great is your faith!' [Matt. 15:28]. 'Do not fear, only believe' [Mark 5:36; Luke 8:50]. 'Not even in Israel have I found such faith ... be it done for you as you have believed' [Matt. 8:10,13; Luke 7:9]. Jesus saw their faith when they brought the paralytic to him [Matt. 9:2; Mark 2:5; Luke 5:20]. 'Your faith has made you well' [Matt. 9:22; Mark 5:34; Luke 8:48]. 'If you have faith as a grain of mustard seed, you will move mountains' [Matt. 17:20]. At times this faith or this trust refers to Jesus as the Messiah. 'When the Son of man comes, will he find faith on earth?' [Luke 18:8], that is, that one may trust in him to establish the kingdom of the Messiah? 'Repent and believe in the gospel' [Mark 1:15], that is, hope and trust in the joyful news that the kingdom of God, the kingdom of the Messiah, is near at hand. 'Do you believe in the Son of man?' said Jesus to the man who was born blind. 'Sir', he said, 'who is he, that I may believe in him?' Jesus said, 'It is he who speaks to you' [John 9:35-37]. Hence, do not worry because you have been expelled from the synagogue: I shall soon found a different kingdom, simply have faith. 'He who believes (in the gospel) and is baptized will be saved; but he who does not believe will be condemned' [Mark 16:16], that is, whoever hopes and trusts that the joyful news of the true kingdom of the Messiah will soon be fulfilled and prepares himself for it by the baptism of repentance, will be saved. This trust is obviously the faith that Jesus demands; no other point of belief or precept is to be found in his discourses. Thus it came about also that the catechism and the creed were so short in the first Christian church. They needed only to believe the gospel or to have confidence that Jesus would soon found the kingdom of God; if in addition they demonstrated repentance they were baptized and were full-fledged Christians. Now since there were many among the Jews who were waiting for the kingdom of God, it was no wonder that several thousand became believers on one day, indeed in a few hours, people to whom nothing more had been announced than that Jesus was the promised prophet and had been proved as such before all the people through deeds and miracles and his resurrection.

§ 9

This catechism is very short, consisting of only one article. And yet we do not even find anywhere in Jesus' discourses that he explains or demonstrates this one main article of the promised Messiah and his kingdom; rather, he merely assumes a common knowledge of the Jews arising from the promises of the prophets according to the interpretation then current. Thus Jesus says as little as John about who or what Christ or Messiah is, or the kingdom of God, the kingdom of heaven, or the gospel. They say simply: The kingdom of heaven or the gospel is near at hand. Jesus sends his disciples out precisely to preach the gospel, but he says nothing about what the kingdom of heaven is to consist of, what the promise was based on, or what the intention of the kingdom was; thus he simply refers to the common belief and hope in such matters. And when Jesus elsewhere describes the kingdom of heaven in parables (it is like a man who sowed good seed on his ground, a grain of mustard seed, leavened dough, a hidden treasure, a merchant who sought fine pearls, a net, a king who would settle accounts with his servant, a house- holder who employs workmen in his vineyard, a king who ar- ranged a wedding for his son), it certainly does not help make the picture much clearer; and if we did not know from the writings of the Jews something more about what then was the idea of the Messiah, the kingdom of heaven, or the kingdom of God, this main article would still be very obscure and unintelli- gible to us. At times Jesus explains his parables, especially to his disciples, and then adds that to them alone it is given to know the secrets of the kingdom of God [Matt. 13:11; Mark 4:11; Luke 8:10]. But since these secrets consist merely of an explana- tion of figurative concepts and the explanation, insofar as it is stripped of parable, in turn contains nothing more than the common knowledge of the promised kingdom of God under the Messiah, one must confess that no really new or incomprehensible precepts are to be found among these secrets. Take note from this, to what extent people let themselves be deceived by words! Today we are accustomed to understanding by the word 'faith' or 'gospel' the whole body of Christian doctrine that we are to believe, or all the articles of the Christian faith in their interconnection, the entire catechism and the creed, and we particularly call 'mysteries' those doctrines that surpass understanding and that are neither to be understood or proved by reason alone. When a person later comes to a reading of the New Testament with such catechetic concepts of the words 'faith', 'gospel', 'mysteries', and finds that Jesus demands belief in the gospel, the phrase makes him think of the whole body of present-day Christian catechetic instruction with all its articles and mysteries that he learned as a child and has become accustomed to, and then he thinks that Jesus meant such a body of doctrine and demanded that it be believed if one wishes to be saved. The above, however, demonstrates that by 'faith in the gospel' Jesus simply meant a trusting in him and in the news that he had proclaimed, that now under him the kingdom of the Messiah was to begin, and that by 'mysteries' he understood the parables about this kingdom, insofar as they were not immediately clear to the common man, but needed some explanation.

Sections 10 to 33 of Part I of Reimarus's discussion are a demonstration that later Christian doctrines, such as the Incarnation and the Trinity, are not to be found in Jesus' teaching. Jesus himself did not claim divine status; his claims remain 'within the bounds of human nature'. Neither did Jesus abolish the ceremonial law of Judaism or seek to introduce any new beliefs or ceremonies to the religion of his own time and people. The Last Supper, for instance, was simply a normal Passover meal. Nor is it likely that Jesus intended his message to go beyond the Jews. Reimarus summarizes these findings in the paragraphs which follow, and then goes on to discuss the meaning of the phrase 'the Kingdom of God'. He argues that this can only represent the hope of a temporal kingdom, a hope that was shared by the disciples, who will change their doctrine only after Jesus' death.

§ 28

Thus we have discussed everything which Jesus ordained and taught which must be believed concerning his kingdom. And if on account of what happened in this part of Jesus' life we simply stay with the report of the four historians or evangelists, we cannot in the least see that Jesus either intended to alter and abolish the Jewish religion and customs ordained in the law, or that he intended to preach new doctrines and mysteries in its place or introduce new ceremonies along with a new religion. Rather, it is much more evident that Jesus himself and his disciples were all full-fledged Jews and that for his own part he taught only that the Jews be truly converted and devote themselves to a better righteousness than the external and hypocritical righteousness of the Pharisees. All his sermons, teachings, and admonitions concentrate on this vital essence and this piety within the heart, and were all stated as parables which even the simplest hearer could grasp and which everyone enjoyed hearing. Thus it is demonstrated in fact that the one part of Jesus' teaching may be summarized briefly in the single word 'repent'. Now we must examine the other part of his teaching which is expressed as a major goal of the foregoing: 'For the kingdom of heaven is near at hand.'

§ 29

The kingdom of heaven for which the repentance thus preached was to be a preparation and a means, and which therefore contained the ultimate purpose of Jesus' undertaking, is not explained by him at all, neither as to what it is nor what it consists of. The parables that he uses about it teach us nothing or certainly not very much if we do not already have some idea that we can connect with the phrase: it is like a sower, a grain of mustard seed, unleavened dough, a hidden treasure, a net, a merchant seeking good pearls, etc. We conclude from this that the term must have been quite clear to the Jews of that day and that Jesus referred to it thus; hence, there is no other way for us to find out what Jesus' intention was concerning the kingdom of heaven than to concern ourselves with the usual meaning of this phrase among the Jews of the time. But in addition to the New Testament other Jewish writings teach us that by 'kingdom of heaven' they understand generally not only the kingdom that God as king established among the Jews and by means of the law, but especially that kingdom that he will reveal much more gloriously under the Messiah. The *Targum* concerning Micah 4:7 explains the passage where in the last days (i.e., in the Jews' speech, in the time of the Messiah) all heathen will come to Jerusalem to the God of Israel and the Lord will be king over them upon Mount Zion forever: the kingdom of heaven will be revealed to them on Mount Zion. Similarly the *Jalkut schimoni*,[3] folio 178, column 1, explains another passage, Zechariah 14:9, which the Jews likewise understand as referring to the time of the Messiah: the time will come when the kingdom of heaven will be revealed. But without referring a great deal to rabbinical writings the New Testament itself makes this meaning perfectly clear to us. For who were those who waited for the kingdom of God except those awaiting the coming and revelation of the Messiah? What sort of kingdom near at hand did John, as a forerunner of Jesus, intend to proclaim except the kingdom of the Messiah? How do the Pharisees understand it otherwise when they ask Jesus in Luke 17:20, 'When is the kingdom of God coming?' or the disciples when they hoped that now he would soon establish his kingdom? The key to this expression is as follows. Since God, according to the Hebrew expression, dwells in heaven and since to the Jews heaven means the same thing as God himself, the kingdom of heaven and the kingdom of God are one and the same thing. Similarly, since the name Father meant the heavenly Father specifically to the Jews and especially so to Jesus, the latter understood specifically by the kingdom of his Father this kingdom of heaven or kingdom of the Messiah which he associates with God or with the heavenly Father to the extent that it would be established by God and

---

[3] *Jalkut Schimoni* [*Yalkut Shimoni*] is a summary of interpretations of the entire Hebrew Bible, consisting of more than fifty writings, some of which are now lost. The summary was apparently made in the thirteenth century by one Simeon of Frankfurt on Main. [Rilla]

God would be supreme in it, although he would have given all power to the Messiah. Thus when Jesus everywhere preached that the kingdom of God and the kingdom of heaven had drawn near and had others preach the same thing, the Jews were well aware of what he meant, that the Messiah would soon appear and that his kingdom would commence. For it was Israel's hope, waiting in longing since the days of oppression and captivity and according to the words of their prophets, that an anointed one or Messiah (a king) would come who would free them from all afflictions and establish a glorious kingdom among them. This Jewish prophecy was known even to the heathen, and to the Jews of that day the time that should be fulfilled had grown long. Thus the proclamation of the kingdom must be the most joyful news or gospel that they could hear. Consequently, 'to preach the gospel' means simply to spread the joyful news that the promised Messiah would appear soon and begin his kingdom. 'Believe the gospel' means no more than to believe that the expected Messiah will come soon for your redemption and to his glorious kingdom.

§ 30

Since these words contain the total intention of Jesus and all his teachings and deeds, it really is expressed quite clearly enough, or as the Jews of that day would put it understandably enough. When John or Jesus or his messengers and apostles proclaimed everywhere, 'The kingdom of heaven is near at hand, believe in the gospel', people knew that the pleasant news of the imminent coming of the expected Messiah was being brought to them. But nowhere do we read that John or Jesus or the disciples added anything to this proclamation concerning what the kingdom of God consists of or its nature and condition. Thus the Jews must necessarily have connected with such words about the kingdom of heaven that was near at hand the concept of it that prevailed among them. But the prevailing idea of the Messiah and his kingdom was that he would be a great temporal king and would establish a powerful kingdom in Jerusalem, whereby he would free them of all servitude and make them masters over other peoples. This was incontestably the general understanding of the Messiah among the Jews and this was the concept that they created among themselves whenever there was mention of the Messiah's coming and of his kingdom. Accordingly, wherever the Jews believed this gospel, where the coming of the kingdom of heaven was proclaimed to them without further explanation of the term, they were bound to expect a temporal Messiah and a temporal kingdom, in accordance with their ideas. Traces of such expectation are seen clearly and often in the words of the disciples and apostles themselves, who had proclaimed this kingdom to others. They quarreled about who would be greatest in this kingdom of heaven, and even though all twelve of them, to be sure, were to sit on twelve thrones to judge the twelve tribes of Israel, yet one of them wishes to sit at the right hand of Jesus the Messiah and another on the left [Mark 10:37; Matt. 19:28; Luke 22:30]. That is, they want to be next in importance to the Messiah and have the most to say, bearing in their minds that this kingdom of God was to be revealed immediately. Now it is good to observe that long before this these disciples of Jesus had received from him the commandment, 'And preach as you go, saying, "The kingdom of heaven is at hand"' [Matt. 10:7]. They had then actually scattered throughout Judea and had gone by twos into all the cities, schools, and homes to preach and to proclaim that the kingdom of heaven was near at hand, after which they returned to Jesus. But naturally nobody can teach people a doctrine and idea different from what he himself knows and believes. Thus since Jesus' disciples as heralds of the kingdom of heaven, not only on that occasion but even long afterwards, were thinking of a temporal kingdom of the Messiah they proclaimed just this in all the cities, schools, and homes of Judea. Thus all Judea got the impression from the disciples that Jesus intended to establish a temporal kingdom. Indeed and what is more, these apostles even after Jesus' death speak in the same way of his intention and plan. 'We had hoped that he (Jesus of Nazareth) was the one to redeem Israel' [Luke 24:21]. Surely there are a great many remarkable things contained in these few words. First of all, it is evident that they are still thinking in terms of a temporal redemption and of an earthly kingdom that they had hoped from Jesus up until that time. Israel or the Jewish people was to be redeemed, but not the human race. It was a redemption that they had hoped for and that was to take place, but that was not fulfilled and had not happened. Now, if a spiritual redemption by means of a suffering savior were meant, then after Jesus' death it would not be a vain and unfulfilled hope and if this redemption was to have been brought about by means of a Passion, they would not have indicated as the basis of their hope Jesus' manifesting himself powerfully before all the people with words and deeds. Thus it was not a savior of the human race who would expiate the sins of the whole world through his Passion and death, but one who would redeem the people of Israel from temporal servitude, whom they invariably presented in Jesus and of whom they hoped that he would be mighty in words and deeds, so regarded by all the people. And here is where their hope went astray. In this connection we should note further that the two disciples are not speaking of themselves alone, but really are speaking of all *per communicationem* ['in general']. For Cleopas speaks of a familiar story on which depended the hope of all Israel; he speaks especially of those who recognized Jesus as a prophet and of those who are frightened by the news of his resurrection, 'Some women of our company amazed us ... Some of those who were with us went to the tomb' [Luke 24:22,24]. Thus all the apostles, all disciples, men and women, thought this way until Jesus' death—that he would apply his mighty deeds and words to redeem the people of Israel from domination by other peoples and would achieve it with good fortune. In the third place, we should note that this is said of all the disciples after Jesus' death, and that consequently all the disciples had thought of him during his lifetime and until his death as nothing other than a worldly ruler and savior, not considering any other purpose of his teaching and deeds. Thus, the next conclusion for us to draw from this is that only after Jesus' death did the disciples grasp the doctrine of a spiritual suffering savior of all mankind. Consequently, after Jesus' death the apostles changed their previous doctrine of his teaching and deeds and only then for the first time ceased hoping in him as a temporal and powerful redeemer of the people of Israel.

§ 31

The evangelists also are to be reckoned with Jesus' disciples and apostles and thus like all the others share this hope in him. Until Jesus' death they too hoped in him as a temporal savior of the people of Israel. After that event and the failure of this hope they conceived for the first time the doctrine of a spiritual suffering savior of all mankind, thus changing their previous doctrine concerning the intention of his teaching and deeds. Now, all the evangelists wrote their accounts of Jesus' teaching and deeds long after his death, after they had changed their idea and doctrine concerning his teaching and deeds. If a person alters his doctrine and idea of another's teaching and deeds he recognizes or pretends to recognize that up until that point he had incorrectly understood and evaluated that person's teaching and deeds. Thus when he composes his narrative in accordance with the altered doctrine he relates the doctrine and deeds differently than he would have done if he had composed the narrative before changing the doctrine. The words of his narrative are intended to express his present thoughts, not the earlier false ones that he has now rejected. Thus, he omits whatever might lead the reader to construct a doctrine similar to the earlier one that is now rejected, and he introduces in much more detail those things from which his present doctrine is drawn. He tells the teaching and deeds not in such a way and with such connections that they may contain the intention of his previous doctrine, but in such a way and with such connections that they show his present doctrine, unless by accident and because of human carelessness he allows some remnants of the previous doctrine to stand. Thus we must not doubt that the evangelists, who wrote their narratives after they changed their idea and doctrine concerning Jesus' intention as expressed in his teaching and deeds and after they rejected their previous doctrine, would have presented his teaching and deeds quite differently than if they had written during his lifetime and before his death. In Jesus' lifetime the narrative would have been so composed that anyone could clearly read and recognize in it the evangelists' hope of those days that Jesus would bring temporal redemption to Israel. In contrast to this their present narrative could not so clearly express their reasons for constructing the previous and now-rejected doctrine. Since they intended to present in the narrative their altered doctrine they must have omitted zealously the things that led them to their earlier conclusions and must have written into the narrative in some detail the things from which their present doctrine is drawn. Moreover, they must have adapted the style and details of the story unless by accident they had let some remnants of their previous doctrine stand.

§ 32

A reading of the evangelists themselves will show that these conclusions are perfectly justifiable, for there the new doctrine of a suffering spiritual savior is clearly and bluntly stated in Jesus' own words. In contrast, there are so few and obscure traces in Jesus' words and deeds of his intention of becoming Israel's temporal savior that one simply cannot grasp from their present telling of the story how all the disciples would always have been able to arrive at the idea expressed in their previous doctrine or how they could have persisted in it if Jesus actually said what they now relate and if he did or said nothing else that would imply a temporal salvation. It is especially difficult to grasp why, if Jesus had spoken so clearly of his death and resurrection in three days, such a vivid promise would not have been remembered by a single disciple, apostle, evangelist, or woman when he really did die and was buried. Here all of them speak and act as if they had never heard of such a thing in their whole lives; they wrap the corpse in a shroud, try to preserve it from decay and putrefaction by using many spices; indeed, they seek to do so even on the third day after his death, even as the promised time of his resurrection was approaching. Consequently, they know nothing of such a promise; they are thinking only that Jesus is dead and will stay dead and that he will decay and stink like anyone else. They completely abandon all hope of salvation through him and do not show the least trace of any other hope of a resurrection or spiritual redemption. They are amazed and horrified when they find the stone rolled away from the entrance to the tomb; they still think the gardener may have carried the body away when they do not find it there, and even when the women bring news of Jesus' resurrection to the disciples they are as frightened as they would be at an unexpected event and do not want to believe it. Is it possible that each and every disciple could act this way if the last words of their master who was going to his death had contained the great promise of the resurrection on a certain day as clearly as the words now state it? According to their present report Jesus said it so clearly and intelligibly that even the Sanhedrin suspects a trick: 'We remember how this impostor said, while he was still alive, "After three days I will rise again"' [Matt. 27:63, 64]. And they actually go in procession on the Sabbath with a guard of soldiers beyond the gate, seal the stone, and set up a guard of mercenaries 'so that the disciples might not come and steal him and afterwards say he had risen'. If Jesus had so openly proclaimed his resurrection that it had become public knowledge as the report of the evangelists now indicates, then it is utterly incomprehensible that it does not even occur to those disciples to whom he had spoken at more length and to whom it had been given to understand the secret of the kingdom of God. Indeed, if they had had any doubts about the promise then they certainly would have thought of it and would have gone all together on the third day to the tomb expecting the thing that even their enemies are supposed to have suspected, to see if he would fulfill his promise and really would rise. But not one of them even thinks of it; they go to the tomb in order to prepare him for his eternal rest in the grave. And what is most significant, they do not even think of the guard keeping watch at the tomb; they go as if they were going to a tomb not barred to them and where the difficulty would be how to roll away the stone from the entrance, not how they would be denied entrance by the guards. Here the guard disappears and the disciples themselves not only fail to think of Jesus' resurrection but also do not even know that the Sanhedrin had reckoned publicly with this resurrection promised by Jesus. Now, if an evangelist in those few days after Jesus' death had been supposed to write down the story of Jesus' deeds and words, how could these narratives have been added concerning his announced redemption by extreme suffering, concerning his resurrection to be expected in three days, and concerning the excitement that this promise had aroused in the whole city? Undoubtedly, since they themselves no longer believed in a redemption and had not thought of a resurrection and acted as if not even the least detail of the care generally shown by the caution of the Sanhedrin had taken place, all of that would have been excluded from their Gospel. On the other hand, since of course there must have been a reason why *all* the disciples *throughout* Jesus' lifetime until his death had hoped in Jesus as a temporal savior of Israel, their telling of the story of Jesus according to their former doctrine would doubtless show us the bases for holding such a persistently unchanging idea and hope. Consequently, since the evangelists changed their doctrine of Jesus' teaching and deeds they added things that they would have omitted previously and omitted things that they would have added previously, and have done this concerning the most important matters upon which their whole new doctrine rests.

§ 33

Since the story of Jesus as told by the disciples differs in its most important points according to the change in doctrine; since the disciples speak of things taking place that are the mainstays of their new doctrine and which they could not possibly have known about before the change; and since they omit other things that they must necessarily have thought of before the change, the new doctrine is not controlled by history, but just the opposite. That is, as long as they had Jesus' actual words and deeds before them they hoped that he would redeem Israel temporally, and their doctrine was based on actual fact. Now, however, that their hope is disappointed, in a few days they alter their entire doctrine and make of Jesus a suffering savior for all mankind; then they change their facts accordingly and Jesus must now say and promise during his lifetime things that they could not have known of before. Indeed, the whole council must also have acted in the same way. Now, where the doctrine is not controlled by the history but vice versa, both history and doctrine are to this extent unfounded; the history because it is not taken from events themselves and the experiences and reminiscences thus brought about, but is told as having happened simply so that it will agree with the new and altered hypotheses or the new doctrine, and the doctrine because it refers to facts that originated in the writers' thinking only after the doctrine was altered and which were simply fabricated and false. Accordingly, to the extent that from the dual and completely altered behavior of Jesus' disciples and especially the evangelists anything can be concluded concerning the actual intention of Jesus in his words and deeds, we can think only that their first doctrine had been based on an intended temporal redemption of Israel and that they invented another doctrine concerning his intention, namely, of his becoming a suffering spiritual savior of men, only when their hopes had been disappointed after his death, and that they afterwards composed the narrative of his words and deeds. Consequently, this story and this doctrine are unfounded and false to this extent.

Part II continues and develops the arguments outlined in Part I. Reimarus argues that the gospels have been rewritten in the light of the disciples' new claim that Jesus was the suffering saviour of humanity. For this reason the original beliefs of Jesus and the disciples can be glimpsed only here and there in the accounts as we have them. Reimarus compares and contrasts the old belief of Jesus and the disciples with the new doctrine put forward after Jesus's death. To test if the new doctrine could have any basis in fact, he analyses the resurrection accounts (the material of Fragment VI), to see if these are trustworthy. He concludes that they are contradictory in many places and therefore unreliable. No legal case today could be established on such conflicting testimony. Nor are the Old Testament passages cited in support of the resurrection any more convincing: the New Testament use of these passages involves distorting their true meaning or offering arguments which are no more than begging the question. As to what really happened, Reimarus argues that the accusation mentioned in Matthew's gospel was probably true: the disciples came and stole Jesus' body to lend support to their new claims. As for the disciples' claim that Jesus would soon return in glory, this was taken from existing Jewish beliefs about the Messiah, and was soon proven to be untrue. Reports of alleged miracles, too, are useless as evidence for the truth of Christianity, since they are at least as doubtful as that they are being used to support. Therefore the new claims made by the disciples after Jesus' death are nothing but 'an intentional, deliberate fabrication'. Reimarus concludes by offering his own reconstruction of the way in which this fraud was perpetrated, in the paragraphs which follow.

Part II

§ 54

After the death of Jesus, great anxiety and fear prevailed among the disciples lest they should be pursued and punished, because they had followed a man who wanted to set himself up as a king, and had incited the people to rebellion. And although they pretended to be so brave and to wish to share danger and death with Jesus, yes, even to be ready to fight with swords for him, they became cowards from the moment they saw that he was taken and likely to be condemned in earnest. 'Then all the disciples forsook him and fled' [Matt. 26:56]; and Peter who had summoned up courage enough to look on from a distance to see what the end of the disturbance might be, denied his master three times, and declared with an oath that he knew him not and knew nothing about him, because, you see, matters were running quite contrary to the desired object. Their twelve seats upon which they meant to sit and judge in the kingdom of Jesus were all at once over-turned, and they no longer desired to sit at his right and at his left!

The alarm of the apostles lasted for some time after the death of Jesus. They left it to Joseph and Nicodemus and the women to attend to his burial, and kept away even from their last duties. They assembled in secret places, locking the doors for fear of the Jews, for their common wants and interests made it advisable that they should hold together and keep of the same mind. By and by, one after another ventures abroad. They find that no further judicial inquiry is being made concerning them. They observe that the magistrates and rulers, after the execution of Jesus as the principal offender, consider his followers of little importance, and trouble themselves no more about them; perhaps also could not take further steps before Pilate. So they soon pluck up their courage, and begin to think of dangers overcome and future prospects of happiness. What was to be done? If they returned to their original occupations and trades, nothing but poverty and disgrace awaited them. Poverty, because they had forsaken all, particularly their nets, ships, and other implements; and, besides, they had grown out of the habit of working. And disgrace, because they had experienced such a tremendous downfall from their high and mighty expectations, and by their adherence to Jesus had become so familiar to all eyes, that everybody would have jeered and pointed at the pretended judges of Israel and intimate friends and ministers of the Messiah, who now had again become poor fishermen and perhaps even beggars. Both of these (poverty and disgrace) being exactly the opposite of their constant and long cherished hopes were highly irritating and repugnant. On the other hand, they had imbibed, while with their master, a little foretaste of the importance to be gained by preaching, and had likewise ascertained that it was not an unremunerative occupation. Jesus himself had nothing. The oldest accounts of him state that he maintained himself by some trade up to the time of his ministry. However, in the thirtieth year of his life, he lays his trade aside and begins to teach. This would by no means necessitate want or starvation, although it did not promise a comfortable income, which, indeed, was not customary with the Jews, who would be all the more prodigal of charitable gifts. When he sojourned at Jerusalem a friend was sure to invite him to be his guest. From this also the saying arose that he was 'a glutton and a drunkard, a friend of tax collectors and sinners' [Matt. 11:19]. It is remarkable, too, that there were many Marthas who put themselves to a vast deal of trouble and pains to prepare delectable dishes for him. When he traveled, he was accompanied by such benevolent women as Mary Magdalene, Joanna, the wife of Chusa, Herod's steward, Susanna, and several others who ministered unto him of their substance, as we are told by Luke [8:1-3]. He was, therefore, provided not only with food but also with money; and Judas, who carried the purse, was the cashier who bought and paid for everything requisite on the journey, and rendered an account of the outlay.

Whenever Jesus had his meals, the disciples did eat with him. Whenever Jesus traveled, their expenses were paid out of the common purse, so that the kind gifts which were bestowed

upon Jesus during his ministry were sufficient for the maintenance of at least thirteen people. And once, as if to ascertain
whether want could be felt in such a course of life, some of the
disciples were sent abroad through all the towns of Judea to an-
nounce the kingdom of God, without purse or script, and when
on their return they were asked whether they had on any occasion suffered from hunger or want, they answered that they had
never experienced either. The apostles then were very well
aware that preaching, and particularly announcing the Messiah,
would not do them any harm, and would not reduce them to
beggary. It was the same with the honor and glory. They had
seen that crowds of people ran after Jesus to listen to his teaching. They themselves had also been to some extent honored and
looked up to by the multitude, because as they were the confi-
dential disciples and allowed to know more than others, their
master had drawn a line between them and the people. They
had also had a little foretaste of honor and glory when they went
about as ambassadors and messengers of the Messiah, announcing
the kingdom of heaven. Above all, they knew how much influence a teacher could gain among the Jews, because the Pharisees, who were the most important and influential of the teachers, had substituted many of their own laws and sayings for those
of the prophets, and had accustomed the people to accept them
blindly. Such influence and importance might rise considerably
if at a time when prophecies and miracles had ceased, someone
were to come forward and pretend to receive divine revelations
and perform miracles, and the highest flight of all could be taken
by one who turned to account the universal expectation of a
Messiah, whose speedy return he would teach the people to
look for, and make them believe that he carried the keys of the
kingdom of heaven. Such is human nature! He who can persuade people and lead them to believe that he can show them
the way to everlasting bliss, a way that others do not know, or
from which all others are shut out, but also a way that he can
close as well as open, becomes thereby master over all else that
man holds dear; over his thoughts, his freedom, his honor, and
his fortune, for everything sinks into insignificance compared
with this great and darling hope!

If we may be allowed to take a premonitory glance at the af-
ter-conduct of the apostles, the sequel shows that they really did
tread in the paths leading to influence and aggrandizement, and
gleaned from them as much power over the minds of ignorant
people as they possibly could. They write to them jointly, as
well as in their council, dictating to all in the name of the Holy
Spirit not only what they are to believe, but also what they are
to do and what they are to avoid, and what they are to eat and
drink. They compel, they threaten, they give people over to
Satan; they appoint bishops, presidents, and elders; they force
people to sell all their property and lay the proceeds at their feet,
so that those to whom the lands belonged must henceforth be
dependent on their charity; to say nothing of others who had no
possessions of the kind, and looked entirely to the beneficent
hands of the apostles for support. Where they could not manage
to introduce this commonwealth, they knew how to urge the
collection of alms with so much religious zeal, that it was considered a small thing for anyone to divide his worldly wealth
with those through whom he had become a participator in
heavenly and spiritual wealth.

§ 55

The apostles, then, had learned by the little foretaste aforemen-
tioned, that by preaching and announcement of the kingdom of
the Messiah, not only a sufficient maintenance, but also power,
honor, and glory were attainable. They also possessed enough
sense (as their future behavior shows) to turn all these things to
the very best advantage. No wonder then that their courage did
not entirely leave them upon the first failure of their hopes of
worldly wealth and power in the Messiah's kingdom, and that
by a bold stroke they succeeded in paving a new way to them.

§ 56

We have already remarked that at that time some of the Jews,
though very few, believed in a twofold coming of the Messiah,
who was first to appear suffering and in misery, and again in
power and glory. This belief exactly suited the purpose of the

apostles. They saw that the game was not yet lost. The expectation of a future Messiah was still universally cherished, and although the Jews had been deceived in such persons as Theudas and Judas Galileus, yet they never ceased to look for a Messiah in others and after a different fashion, as is shown by the later history of the Jews. The apostles could also feel sure that a great many of those who looked upon Jesus as a prophet, mighty in words and deeds, would henceforth catch at this doctrine, and would consider his suffering to have been part of his ministry, and the consequence of his first coming; and would, therefore, believe and expect his glorious second coming from heaven to be all the nearer at hand. Neither could they doubt that many of the former adherents of Jesus, from the same fear of poverty and disgrace which had influenced themselves, would embark in the same boat with them, and would gladly believe whatever the apostles wished, so they could only convince them that they had not been mistaken and deceived. Behind locked doors, and so long as they were unanimous as to their common anxiety, they had good opportunities for deliberating and consulting one with another as to the best method of utilizing their idea to their own advantage. Above all things, it was necessary to get rid of the body of Jesus as speedily as possible, in order that they might say he had arisen and ascended into heaven, and would promptly return from thence with great power and glory. This design of disposing of the body of Jesus was easy to carry out. It lay entombed in a rock situated in Joseph's garden. Both the master and the gardener allowed the apostles to visit the grave by day or by night. They betray themselves by owning that anyone might have secretly removed the body. They bore the accusation made by the rulers and magistrates of having actually done it themselves by night, and nowhere did they dare to contradict the common report. In short, all circumstances combine to show that they really did carry out their undertaking, and added it later on to the foundation stone of their new doctrine. It appears in the sequel, also, that they were not very long about it, for they made away with the corpse in little more than twenty-four hours, before corruption had well set in; and when it became known that the body of Jesus was gone, they pretended to be full of astonishment, and ignorant of any resurrection, and proceeded with others to the spot in order to survey the empty tomb. As yet, it was too soon to make their assertion. They wait a full fifty days before they attempt it, so that by and by the time might be past for an examination of the body, and for requiring them to produce openly the Jesus who had arisen. They wait fifty days that they may be able the more confidently to insist that they have seen him here and there, that he had been with them, had spoken to them, had eaten with them, and, lastly, had parted from them, and had ascended into heaven that he might soon return in glory.

§ 57

What chance of success could they promise themselves by such an undertaking? Decidedly a good one. No one could now accuse them manifestly of fraud or falsehood. The *corpus delicti* was not to be found, and even if anyone should come and point out that it was somewhere to be found, more than fifty days had passed over since the death of Jesus, and decay must have done its work. Who would be able to recognize him now, and say, 'This is the body of Jesus'? The lapse of time secured them from detection, and made investigation useless. It also helped them to tell crowds of people how often and in what manifold ways he had appeared to them in the meanwhile, and what he had said to them; so that they could teach and arrange whatever seemed most desirable, as though they were doing it according to the sayings and commands of Jesus; and if anyone after the fifty days should happen to ask, 'Where is this Jesus who has arisen? Show him to me', the answer was all ready, 'He has now ascended into heaven'. All depended on showing a bold front, and in affirming confidently that they had seen Jesus, had spoken with him, felt him, eaten and walked with him; and in these declarations they were all unanimous.

Such evidence could not easily be rejected, because truth, according to law, consisted in the evidence of two or three witnesses, and here there were eleven who stated one and the same thing. The resurrection in itself was not incredible to the greater mass, that is to say, to the Pharisees; and the people, who believed that others had been raised from death by the prophets,

consequently were forced to allow the possibility of the resurrection of Jesus in accordance with their own doctrine. The
apostles, or rather Paul, as the cleverest of them, knew how to
turn this to account for his defense and acquittal in a masterly
style, when he stood upon his trial before the council. In order
to set the Pharisees and Sadducees (who both sat in judgment) at
each other's throats and thereby to escape, he pretended at the
time not to lay any particular stress upon the resurrection of Jesus, but he distorted the accusation brought against him, making
it appear as though it referred to a common dogma. When he
stood before the judges at Jerusalem and 'Paul perceived that
one part were Sadducees and the other Pharisees, he cried out in
the council, "Brethren, I am a Pharisee, a son of Pharisees; with
respect to the hope and the resurrection of the dead I am on
trial." And when he had said this, a dissension arose between the
Pharisees and the Sadducees; and the assembly was divided ...
Then a great clamor arose; and some of the scribes of the Pharisees' party stood up and contended, "We find nothing wrong in
this man. What if a spirit or an angel spoke to him"' [Acts
23:6-7, 9]. Paul speaks afterwards in the same manner at Cae-
sarea before the governor, 'Let these men themselves say what
wrongdoing they found when I stood before the council, except
this one thing which I cried out while standing among them,
"With respect to the resurrection of the dead I am on trial before you this day"' [Acts 24:20-21]. He speaks again in the same
way before King Agrippa, and rebukes the Jews in his presence,
'Why is it thought incredible by any of you that God raises the
dead?' [Acts 26:8]. What he meant was, 'Why, it is your own
confession of faith that there is a resurrection of the dead! There
are examples of it in the Scriptures.' Paul knew how to catch the
Jews with their own dogmas; and when he comes upon the particular resurrection of Jesus, he has recourse to a *bath qol*, a voice
which had called to him from heaven. Now for such a *bath qol*,
at that time, all honor was felt, so they were perforce bound to
show it due respect: 'If a spirit or an angel has spoken to him, let
us not fight against God' [Acts 23:9].

In a similar way the apostles often have recourse to heavenly
voices, the Holy Spirit, angels, visions, ecstasies as high up as the

third heaven, whenever they want to give force to their pretences.

Those who still entertained regard and esteem for the person of Jesus, and who had heard of his many miracles, and of his having even reawakened people from death, were all the more ready to believe that he had himself arisen from the dead. The apostles had besides learned from their master how to perform miracles, or rather how to give the semblance of them to spectators, and I have shown elsewhere that it requires no skill whatever to relate miracles, or even to perform them, so there be plenty of confederates to assist by dexterity of speech and hand, especially where one deals with a people accustomed from youth up to believe in miracles. The apostles took pains to strengthen this readiness to believe, by recommending and urging the faith as an advantageous and a saving one, and denouncing unbelief by damnation. And when there was a question of proof, they had Moses and all the prophets to back them; for having acquired all the tricks of allegorical adaptation, it was not difficult for them to find passages applicable to Jesus as Messiah, to his birth, to his flight into Egypt, his sojourn at Nazareth, his deeds, his miracles, his crucifixion, burial, resurrection, ascension, second coming, and, in short, to anything else they wanted.

This pharisaical art of reasoning was, in those days, looked upon as displaying the greatest cleverness, the deepest science, and, in short, as irresistible; where conviction was lacking, the apostles inclined people's minds to faith by the promise of rich rewards on the speedy return of Jesus to his glorious kingdom. For this kingdom, according to the opinion of the Jews and early Christians, was not to be merely an invisible kingdom of spiritual wealth in heaven, which probably would have made less impression, but it was to be a visible kingdom lasting a thousand years upon earth, in which people were to eat and drink and live as before, only everything was to be in profusion, pleasure and happiness were to be boundless, and all enemies conquered and kept in subjection. Such promises could not fail to touch the senses. Such bright representations dazzle the desires (and thereby the mind) to such a degree that people utterly neglect and despise all investigation, all searching after truth, and even present interests in the lively hope of a future abundance of wealth and happiness. In this way the apostles found opportunities of persuading many to give up their money and property to the common use for the sake of the immense reward awaiting them hereafter. This was a savings bank in which everyone with whatever little fortune he possessed strove to buy shares in the speedily expected kingdom of heaven; and the division of these properties into alms enabled the apostles not only to exchange their poverty for affluence, but to allure to them thousands of poor people by relieving their immediate wants and promising them future plenty.

Reimarus concludes his discussion by showing how the new message created by the disciples was spread and became firmly established in the Jewish and Roman world. It is in this way that the life of the Christian church begins.

2

History and Myth

David Friedrich Strauss (1808-74)

A century after the time of Reimarus, David Friedrich Strauss wrote with appreciation of his predecessor's work, noting that the eighteenth century had needed a radical break with the supernaturalist traditions of biblical interpretation. Reimarus's *Apology* had provided that break, and Strauss was happy to occupy the territory which had been cleared by his predecessor's bold assault. Yet, if Reimarus had cleared the ground, Strauss intended to build on it. His interpretation of the Gospels stood in opposition, on the one hand, to the traditional claim that these were accurate historical reports and, on the other, to the idea that they were the product of a deliberate deception. Strauss's claim was that much of what we find in the Gospels is neither history nor deception but 'myth' and needed to be interpreted accordingly.

Strauss's scholarly career was in many ways a tragic one. Born in the town of Ludwigsburg in the German province of Württemberg the young Strauss received his earliest education at his local school and at a preparatory school for ministerial candidates in nearby Blaubeuren. In 1825 he gained admission to the Lutheran seminary at the University of Tübingen, where he and his colleagues began their study with classical philology and philosophy. During the following years of his theological training, Strauss studied under Ferdinand Christian Baur (1792-1860), although at an early stage of the latter's distinguished career. Baur introduced his students to the philosophy of Friedrich Schleiermacher (1768-1834), but Strauss's attention was particularly attracted by the work of the great idealist philosopher G.W.F. Hegel (1770-

1831). After graduating in 1830 Strauss spend a short time in parish ministry before undertaking further studies in Berlin (where he managed to meet Hegel in person, shortly before the latter's death). In 1832 he returned to the Tübingen seminary as an instructor in philosophy. It was there that he wrote the first edition of his *Life of Jesus Critically Examined*, published in 1835. As Albert Schweitzer would later remark, the book 'rendered him famous in a moment—and utterly destroyed his prospects'. He lost his post in Tübingen and taught classical languages for a short time in a secondary school. An appointment in 1839 to a chair of theology in Zurich was thwarted when his opponents arranged a popular petition which resulted in the overturning of the decision. It was at this time that Strauss produced his major theological work, entitled *The Doctrine of the Christian Faith* (1840-41), but shortly after this he turned away from theology and wrote on politics, music, and literature. An ill-advised marriage broke up in 1847, and a short-lived political career was equally unsuccessful. In 1864 Strauss returned to biblical scholarship, with the publication of his *Life of Jesus for the German People*, which recapitulated many of his previous views but also offered a reconstruction of Jesus' life and work. Strauss also published in 1865 an attack on the Christology of Friedrich Schleiermacher entitled *The Christ of Faith and the Jesus of History*. In his last work, *The Old Faith and the New*, published in 1872, Strauss asks, with great honesty, 'Are we still Christians', and comes to the conclusion that he could only reply 'No'. In a way which is consistent with that conclusion he leaves instructions that his funeral is to be an entirely secular affair, marked by no prayers or Christian ceremonies.

In his *Life of Jesus Critically Examined,* Strauss has not yet arrived at his final estrangement from Christianity. Throughout the work he engages with two sets of opponents, but with Reimarus's more radical critique never far from his mind. His two sets of opponents he describes as the supernaturalists and the rationalists. The supernaturalists were those who held to the traditional Christian view: the history of Israel was set apart from that of any other people by the immediate involvement of God in the events narrated by the Bible. For the supernaturalists, therefore, accounts of miraculous divine actions were to be accepted as literally true, indeed guaranteed as true by the inspired status of the Scriptures. The naturalists, on the other hand, shared the eighteenth century's scepticism of miracles, but wished to maintain that the biblical narratives were accurate historical reports. They reconciled these two positions by arguing that the events narrated in the Bible actually occurred, but that they had natural causes. It was only the ignorance of the witnesses which led them to be reported as miraculous events. Thus, for instance, the voice from heaven at Jesus' baptism was in fact a clap of thunder and Jesus himself fed the multitude, not by divine power, but by inspiring them to share what they had with one another. Strauss rejects both positions, and in their place he substitutes what he describes as the 'mythical interpretation'.

For Strauss believed, not only that the supernaturalist and naturalist positions were untenable, but that Reimarus's accusation of fraud sprang from an anachronistic reading of history. The disciples did not belong to an age of cool and sober reason, but to an age of unquenchable religious enthusiasm. There was no need to assume that behind the discredited claims of the Gospel there lay an act of deliberate deception. Rather, the new message about Jesus was the product of the disciples' religious imagination, an imagination which clothed spiritual truths in narrative form. The clothing of religious truths in narrative garb Strauss described as the formation of 'myth', and it is this insight which represents Strauss's lasting contribution to the world of biblical scholarship. It was the task of the modern interpreter to understand the process by which this had occurred and then to separate once again the religious message from the rather naïve terms in which that message is expressed.

The following extracts come from the fourth edition of Strauss's *Life of Jesus Critically Examined*, published in 1840, and translated by Mary Ann Evans (better known as the novelist George Eliot). The first readings come from the introduction to the book, and trace the development in Christian history of something resembling the 'mythical interpretation' of the Gospels which Strauss is about to put forward. For Strauss argues that his understanding of myth resembles the allegorical interpretations of ancient Jewish and patristic exegesis. The figures singled out here are the great first-century Jewish scholar, Philo of Alexandria (ca. 20 BCE–50 CE), and the early Christian interpreter Origen (ca. 185–254 CE). Strauss sees Origen as a figure of particular significance, since he is occasionally prepared to hold to an allegorical interpretation at the expense of the literal.

The Life of Jesus Critically Examined

§ 3
Allegorical Interpretations among the Hebrews—Philo

Whilst, on the one hand, the isolation and stability of the Hebrews served to retard the development of similar manifestations amongst this people, on the other hand, when once actually developed, they were the more marked; because, in proportion to the high degree of authority ascribed to the sacred records, was the skill and caution required in their interpretation. Thus, even in Palestine, subsequent to the exile, and particularly after the time of the Maccabees, many ingenious attempts were made to interpret the Old Testament so as to remove offensive literalities, supply deficiencies, and introduce the notions of a later age. Examples of this system of interpretation occur in the writings of the Rabbins, and even in the New Testament;[1] but it was at that place where the Jewish mind came into contact with Greek civilization, and under its influence was carried beyond the limits of its own national culture—namely at Alexandria—that the allegorical mode of interpretation was first consistently applied to

---

[1] Döpke, *Die Hermeneutik der neutestamentlichen Schriftsteller*, 123ff.

the whole body of historical narrative in the Old Testament. Many had prepared the way, but it was Philo who first fully developed the doctrine of both a common and a deeper sense of the Holy Scriptures. He was by no means inclined to cast away the former, but generally placed the two together, side by side, and even declared himself opposed to those who, everywhere and without necessity, sacrificed the literal to the higher signification. In many cases, however, he absolutely discarded the verbal meaning and historical conception, and considered the narrative merely as the figurative representation of an idea. He did so, for example, whenever the sacred story appeared to him to present delineations unworthy of Deity, tending either to materialism or anthropomorphism, or otherwise to contain contradictions.[2]

The fact that the Jews, whilst they adopted this mode of explaining the Old Testament, (which, in order to save the purity of the intrinsic signification, often sacrificed the historical form), were never led into the opposite system of Evemerus (which preserved the historical form by divesting the history of the divine, and reducing it to a record of mere human events), is to be ascribed to the tenacity with which that people ever adhered to the supernatural point of view. The latter mode of interpretation was first brought to bear upon the Old Testament by the Christians.

§ 4
Allegorical Interpretations among the Christians—Origen

To the early Christians who, antecedent to the fixing of the christian canon, made especial use of the Old Testament as their principal sacred record, an allegorical interpretation was the more indispensable, inasmuch as they had made greater advances beyond the views of the Old Testament writers than even the most enlightened of the Jews. It was no wonder therefore that this mode of explanation, already in vogue among the Jews, was almost universally adopted by the primitive christian churches. It

---

[2] Gfrörer. Dähne.

was however again in Alexandria that it found the fullest application amongst the Christians, and that in connexion with the
name of Origen. Origen attributes a threefold meaning to the
Scriptures, corresponding with his distribution of the human
being into three parts: the literal sense answering to the body;
the moral, to the soul; and the mystical, to the spirit.[3] The rule
with him was to retain all three meanings, though differing in
worth; in some particular cases, however, he was of opinion that
the literal interpretation either gave no sense at all, or else a perverted sense, in order the more directly to impel the reader to
the discovery of its mystical signification. Origen's repeated observation that it is not the purpose of the biblical narratives to
transmit old tales, but to instruct in the rules of life;[4] his assertion
that the merely literal acceptation of many of the narratives
would prove destructive of the christian religion,[5] and his application of the passage 'The letter killeth, but the spirit giveth
life',[6] to the relative worth of the allegorical and the literal
modes of biblical interpretation, may be understood as indicating
only the inferiority of the literal to the deeper signification. But
the literal sense is decidedly given up when it is said, 'Every
passage of Scripture has a spiritual element, but not every one
has a corporeal element';[7] 'A spiritual truth often exists embod-

---

[3] Homil. 5. in Levit. § 5.

[4] Homil. 2. in Exod. iii: *Nolite putare, ut saepe jam diximus, veterum vobis
fabulas recitari, sed doceri vos per haec, ut agnoscatis ordinem vitae* ['Do not think, as
we have often said already, that tales of the ancients are being recited to you,
but (rather) that you are being taught through these things, that you may recognize the pattern of life.' I have been unable to find the quotation which
Strauss cites here, but at the beginning of the homily to which he refers we
find this comment: *Sed nos, qui omnia quae scripta sunt, non pro narrationibus an-
tiquitatum, sed pro disciplina et utilitate nostra scripta didicimus...* 'But we, who have
learned that all the things which have been written (were) written, not (to
recount) the tales of the ancients, but for our instruction and to be useful to
us...' The phrase *sicut saepe iam dicimus* is found near the beginning of Homily
5 on Leviticus (see following note).]

[5] Homil. 5. in Levit. i.: *Haec omnia, nisi alio sensu accipiamus quam literae
textus ostendit, obstaculum magis et subversionem Christianae religioni, quam hortatio-
nem aedificationemque praestabunt.* ['Unless we accept them in a sense other than
the text of the letter shows, all these things would offer more of an obstacle to
the Christian religion and its subversion than exhortation and edification.']

[6] *Contra Cels.* vi. 70.

ied in a corporeal falsehood';[8] 'The Scriptures contain many things which never came to pass, interwoven with the history, and he must be dull indeed who does not of his own accord observe that much which the Scriptures represent as having happened never actually occurred.'[9] Among the passages which Origen regarded as admitting no other than an allegorical interpretation, besides those which too sensibly humanised the Deity[10] he included those which attributed unworthy action to individuals who had held intimate communion with God.[11]

It was not however from the Old Testament views alone that Origen had, in consequence of his christian training, departed so widely that he felt himself compelled, if he would retain his reverence for the sacred records, to allegorize their contents, as a means of reconciling the contradiction which had arisen between them and his own mind. There was much likewise in the

---

[7]*De princpp.* L. iv. ß 20: πᾶσα μὲν (γραφὴ) ἔχει τὸ πνευματικὸν, οὐ πᾶσα δὲ τὸ σωματικόν ['All (Scripture) has the spiritual (sense), but not all has the bodily.']

[8] *Comm. in Joann.*, Tom. x. §4: σωζομένου πολλάκις τοῦ ἀλπθοῦς [*sic*; read: ἀληθοῦς] πνευματικοῦ ἐν τῷ σωματικῷ ὡς ἄν εἴποι τις, ψεύδει. ['... often the true spiritual (sense) being preserved in the bodily—as one might say—falsehood'].

[9] *De princpp.* iv. 15: συνύφηνεν ἡ γραφὴ τῇ ἱστορίᾳ τὸ μὴ γενόμενον, πῆ [*sic*; read: πῇ] δὲ δύνατον μὲν γενέσθαι, οὐ μὴν γεγενημένον. ['The Scripture wove together with the history that which did not occur, in one place that which is not able to occur, in another that which is able to occur, but certainly did not.'] *De princpp.* iv. 16: καὶ τί δεῖ πλείω λέγειν; τῶν μὴ πάνυ ἀμβλέων μυρία ὅσα τοιαῦτα δυναμένων συναγαγεῖν, γεγραμμένα [*sic*; read: ἀναγεγραμμένα] μὲν ὡς γεγονότα, οὐ γεγενημένα δὲ κατὰ τὴν λέξιν. ['And what more is it necessary to say? Those who are not altogether dull are able to infer a great number of things of this sort, written down as if they occurred, but (which) have not occurred in the manner related.']

[10] *De princpp.* iv. 16.

[11] Homil. 6, in Gen. iii.: *Quae nobis aedificatio erit, legentibus, Abraham, tantam patriarcham, non solum mentitum esse Abimelech regi, sed et pudicitiam conjugis prodidisse? Quid nos aedificat tanti patriarchae uxor, si putetur contaminationibus exposita per conniventiam maritalem? Haec Judaei putent et si qui cum eis sunt literae amici, non spiritus.* ['What edification will it be to us to read that Abraham, so great a patriarch, not only lied to Abimelech the king but betrayed the chastity of his spouse? In what way would the wife of so great a patriarch edify us, if she were thought to be exposed to contamination through marital connivance? Let the Jews think these things and those who with them are friends of the letter, not the spirit.']

New Testament writings which so little accorded with his philosophical notions, that he found himself constrained to adopt a similar proceeding in reference to them. He reasoned thus:—the New Testament and the Old are the work of the same spirit, and this spirit would proceed in the same manner in the production of the one and of the other, interweaving fiction with reality, in order thereby to direct the mind to the spiritual signification.[12] In a remarkable passage of his work against Celsus, Origen classes together, and in no ambiguous language, the partially fabulous stories of profane history, and of heathen mythology, with the gospel narratives.[13] He expresses himself as follows: 'In almost every history it is a difficult task, and not unfrequently an impossible one, to demonstrate the reality of the events recorded, however true they may in fact be. Let us suppose some individual to deny the reality of a Trojan war on account of the incredibilities mixed up with the history; as, for example, the birth of Achilles from a goddess of the sea. How could we substantiate the fact, encumbered as it is with the numerous and undeniable poetical fictions which have, in some unascertainable manner, become interwoven with the generally admitted account of the war between the Greeks and the Trojans? There is no alternative: he who would study history with understanding, and not suffer himself to be deluded, must weigh each separate detail, and consider what is worthy of credit and may be believed without further evidence; what, on the contrary, must be regarded as merely figurative; (τίνα δὲ τροπολογήσει ['and what, on the contrary, he will interpret figuratively']) always bearing in mind the aim of the narrator—and what must be wholly mistrusted as being written with intent to please certain individuals.' In conclusion Origen says, 'I was desirous of making these preliminary observations in relation to the entire

---

[12] *De principp.* iv. 16: οὐ μόνον δὲ περὶ τῶν πρὸ τῆς παρουσίας ταῦτα τὸ πνεῦμα ᾠκονόμησεν, ἀλλ᾽, [*sic*; read: ἀλλὰ γὰρ] ἅτε τὸ αὐτὸ τυγχάνον καὶ ἀπὸ ἑνὸς θεοῦ, τὸ ὅμοιον καὶ ἐπὶ τῶν εὐαγγελίων πεποίηκε καὶ ἐπὶ τῶν ἀποστόλων, οὐδὲ τούτων πάντη ἄκρατον τὴν ἱστορίαν τῶν προσυφασμένων κατὰ τὸ σωματικόν ἐχόντων μὴ γεγενημένων ['The Spirit arranged these things, not only regarding the (books) before the coming (of Christ), but, as it is the same (Spirit) and from the one God, has done a similar thing regarding the gospels and the apostles, not even these having a history altogether unmixed with interwoven matters (which) according to the bodily (sense) did not occur.']
[13] *Contra Celsum*, i. 40 [*sic*; read: 42].

history of Jesus given in the Gospels, not with the view of ex-
acting from the enlightened a blind and baseless belief, but with
design to show how indispensable to the study of this history are
not only judgment and diligent examination, but, so to speak,
the very penetrating into the mind of the author, in order to
discover the particular aim with which each narrative may have
been written.'

We here see Origen almost transcending the limits of his
own customary point of view, and verging towards the more
modern mythical view. But if his own prepossessions in favour
of the supernatural, and his fear of giving offence to the orthodox church, combined to hinder him from making a wider application of the allegorical mode of interpretation to the Old
Testament, the same causes operated still more powerfully in
relation to the New Testament; so that when we further inquire
of which of the gospel histories in particular did Origen reject
the historical meaning, in order to hold fast a truth worthy of
God? the instances will prove to be meagre in the extreme. For
when he says, in illustration of the above-mentioned passage,
that amongst other things, it is not to be understood literally that
Satan showed to Jesus all the kingdoms of the earth from a
mountain, because this is impossible to the bodily eye; he here
gives not a strictly allegorical interpretation, but merely a different turn to the literal sense, which, according to him, relates not
to an external fact, but to the internal fact of a vision. Again,
even where the text offers a tempting opportunity of sacrificing
the literal to the spiritual meaning, as, for example, the cursing
of the fig-tree,[14] Origen does not speak out freely. He is most
explicit when speaking of the expulsion of the buyers and sellers
from the temple; he characterizes the conduct of Jesus, according to the more literal interpretation, as assuming and seditious.[15]
He moreover expressly remarks that the Scriptures contain many
more historical than merely scriptural truths.[16]

---

[14] *Comm. in Matth.*, Tom. xvi. 26.

[15] *Comm. in Joann.*, Tom. x. 17.

[16] *De princip.* iv. 19. After Origen, that kind of allegory only which left
the historical sense unimpaired was retained in the church; and where, subsequently, a giving up of the verbal meaning is spoken of, this refers merely to a
trope or a simile.

In the passages which follow his discussion of Philo and Origen, Strauss surveys the differing approaches to the interpretation of the Bible in modern times, from the Deists and Naturalists of the 17th and 18th century, through the work of Reimarus, to that of the Rationalists. He devotes a short discussion to the understanding of Jesus found in the work of Immanuel Kant (1724-1804), before turning to the origins of the approach he himself favours, namely the mythical interpretation. After looking at some early discussions of myth (Strauss uses the Latin term *mythus*) within the broader study of religions and cultures, he goes on to defend the use of this term with regard to the Gospels. In the section reproduced below Strauss discusses how one might distinguish Gospel material which is 'mythical' from that which may still be considered 'historical'. The criteria are both negative and positive. Negatively, an account may be regarded as mythical, firstly when it describes events which contradict the known laws by which the world operates, and secondly when it is internally inconsistent or irreconcilable with other accounts. Positively, an account may be thought of as mythical, firstly when it portrays characters as speaking in a more elevated style than one might expect in similar situations, and secondly when it depicts scenes which seem to have been shaped by existing religious exemplars (such as the Old Testament stories). After adding some qualifications, Strauss offers illustrations of the application of these principles, drawn particularly from the accounts of the birth and infancy of Jesus.

§16
Criteria by which to Distinguish the Unhistorical in the Gospel Narrative

Having shown the possible existence of the mythical and the legendary in the Gospels, both on extrinsic and intrinsic grounds, and defined their distinctive characteristics, it remains in conclusion to inquire how their actual presence may be recognised in individual cases?

The mythus presents two phases: in the first place it is not history; in the second it is fiction, the product of the particular mental tendency of a certain community. These two phases afford the one a negative, the other a positive criterion, by which the mythus is to be recognised.

I. *Negative.* That an account is not historical—that the matter related could not have taken place in the manner described is evident,

First. When the narration is irreconcilable with the known and universal laws which govern the course of events. Now according to these laws, agreeing with all just philosophical conceptions and all credible experience, the absolute cause never disturbs the chain of secondary causes by single arbitrary acts of interposition, but rather manifests itself in the production of the aggregate of finite causalities, and of their reciprocal action. When therefore we meet with an account of certain phenomena or events of which it is either expressly stated or implied that they were produced immediately by God himself (divine apparitions—voices from heaven and the like), or by human beings possessed of supernatural powers (miracles, prophecies), such an account is *in so far* to be considered as not historical. And inasmuch as, in general, the intermingling of the spiritual world with the human is found only in unauthentic records, and is irreconcilable with all just conceptions; so narratives of angels and of devils, of their appearing in human shape and interfering with human concerns, cannot possibly be received as historical.

Another law which controls the course of events is the law of succession, in accordance with which all occurrences, not excepting the most violent convulsions and the most rapid changes, follow in a certain order of sequence of increase and decrease. If therefore we are told of a celebrated individual that he attracted already at his birth and during his childhood that attention which he excited in his manhood; that his followers at a single glance recognized him as being all that he actually was; if the transition from the deepest despondency to the most ardent enthusiasm after his death is represented as the work of a single hour; we must feel more than doubtful whether it is a real history which lies before us. Lastly, all those psychological laws, which render it improbable that a human being should feel, think, and act in a manner directly opposed to his own habitual mode and that of men in general, must be taken into considera-

tion. As for example, when the Jewish Sanhedrim are represented as believing the declaration of the watch at the grave that
Jesus was risen, and instead of accusing them of having suffered
the body to be stolen away whilst they were asleep, bribing
them to give currency to such a report. By the same rule it is
contrary to all the laws belonging to the human faculty of memory, that long discourses, such as those of Jesus given in the
fourth Gospel, could have been faithfully recollected and reproduced.

It is however true that effects are often far more rapidly produced, particularly in men of genius and by their agency, than
might be expected; and that human beings frequently act in-
consequently, and in opposition to their general modes and
habits; the two last mentioned tests of the mythical character
must therefore be cautiously applied, and in conjunction only
with other tests.

Secondly. An account which shall be regarded as historically
valid, must neither be inconsistent with itself, nor in contradiction with other accounts.

The most decided case falling under this rule, amounting to a
positive contradiction, is when one account affirms what another denies. Thus, one gospel represents the first appearance of
Jesus in Galilee as subsequent to the imprisonment of John the
Baptist, whilst another Gospel remarks, long after Jesus had
preached both in Galilee and in Judea, that 'John was not yet
cast into prison.'

When on the contrary, the second account, without absolutely contradicting the first, differs from it, the disagreement
may be merely between the incidental particulars of the narrative; such as *time*, (the clearing of the Temple,) *place*, (the original residence of the parents of Jesus;) number, (the Gadarenes,
the angels at the sepulchre;) *names*, (Matthew and Levi;) or it
may concern the essential substance of the history. In the latter
case, sometimes the character and circumstances in one account
differ altogether from those in another. Thus, according to one
narrator, the Baptist recognizes Jesus as the Messiah destined to
suffer; according to the other, John takes offence at his suffering
condition. Sometimes an occurrence is represented in two or
more ways, of which one only can be consistent with the reality;

as when in one account Jesus calls his first disciples from their nets whilst fishing on the sea of Galilee, and in the other meets them in Judea on his way to Galilee. We may class under the same head instances where events or discourses are represented as having occurred on two distinct occasions, whilst they are so similar that it is impossible to resist the conclusion that both the narratives refer to the same event or discourse.

It may here be asked: is it to be regarded as a contradiction if one account is wholly silent respecting a circumstance mentioned by another? In itself, apart from all other considerations, the argumentum ex silentio is of no weight; but it is certainly to be accounted of moment when, at the same time, it may be shown that had the author known the circumstance he could not have failed to mention it, and also that he must have known it had it actually occurred.

II. *Positive.* The positive characters of legend and fiction are to be recognized sometimes in the form, sometimes in the substance of a narrative.

If the form be poetical, if the actors converse in hymns, and in a more diffuse and elevated strain than might be expected from their training and situations, such discourses, at all events, are not to be regarded as historical. The absence of these marks of the unhistorical do not however prove the historical validity of the narration, since the mythus often wears the most simple and apparently historical form: in which case the proof lies in the substance.

If the contents of a narrative strikingly accords with certain ideas existing and prevailing within the circle from which the narrative proceeded, which ideas themselves seem to be the product of preconceived opinions rather than of practical experience, it is more or less probable, according to circumstances, that such a narrative is of mythical origin. The knowledge of the fact, that the Jews were fond of representing their great men as the children of parents who had long been childless, cannot but make us doubtful of the historical truth of the statement that this was the case with John the Baptist; knowing also that the Jews saw predictions everywhere in the writings of their prophets and poets, and discovered types of the Messiah in all the lives of holy men recorded in their Scriptures; when we find details in the life of Jesus evidently sketched after the pattern of these prophecies and prototypes, we cannot but suspect that they are rather mythical than historical.

The more simple characteristics of the legend, and of additions by the author, after the observations of the former section, need no further elucidation.

Yet each of these tests, on the one hand, and each narrative on the other, considered apart, will rarely prove more than the possible or probable unhistorical character of the record. The concurrence of several such indications, is necessary to bring about a more definite result. The accounts of the visit of the Magi, and of the murder of the innocents at Bethlehem, harmonize remarkably with the Jewish Messianic notion, built upon the prophecy of Balaam, respecting the star which should come out of Jacob; and with the history of the sanguinary command of Pharaoh. Still this would not alone suffice to stamp the narratives as mythical. But we have also the corroborative facts that the described appearance of the star is contrary to the physical, the alleged conduct of Herod to the psychological laws; that Josephus, who gives in other respects so circumstantial an account of Herod, agrees with all other historical authorities in being silent concerning the Bethlehem massacre; and that the visit of the Magi together with the flight into Egypt related in the one Gospel, and the presentation in the temple related in another Gospel, mutually exclude one another. Wherever, as in this instance, the several criteria of the mythical character concur, the result is certain, and certain in proportion to the accumulation of such grounds of evidence.

It may be that a narrative, standing alone, would discover but slight indications, or perhaps, might present no one distinct feature of the mythus; but it is connected with others, or proceeds from the author of other narratives which exhibit unquestionable marks of a mythical or legendary character; and consequently suspicion is reflected back from the latter, on the former. Every narrative, however miraculous, contains some details which might in themselves be historical, but which, in consequence of their connexion with the other supernatural incidents, necessarily become equally doubtful.

In these last remarks we are, to a certain extent, anticipating the question which is, in conclusion, to be considered: viz., whether the mythical character is restricted to those features of the narrative, upon which such character is actually stamped; and whether a contradiction between two accounts invalidate one account only, or both? That is to say, what is the precise boundary line between the historical and the unhistorical?—the most difficult question in the whole province of criticism.

In the first place, when two narratives mutually exclude one another, one only is thereby proved to be unhistorical. If one be true the other must be false, but though the one be false the other may be true. Thus, in reference to the original residence of the parents of Jesus, we are justified in adopting the account of Luke which places it at Nazareth, to the exclusion of that of Matthew, which plainly supposes it to have been at Bethlehem; and, generally speaking, when we have to choose between two irreconcilable accounts, in selecting as historical that which is the least opposed to the laws of nature, and has the least correspondence with certain national or party opinions. But upon a more particular consideration it will appear that, since one account is false, it is possible that the other may be so likewise: the existence of a mythus respecting some certain point, shows that the imagination has been active in reference to that particular subject; (we need only refer to the genealogies;) and the historical accuracy of either of two such accounts cannot be relied upon, unless substantiated by its agreement with some other well authenticated testimony.

Concerning the different parts of one and the same narrative: it might be thought for example, that though the appearance of an angel, and his announcement to Mary that she should be the Mother of the Messiah, must certainly be regarded as unhistorical, still, that Mary should have indulged this hope before the birth of the child, is not in itself incredible. But what should have excited this hope in Mary's mind? It is at once apparent that that which is credible in itself is nevertheless unhistorical when it is so intimately connected with what is incredible that, if you discard the latter, you at the same time remove the basis on which the former rests. Again, any action of Jesus represented as a miracle, when divested of the marvellous, might be thought to exhibit a perfectly natural occurrence; with respect to some of the miraculous histories, the expulsion of devils for instance, this might with some limitation, be possible. But for this reason alone: in these instances, a cure, so instantaneous, and effected by a few words merely, as it is described in the Gospels, is not psychologically incredible; so that, the essential in these narratives remains untouched. It is different in the case of the healing of a man born blind. A natural cure could not have been effected otherwise than by a gradual process; the narrative states the cure to have been immediate; if therefore the history be understood to record a natural occurrence, the most essential particular is incorrectly represented, and consequently all security for the truth of the otherwise natural remainder is gone, and the real fact cannot be discovered without the aid of arbitrary conjecture.

The following examples will serve to illustrate the mode of deciding in such cases. According to the narrative, as Mary entered the house and saluted her cousin Elizabeth, who was then pregnant, the babe leaped in her womb, she was filled with the Holy Ghost, and she immediately addressed Mary as the mother of the Messiah. This account bears indubitable marks of an unhistorical character. Yet, it is not, in itself, impossible that Mary should have paid a visit to her cousin, during which everything went on quite naturally. The fact is however that there are psychological difficulties connected with this journey of the betrothed; and that the visit, and even the relationship of the two women, seem to have originated entirely in the wish to exhibit a connexion between the mother of John the Baptist, and the mother of the Messiah. Or when in the history of the transfiguration it is stated, that the men who appeared with Jesus on the Mount were Moses and Elias: and that the brilliancy which illuminated Jesus was supernatural; it might seem here also that, after deducting the marvellous, the presence of two men and a bright morning beam might be retained as the historical facts. But the legend was predisposed, by virtue of the current idea concerning the relation of the Messiah to these two prophets, not merely to make any two men (whose persons, object and conduct, if they were not what the narrative represents them, remain in the highest degree mysterious) into Moses and Elias, but to create the whole occurrence; and in like manner not merely to conceive of some certain illumination as a supernatural effulgence (which, if a natural one, is much exaggerated and misrepresented), but to create it at once after the pattern of the brightness which illumined the face of Moses on Mount Sinai.

Hence is derived the following rule. Where not merely the particular nature and manner of an occurrence is critically suspicious, its external circumstances represented as miraculous and the like; but where likewise the essential substance and groundwork is either inconceivable in itself, or is in striking harmony with some Messianic idea of the Jews of that age, then not the particular alleged course and mode of the transaction only, but the entire occurrence must be regarded as unhistorical. Where on the contrary, the form only, and not the general contents of the narration, exhibits the characteristics of the unhistorical, it is at least possible to suppose a kernel of historical fact; although we can never confidently decide whether this kernel of fact actually exists, or in what it consists; unless, indeed, it be discoverable from other sources. In legendary narratives, or narratives embellished by the writer, it is less difficult, —by divesting them of all that betrays itself as fictitious imagery, exaggeration, etc.— by endeavouring to abstract from them every extraneous adjunct and to fill up every hiatus—to succeed, proximately at least, in separating the historical groundwork.

The boundary line, however, between the historical and the unhistorical, in records, in which as in our Gospels this latter element is incorporated, will ever remain fluctuating and unsusceptible of precise attainment. Least of all can it be expected that the first comprehensive attempt to treat these records from a critical point of view should be successful in drawing a sharply defined line of demarcation. In the obscurity which criticism has produced, by the extinction of all lights hitherto held historical, the eye must accustom itself by degrees to discriminate objects with precision; and at all events the author of this work, wishes especially to guard himself in those places where he declares he knows not what happened, from the imputation of asserting that he knows that nothing happened.

Our final extract comes from Strauss's Concluding Dissertation, in which he discusses 'The Dogmatic Import of the Life of Jesus'. Here he addresses the issue of what Christians might continue to believe about Jesus once the critical examination of the Gospels is complete. Strauss outlines and rejects the Christology of historic, orthodox Christianity, before looking at the Christological formulations offered by the Rationalists. These, too, he rejects, because they cannot do justice to the demands of Christian faith. The Christology of Schleiermacher is also examined and rejected, as is the interpretation of Christ in terms of a simple religious ideal. Finally Strauss comes to his own interpretation, which sees in the doctrine of the Incarnation a symbol of the union of the divine Spirit and humanity which is brought about, not (as Christian faith traditionally maintained) in a particular individual, but in the spiritual development of humanity as a whole. In this respect Strauss is particularly influenced (as he himself notes) by the philosophy of Hegel.

§ 150
The Speculative Christology

Kant had already said that the good principle did not descend from heaven merely at a particular time, but had descended on mankind invisibly from the commencement of the human race; and Schelling laid down the proposition: the incarnation of God is an incarnation from eternity.[17] But while the former understood under that expression only the moral instinct, which, with its ideal of good, and its sense of duty, has been from the beginning implanted in man; the latter understood under the incarnate Son of God the finite itself, in the form of the human consciousness, which in its contradistinction to the infinite, wherewith it is nevertheless one, appears as a suffering God, subjected to the conditions of time.

In the most recent philosophy this idea has been further developed in the following manner.[18] When it is said of God that

---

[17] *Vorlesungen über die Methode des akademischen Studiums*, 192.
[18] Hegel's *Phänomenologie des Geistes*, 561ff., *Vorlesungen über die Philos. der Relig.* 2, 234ff. Marheineke, *Grundlehren der christl. Dogmatik.* 174ff. Rosenk-

he is a Spirit, and of man that he also is a Spirit, it follows that
the two are not essentially distinct. To speak more particularly, it
is the essential property of a spirit, in the distribution of itself
into distinct personalities, to remain identical with itself, to possess itself in another than itself. Hence the recognition of God as
a spirit implies, that God does not remain as a fixed and immutable Infinite encompassing the Finite, but enters into it, produces the Finite, Nature, and the human mind, merely as a limited manifestation of himself, from which he eternally returns
into unity. As man, considered as a finite spirit, limited to his
finite nature, has not truth; so God, considered exclusively as an
infinite spirit, shut up in his infinitude, has not reality. The infinite spirit is real only when it discloses itself in finite spirits; as
the finite spirit is true only when it merges itself in the infinite.
The true and real existence of spirit, therefore, is neither in God
by himself, nor in man by himself, but in the God-man; neither
in the infinite alone, nor in the finite alone, but in the inter-
change of impartation and withdrawal between the two, which
on the part of God is revelation, on the part of man religion.

If God and man are in themselves *one*, and if religion is the
human side of this unity: then must this unity be made evident
to man in religion, and become in him consciousness and reality.
Certainly, so long as man knows not that he is a spirit, he cannot
know that God is man: while he is under the guidance of nature
only, he will deify nature; when he has learned to submit himself to law, and thus to regulate his natural tendencies by external means, he will set God before him as a lawgiver. But when,
in the vicissitudes of the world's history, the natural state discloses its corruptions, the legal its misery; the former will experience the need of a God who elevates it above itself, the latter, of
a God who descends to its level. Man being once mature
enough to receive as his religion the truth that God is man, and
man of a divine race; it necessarily follows, since religion is the
form in which the truth presents itself to the popular mind, that
this truth must appear, in a guise intelligible to all, as a fact obvious to the senses: in other words, there must appear a human
individual who is recognised as the visible God. This God-man

ranz, *Encyklopädie der theol. Wissenschaften*, 38ff, 148ff.; comp. my *Streitschriften*,
3tes. Heft, 76ff.

uniting in a single being the divine essence and the human personality, it may be said of him that he had the Divine Spirit for a
father and a woman for his mother. His personality reflecting
itself not in himself, but in the absolute substance, having the
will to exist only for God, and not at all for itself, he is sinless
and perfect. As a man of Divine essence, he is the power that
subdues nature, a worker of miracles; but as God in a human
manifestation, he is dependent on nature, subject to its necessities and sufferings—is in a state of abasement. Must he even pay
the last tribute to nature? does not the fact that the human nature is subject to death preclude the idea that that nature is one
with the divine? No: the God-man dies, and thus proves that
the incarnation of God is real, that the infinite spirit does not
scorn to descend into the lowest depths of the finite, because he
knows how to find a way of return into himself, because in the
most entire alienation of himself, he can retain his identity.
Further, the God-man, in so far as he is a spirit reflected in his
infinity, stands contrasted with men, in so far as they are limited
to their finiteness: hence opposition and contest result, and the
death of the God-Man becomes a violent one, inflicted by the
hands of sinners; so that to physical degradation is added the
moral degradation of ignominy and accusation of crime. If God
then finds a passage from heaven to the grave, so must a way be
discoverable for man from the grave to heaven: the death of the
prince of life is the life of mortals. By his entrance into the
world as God-man, God showed himself reconciled to man; by
his dying, in which act he cast off the limitations of mortality, he
showed moreover the way in which he perpetually effects that
reconciliation: namely, by remaining, throughout his manifestation of himself under the limitations of a natural existence, and
his suppression of that existence, identical with himself. Inasmuch as the death of the God-man is merely the cessation of his
state of alienation from the infinite, it is in fact an exaltation and
return to God, and thus the death is necessarily followed by the
resurrection and ascension.

The God-man, who during his life stood before his contemporaries as an individual distinct from themselves, and perceptible by the senses, is by death taken out of their sight; he enters
into their imagination and memory: the unity of the divine and

human in him, becomes a part of the general consciousness; and the church must repeat spiritually, in the souls of its members, those events of his life which he experienced externally. The believer, finding himself environed with the conditions of nature, must, like Christ, die to nature—but only inwardly, as Christ did outwardly, —must spiritually crucify himself and be buried with Christ, that by the virtual suppression of his own sensible existence, he may become, in so far as he is a spirit, identical with himself, and participate in the bliss and glory of Christ.

§ 151
The Last Dilemma

Thus by a higher mode of argumentation, from the idea of God and man in their reciprocal relation, the truth of the conception which the church forms of Christ appears to be confirmed, and we seem to be reconducted to the orthodox point of view, though by an inverted path: for while there, the truth of the conceptions of the church concerning Christ is deduced from the correctness of the evangelical history; here, the veracity of the history is deduced from the truth of those conceptions. That which is rational is also real; the idea is not merely the moral imperative of Kant, but also an actuality. Proved to be an idea of the reason, the unity of the divine and human nature must also have an historical existence. The unity of God with man, says Marheineke,[19] was really and visibly manifested in the person of Jesus Christ; in him, according to Rosenkranz,[20] the divine power over nature was concentrated, he could not act otherwise than miraculously, and the working of miracles, which surprises us, was to him natural. His resurrection, says Conradi,[21] is the necessary sequel of the completion of his personality, and so little ought it to surprise us, that, on the contrary, we must rather have been surprised if it had not happened.

---

[19] *Dogmatik,* § 326.

[20] *Encyklopädie,* 160.

[21] *Selbstbewusstsein und Offenbarung,* 29f. Comp. Bauer, 'Recens. des L. J.', *Jahrbücher f. wiss. Kritik,* 1836, Mai, 699ff.

But do these deductions remove the contradictions which have exhibited themselves in the doctrine of the church, concerning the person and work of Christ? We need only to compare the structures, which Rosenkranz in his Review has passed on Schleiermacher's criticism of the Christology of the church, with what the same author proposes as a substitute in his Encyclopaedia, in order to perceive, that the general propositions on the unity of the divine and human natures, do not in the least serve to explain the appearance of a person, in whom this unity existed individually, in an exclusive manner. Though I may conceive that the divine spirit in a state of renunciation and abasement becomes the human, and that the human nature in its return into and above itself becomes the divine; this does not help me to conceive more easily, how the divine and human natures can have constituted the distinct and yet united portions of an historical person. Though I may see the human mind in its unity with the divine, in the course of the world's history, more and more completely establish itself as the power which subdues nature; this is quite another thing, than to conceive a single man endowed with such power, for individual, voluntary acts. Lastly, from the truth, that the suppression of the natural existence is the resurrection of the spirit, can never be deduced the bodily resurrection of an individual.

We should thus have fallen back again to Kant's point of view, which we have ourselves found unsatisfactory: for if the idea have no corresponding reality, it is an empty obligation and ideal. But do we then deprive the idea of all reality? By no means: we reject only that which does not follow from the premises.[22] If reality is ascribed to the idea of the unity of the divine and human natures, is this equivalent to the admission that this unity must actually have been once manifested, as it never had been, and never more will be, in one individual? This is indeed not the mode in which Idea realizes itself; it is not wont to lavish all its fulness on one exemplar, and be niggardly towards all others[23]—to express itself perfectly in that one individual, and imperfectly in all the rest: it rather loves to distribute

---

[22] Compare with this my *Streitschriften*, 3 Heft, 68ff., 125.

[23] With this should be compared the explanation in the *Streitschriften*, ut sup. 119.

its riches among a multiplicity of exemplars which reciprocally complete each other—in the alternate appearance and suppression of a series of individuals. And is this no true realization of the idea? Is not the idea of the unity of the divine and human natures a real one in a far higher sense, when I regard the whole race of mankind as its realization, than when I single out one man as such a realization? Is not an incarnation of God from eternity, a truer one than an incarnation limited to a particular point of time?

This is the key to the whole of Christology, that, as subject of the predicate which the church assigns to Christ, we place, instead of an individual, an idea; but an idea which has an existence in reality, not in the mind only, like that of Kant. In an individual, a God-man, the properties and functions which the church ascribes to Christ contradict themselves; in the idea of the race, they perfectly agree. Humanity is the union of the two natures—God become man, the infinite manifesting itself in the finite, and the finite spirit remembering its infinitude; it is the child of the visible Mother and the invisible Father, Nature and Spirit; it is the worker of miracles, in so far as in the course of human history the spirit more and more completely subjugates nature, both within and around man, until it lies before him as the inert matter on which he exercises his active power;[24] it is the sinless existence, for the course of its development is a blameless one, pollution cleaves to the individual only, and does not touch the race or its history. It is Humanity that dies, rises, and ascends to heaven, for from the negation of its phenomenal life there ever proceeds a higher spiritual life; from the suppression of its mortality as a personal, national, and terrestrial spirit, arises its union with the infinite spirit of the heavens. By faith in this Christ, especially in his death and resurrection, man is justified before God; that is, by the kindling within him of the idea of Humanity, the individual man participates in the divinely human life of the species. Now the main element of that idea is, that the negation of the merely natural and sensual life, which is

---

[24] Of this also there is an explanation in the *Streitschriften*, 3, 166 f.

itself the negation of the spirit (the negation of negation, therefore), is the sole way to true spiritual life.[25]

This alone is the absolute sense of Christology: that it is an-
nexed to the person and history of one individual, is a necessary
result of the historical form which Christology has taken.
Schleiermacher was quite right when he foreboded, that the
speculative view would not leave much more of the historical
person of the Saviour than was retained by the Ebionites. The
phenomenal history of the individual, says Hegel, is only a
starting point for the mind. Faith, in her early stages, is governed
by the senses, and therefore contemplates a temporal history;
what she holds to be true is the external ordinary event, the evidence for which is of the historical, forensic kind—a fact to be
proved by the testimony of the senses, and the moral confidence
inspired by the witnesses. But mind having once taken occasion
by this external fact, to bring under its consciousness the idea of
humanity as one with God, sees in the history only the presentation of that idea; the object of faith is completely changed;
instead of a sensible, empirical fact, it has become a spiritual and
divine idea, which has its confirmation no longer in history but
in philosophy. When the mind has thus gone beyond the sensible history, and entered into the domain of the absolute, the
former ceases to be essential; it takes a subordinate place, above
which the spiritual truths suggested by the history stand self-
supported; it becomes as the faint image of a dream which belongs only to the past, and does not, like the idea, share the
permanence of the spirit which is absolutely present to itself.[26]
Even Luther subordinated the physical miracles to the spiritual,
as the truly great miracles. And shall we interest ourselves more
in the cure of some sick people in Galilee, than in the miracles

[25] Herein lies the answer to the objection which Schaller (*Der historische
Christus und die Philosophie*, 64ff.) has made to the above view; namely, that it
teaches only a substantial not a personal unity of man with God. That unity
which exists in the determination of the race has already been present in individuals separately, according to the different measure of their religious development, and thus the substantial unity has become, in different degrees, a personal unity.

[26] *Vorlesungen über die Philosophie der Religion*, 2, 263ff. Compare the collection of the several propositions of Hegel on the person of Christ and the evangelical history, in my *Streitschriften*, 3 Heft, 76.

of intellectual and moral life belonging to the history of the world—in the increasing, the almost incredible dominion of man over nature—in the irresistible force of ideas, to which no unintelligent matter, whatever its magnitude, can oppose any enduring resistance? Shall isolated incidents, in themselves trivial, be more to us than the universal order of events, simply because in the latter we presuppose, if we do not perceive, a natural cause, in the former the contrary? This would be a direct contravention of the more enlightened sentiments of our own day, justly and conclusively expressed by Schleiermacher. The interests of pity [*sic*; read 'piety' (*Frömmigkeit*)], says this theologian, can no longer require us so to conceive a fact, that by its dependence on God it is divested of the conditions which would belong to it as a link in the chain of nature; for we have outgrown the notion, that the divine omnipotence is more completely manifested in the interruption of the order of nature, than in its preservation.[27] Thus if we know the incarnation, death and resurrection, the *duplex negatio affirmat* ['double negation affirms'], as the eternal circulation, the infinitely repeated pulsation of the divine life; what special importance can attach to a single fact, which is but a mere sensible image of this unending process? Our age demands to be led in Christology to the idea in the fact, to the race in the individual: a theology which, in its doctrines on the Christ, stops short at him as an individual, is not properly a theology, but a homily.

---

[27] *Glaubenslehre*, I, 47.

3

Consistent Scepticism

William Wrede (1859-1906)

Hermann Samuel Reimarus and David Friedrich Strauss
represent a first stage in the historical Jesus quest. That first
stage involved calling into question the assumption that the
Gospels were accurate reports of Jesus' words and deeds,
which could be called upon in support of the claims of
Christian faith. Reimarus fired the opening salvos, claiming
that the ideas put forward by the disciples after Jesus' death
were quite different from what they had believed during
their Master's lifetime. Strauss effectively agreed, undermining both traditional 'supernaturalist' and modern 'rationalist'
assumptions about the accuracy of the Gospels. He differed
from Reimarus only in his interpretation of these claims, in
particular rejecting Reimarus's assumption that the Gospels as
we have them represent a deliberate act of fraud. For Strauss
the Gospel stories represent, not fraud, but a (for the most
part) unconscious process of mythologization, whereby the
disciples' genuine religious convictions were clothed in the
form of a historical narrative. Yet both Reimarus and Strauss
believed that the Gospels could be used as a historical source.
They assumed that it was possible to sift through the Gospel
material, separating the earlier from the later, the mythical
from the historical, in order to arrive at a reconstruction of
Jesus' life. It fell to William Wrede to call into question even
this assumption.

Wrede was born into a conservative Lutheran family who
lived at Bücken in Hannover, and received his secondary
education in the nearby town of Celle. He began his theo-

logical education at Leipzig, where he soon became disappointed with the dominant school of confessional Lutheran
theology. Along with other liberally-minded students, Wrede
found intellectual stimulation in the company of the young
Adolf von Harnack (1851-1930), at that time beginning his
career in Leipzig. It was under von Harnack's guidance that
Wrede read the theology of Albrecht Ritschl (1822-89), and
this in turn led him to a period of study in Göttingen, where
Ritschl was lecturing. After a short spell teaching in a private
school, Wrede studied at a prestigious Lutheran theological
seminary at Loccum (west of Hannover), from where he
returned to a tutor's post at a theological college in Göttingen. In a way which resembles the theological career of Ernst
Troeltsch, Wrede moved away from Ritschl's position as he
began to view the rise of Christianity in the broader context
of the 'history of religions'. Thus began Wrede's association
with the group of scholars (including Troeltsch, Johannes
Weiss, and Wilhelm Bousset), who would come to be
known as the 'history of religions school'. After a very successful period of parish ministry (from 1886-89), Wrede began his formal university career with a dissertation and
teaching post at Göttingen, from where he was called in
1892 to be associate professor at the University of Breslau
(today Wroclaw in Poland). He worked in Breslau until his
death, publishing the work for which he is best remembered,
The Messianic Secret in the Gospels, in 1901.

The following extracts are taken from that work. The first
deals with the Gospel of Mark, already widely recognized as
the earliest of the four Gospels. Wrede argues that, despite its
priority, the Gospel of Mark cannot be regarded as a reliable
source for the life of Jesus. In other words, one cannot produce a portrait of Jesus by taking Mark's story-line and filling
in the gaps with assumptions about the historical context and
the psychological development of Jesus himself and the disciples. For the Gospel of Mark can only be understood as a
document of faith: it belongs already to the history of Christian dogma. As an author Mark shows no interest in historical
causation or psychological development, but merely presents
early Christian belief about Jesus in the form of a series of in-

dividual stories. These stories have little connection with each other, and Mark himself shows little or no ability to enter imaginatively into the original context of Jesus' life. It is true that the Gospel does take a particular historical context for granted, but this 'warp' of history is so interwoven with a 'weft' of dogmatic considerations that the Gospel as we have it can no longer function as an outline for a reconstruction of the life and work of the historical Jesus.

The Messianic Secret

Reprinted from *The Messianic Secret* William Wrede, copyright ©1971 James Clarke and Co. Ltd. Used by permission of James Clarke and Co.

Mark as an Author

Present-day investigation of the Gospels is entirely governed by the idea that Mark in his narrative had more or less clearly before his eyes the actual circumstances of the life of Jesus, even if not without gaps. It presupposes that he is *thinking from the standpoint of the life of Jesus,* and is motivating the individual features of his story in accordance with the actual circumstances of this life and in accordance with the actual thoughts and feelings of Jesus, and is linking together the events he describes in the historical psychological sense.

This is its criterion for the investigation and criticism of the Gospel in particular. It does, to be sure, assume chronological displacements and inaccuracies in matters of fact, alterations in the wording of pronouncements ascribed to Jesus and even an accretion of later dogmatic views. But everywhere it operates with the psychological necessities and probabilities which existed in the given situations for the persons taking part. This is where it finds its motivation, supplementing the information by the consequences which might naturally be expected to follow from them, and so clothing the skeleton of dry data with flesh.

This view and this procedure must be recognised as wrong in principle. It must frankly be said that *Mark no longer has a real view of the historical life of Jesus.*

In this I am not at all intending to pass judgement on the historical character of the materials I have not examined. These may be entirely disregarded here. What we have inspected more closely is an adequate basis for our verdict.

It is axiomatic that Mark has a whole series of historical ideas, or ideas in a historical form.

Jesus came on the scene as a teacher first and foremost in Galilee. He is surrounded by a circle of disciples and goes around with them and gives instruction to them. Among them some are his special confidants. A larger crowd sometimes joins itself to the disciples. Jesus likes to speak in parables. Alongside his teaching there is his working of miracles. This is sensational and he is mobbed. He was specially concerned with those whose illnesses took the form of demon possession. In so far as he encountered the people he did not despise associating with publicans and sinners. He takes up a somewhat free attitude towards the Law. He encounters the opposition of the Pharisees and the Jewish authorities. They lie in wait for him and try to entrap him. In the end they succeed after he has not only walked on Judaean soil but even entered Jerusalem. He suffers and is condemned to death. The Roman authorities co-operate in this.

We may say that these will be the main features. To them may be added indeed many a detail as to the miracles, the discourses and the locations, and it may be possible to abstract features of significance from them. But for Mark's *view* and thus for his presentation as a whole this is not of importance. For in these questions of detail we are concerned not with actual factors and dominant characteristics of history. In so far as these come under consideration, almost all the ideas are quite general and undefined. On no account can we say that with them a concrete picture of his life is given. We only get the external framework or as I see it a few trivial sketches.

But the real texture of the presentation becomes apparent only when to the warp of these general historical ideas is added a strong thread of thoughts that are dogmatic in quality.[1] In part

---

[1] Cf. also 71ff. [The footnotes are original, although the page references are to the English translation of Wrede's book, to which the reader of this anthology is referred.]

they merge with the historical motifs and in part they stand alongside and between them.

The person of Jesus is dogmatically conceived. He is the bearer of a definite dignity bestowed by God, or, which comes to the same thing, he is a higher supernatural being. Jesus acts with divine power and he knows the future in advance. The motives for his actions do not derive from human peculiarity, human objectives and human necessities. The one pervasive motive rather takes the form of a divine decree lying above and beyond human comprehension. This he seeks to realise in his actions and his suffering. The teaching of Jesus is correspondingly supernatural. His knowledge is such as no man can possess on his own account but he conceals it and conceals his own being because from the beginning his gaze is directed to the point of the whole story, i.e. the resurrection, which is the event that will make manifest for men what is secret. For he is known in the world beyond and already on earth he has a link with that world when he proves his power to the spirits or sees the heavens opening.

But the other main factors of the story are also theologically or dogmatically conceived. The disciples are by nature receivers of the highest revelation and are naturally and indeed by a higher necessity lacking in understanding. The people are by nature non-recipients of revelation, and the actual enemies of Jesus from the beginning are as it were essentially full of evil and contrariety and so far as men come into it bring about the end but thereby also the glory.

These motifs and not just the historical ones represent what actually motivates and determines the shape of the narrative in Mark. They give it its colouring. The interest naturally depends on them and the actual thought of the author is directed towards them. It therefore remains true to say that as a whole the Gospel no longer offers a historical *view* of the real life of Jesus. Only pale residues of such a view have passed over into what is a suprahistorical view for faith. In this sense the Gospel of Mark belongs to the history of dogma.

Exegesis of Mark must therefore take this into account. For in the last resort the formal nature of its presentation of history rests on this. In this respect I shall single out only two features as characteristic.

If one considers together the *different portions* of the account one discovers that in general no internal sequence is provided. Several stories are indeed often held together by the same situation, by a chronological or other type of remark; smaller sections complete in themselves can be isolated; and we even get references back to something said earlier, such as in 6.52, 8.17ff. But on the whole one portion stands next to the other with a piecemeal effect. There is naturally a connection, but it is the connection of ideas and not of historical developments. It could indeed be conceived that Mark might have given a sort of historical life to the dogmatic or semi-dogmatic ideas which he presents formally as historical motifs and that in his own way he might have thought historically in them. For a painfully naïve author of antiquity this is, of course, extremely improbable, and in any event Mark does not do it. We saw that he did not establish any connection between the many kinds of prohibition, the different prophecies about death and resurrection and the various expressions of incomprehension on the part of the disciples. In actual fact he did not think through from one point in his presentation to the next.

It follows from this that we must not draw conclusions from what he says which he has not himself drawn, or establish connections which are not manifest. B. Weiss on one occasion remarks[2] on the statement in 6.14, according to which Jesus' name was also known at the court of Herod, that this was the result of the previous mission of the disciples which had directed attention to Jesus in much wider circles. This remark certainly does not merit special censure, for such connections are made in dozens in the gospels, nor is the example specially glaring. But it is all the more typical for that. At the bottom of such connections there lies a false overall view of the type of authorship that we have in Mark. Not by a single syllable does he indicate that he desires to see two facts brought into connection which he hap-

---

[2] *Das Markusevangelium*, p.213.

pens to tell one after the other. For this reason it is not legitimate to manufacture such a connection.

A second point concerns the *individual accounts* and this is
even more instructive. It is demonstrable that this author *only has
a limited capacity for transposing himself into the historical situation with
which he is dealing*. His presentations of material are of the utmost
brevity. Otherwise it would not be possible for such strange
things, which from a realistic standpoint are quite inconceivable,
to be found in the individual accounts.

There was no difficulty in seeing that the prohibition to
speak about the raising of the young girl could not be imple-
mented.[3] But Mark does not notice this. Here, however, the
inconceivable nature of the item is to an extent concealed
whereas it lies open to our gaze when, following upon the
command to keep quiet, the person healed spreads the news of
his cure. Mark does *not* ask himself what then becomes of the
secret. A similar point presses itself upon us in the passage
1.24-27. Jesus' power over the demons is marvelled at and this
presupposes that those who marvelled were witnesses of the preceding exorcism and so also witnesses of Jesus' conversation with
the demon. But the demon has cried out the secret of the holy
God and according to Mark no-one was to hear this. One can
gain the same impression from 3.11, 12 and this has actually
happened.[4]

Thus Mark seems very quickly to forget his own presuppositions. According to 7.33 Jesus is alone with the deaf-mute but in
7.36 we read: 'and he charged them to tell no-one; but the
more he charged them the more zealously they proclaimed it'.[5]
The second sentence shows that here the disciples are not tacitly
regarded as witnesses. It is certainly not they who proclaim the
miracle. One expedient in dealing with this is to suggest that the
people who bring the sick man to Jesus (verse 32) are not to be
reckoned with the *ochlos* ['crowd'] from which Jesus isolates him
in verse 33. But these are the only people who can be the *ochlos*

---

[3] Cf. above p.50f.

[4] Hilgenfeld, *die Evangelien*, p.131; but also Holtzmann, HC, p.7: the demons proclaim him Messiah before a great crowd.

[5] Br. Bauer in his *Kritik der Evangelien*, III, p.136, has already emphasised
this contradiction.

if verse 33 is explained naturally—or at least they must belong to the *ochlos*. For the text does only say 'taking him aside from the multitude privately'. In reality Mark has displaced the situation introduced at the start. To begin with he is thinking of the sick man as being alone with Jesus. Then, while he does hold on to the idea of isolation, as the prohibition shows, he thinks of the others as being together with the sick man without perceiving that the prohibition to the multitude does not improve matters.

If one takes note of such features then even some earlier expositions which at first sight might strike one as odd will seem justified.

Mark in fact[6] is not, in the story of the blind man at Bethsaida, thinking that the man's house lay outside the *kōmē* ['town'] mentioned in the text. According to 8.23 Jesus has led him out of the town—consequently the town is regarded as his home. Thus we do not here have any data to fill in which Mark does not divulge to us but we have simply to learn that in the way he presents his material he can overlook the simplest conclusions. The house implies isolation. The town implies publicity. Therefore the blind man is supposed to go into his house and not into the town. This is enough for Mark. The further conclusion that the house lies *in* the town is no problem to him.

In the same way it is enough for the evangelist when he says that Jesus concealed himself in Galilee, 9.30. How Jesus began to do thus in the very act of going through Galilee he did not consider. He even quite casually reports that Jesus came to Capernaum, 9.33, on this journey, where according to his own account he was best known. But there too isolation is quickly established in that we are told that Jesus came 'into the house'. In the house he then places a child in the midst of the disciples. How does this come about if he is trying to hide himself? The child suits the *idea*, for Jesus is speaking about wanting to be great: but it does *not* suit the situation.

I would also draw attention to the fact that during the journey Jesus does not go into the discussion of the disciples about the question of who is the greatest but then at once asks in the

---

[6] Cf. p.51.

house, 'What were you discussing on the way?' (verse 33). Mark
does not consider it is possible to give secret instruction even 'on
the way'. 'On the way' is to all appearances, however, the same
for him as 'publicly'. In the same context we had the idea that
Jesus altogether hides himself from the world (9.30f.) in order to
speak of the secret of his suffering, dying and resurrection, to the
disciples. We rejected the supplementation by accommodating
ideas[7] and we adhere to this. Mark is thinking quite simply that
if a secret is to be imparted people are to be avoided. But he
does not notice that the apparatus for the idea he has in mind—
namely, travelling secretly through Galilee—is too elaborate, not
to say too monstrous altogether.

In the individual tales the internal verisimilitude is in many
respects different. But it is not surprising that offence is most
obviously taken in those places where the ideas of the author
which we came to know find particular expression. Mark has in
fact absolutely no other purpose than to enunciate these ideas in
the story. He injects the dogmatic motif offhandedly into the
tale—and he can switch on those lights anywhere he wants. He
is little concerned with how it looks as a historical feature in its
environment. This is his procedure. Those who understand it
will, however, at the same time excuse him. Seen from the historical standpoint Mark contains a whole heap of bad, pointless
features. If one regards as an idea what in fact is an idea one frees
him from this; that is to say, no weight will be laid upon these.
They will perhaps be regarded as understandable concomitants
of a type of authorship which somewhat gauchely tries to fashion history out of ideas.

As to what particularly concerns the idea of the secret, Mark
has expressed it most forcibly in the prohibitions, and, alongside
these, in a whole series of vivid ideas—whether he invented
these himself or found them already in his sources. As such, we
have become familiar with the idea of Jesus' being alone with his
disciples and especially with his confidants; his secret journeying;
his withdrawal from the people into isolation; and his visiting
the house or sending sick people home to their houses. I refer
also to the notes collected together earlier.[8]

---

[7] p.81.
[8] p.53ff.

That most of them belong to this context will no longer now require demonstration. We need have reservations only about the fact that some individual instances of these features such as the representation of withdrawal and of the search for isolation or for the house are also on occasion given a less idealised motivation: Jesus is burdened by the people or his opponents are lying in wait for him.

By way of supplement we may mention here too the climbing of the 'mountain' or of 'a high mountain'. At times this does also seem to be relevant here. After Jesus in 3.12 has pronounced the prohibition he climbs 'the' mountain in 3.13 and here undertakes the choice of his disciples which is, to be sure, solemnly conceived. This mountain is not to be sought on the map. Indeed, exegetes also consider, on account of what happens before this, that we are not to think of a single mountain but rather of mountainous terrain, the uplands as opposed to the seashore. But this is not the meaning of *to oros* ['the mountain']. It is an ideal mountain.[9] The mountain or a mountain is always ready to hand for Mark's use when he needs it, just as is 'a desert place'—*erēmos topos*—and just as is 'the house' or 'a house'. Similar to 3.12 is 9.2, where by the mention of the confidants and the emphasis on his being alone with them the mystery is so strongly emphasised that Jesus led the disciples to a high mountain.[10] Behind this, of course, there may lie the idea that a high mountain is the appropriate place for such a revelation as the Transfiguration, rather than the idea of its being a lonely place. But the two points bear on each other.

All these vivid ideas are scattered by Mark wherever and however he chooses in his presentation. In this one can indeed see very well how he operates. On occasion one also sees that in the teaching of Jesus what is stamped as secret has nothing particularly mysterious about it so far as content is concerned—at all events no more than other material which is imparted to everybody. An instance of this is to be found at 10.10 where he speaks 'specially' to his disciples about divorce, while he has al-

---

[9] Thus Volkmar, to whose discussion on pp.240ff. I refer, without appropriating every single detail of his.

[10] II Peter 1.18, *en tē orei tē agiō* ['on the holy mountain']—an apt explanation of 'the mountain' (Volkmar, p.462).

ready given utterance on the same theme previously to the Pharisees. Here the idea of secret instruction has manifestly become a mannerism.

Perhaps it may be permitted by way of appendix to discuss here a few other isolated passages which become all the more comprehensible at this very point, and which I would be loath to leave out of account.

I refer first of all once again to the passage in 1.32ff. It is uncommonly characteristic. Within short compass the two motifs of secrecy and manifestation alternate three times:

(1) verses 32-34, Jesus is known as a wonder-worker and is mobbed; verses 35-39, he retreats into isolation and into the neighbourhood (in verse 34 we already have the prohibition to the demons);

(2) verse 44, the prohibition to the leper; 45a, the leper makes the news public;

(3) verse 45b, the town is avoided and isolation is sought; however, once again the crowd rushes to him.

Thus the one idea again and again changes into the other. On the first occasion the matter is naturally somewhat veiled. In verse 35 we have it that Jesus prayed in isolation and in verse 38 he provides a motive for his departure into other towns by saying that he has come in order to preach there too. But the idea that he wants to hide himself from the public nonetheless seems to me to lie plainly in the text. We may note how the two ideas of retreat into isolation and looking for other towns have their common element in this idea; how the saying of the disciples ('all seek thee', verse 37) precedes the second notion; and how at verse 35 avoidance of the town and the search for isolation recur. If we are thinking about Jesus' prayer, this is to be looked upon as a motivation which is also current in Mark even if not so much so as in Luke, and which is inserted here as if in an apt place. And the saying about Jesus's vocation to preach elsewhere too, which indeed, on account of the *eis touto gar exēlthon* ['for that I came out'], can be recognised straight away as the retrospective observation of people who came later, is in my view meant only to be to the disciples a plausible reason for Jesus' failure to accede to their request, but leaves open the idea that his real motivation lies in going where he is unknown.

It is also worth noting that in 2.1 Jesus does again come into Capernaum. Of course, the evangelist adds *di' hēmerōn* ['after (some) days'] but this does not make it essentially more natural that Jesus should again seek out the town which he has just avoided. According to verse 39 Jesus is supposed to have visited the synagogues of all Galilee in these 'days'.

There is a second passage in 8.34: 'and he called to him the multitude with his disciples and said to them "If any man would come after me let him deny himself and take up his cross and follow me"'. Why does Jesus call upon the crowd after the scene with Peter and direct such an admonition to them? I am not aware of a satisfying explanation. The following are my suppositions on the subject.

We have here a correlative to the phenomenon that Jesus together with his disciples separates himself from the people and then gives teaching of a mysterious character. The scene containing the confession of Peter and the prophecy of the Passion is thought of as a secret scene. Now just as it has previously been let down through isolation the curtain is again opened with the restoration of contact with the public. This and this alone could be the meaning of the fact that the crowd is mentioned. No success will attend our efforts to discover something which made this speech seem to be the very thing for the crowd. I quote Holtzmann. His view is that emphasis on the readiness to suffer 'as a precondition for any following of him intended for the future' is easier to understand 'in relation to a larger circle of hearers *some of whom still seemed disposed to take the risk with him,* than it would be in relation to such as had already been initiated for a longer time'.[11] This is said on the supposition that Mark is here making a historical statement but the idea of these being some who were disposed to follow Jesus is absolutely remote. According to Mark what one must rather say is that so far as its content goes the speech simply does not suit the situation of the *ochlos* ['crowd'], for following Jesus and taking up one's cross presupposes the idea of suffering which is only for the disciples. Only, here Mark was not thinking of this. The explanation of

---

[11] HC, in loc. Similarly B. Weiss, *Das Markusevangelium*, in loc.

the speech for the benefit of the public is entirely in what lies before.

But if nothing has previously been said about the *ochlos*[12] no considerations arising out of the situation are required in order to put it in the picture in verse 34. The explanation given is that as the disciples previously were on the road with Jesus he must now be conceived of as being in a township, yet the change of situation has no effect on the narrator![13] To be sure Jesus 'must' be thought of as being in a place where there is no crowd if a historically possible situation is really being given, but perhaps the passage does contain some challenge not to forget this little 'if' in favour of the 'must', entirely. In Mark the same thing holds good for the crowd as for the house and similar ideas: he always has them to hand when he needs them. And the crowd is never far away as soon as he starts thinking about the disciples.

We may in addition compare 7.14.[14] Jesus enters into conversation with the Pharisees and some scribes on the subject of handwashing (7.1ff.) then he 'again calls the crowd to him' and lets them hear a parable. Thereafter he retires into the house away from the crowd and we have the parable explained for the disciples. Here we have the opposite of what was in the previous context. But that 'the crowd' appears is not much less surprising than in 8.34. To be sure Mark is here thinking of the fact that he has previously (6.53ff.) spoken of a crowd (cf. the *palin* ['again']; but the scene in 7.1ff. is nonetheless an independent one with a new situation. Manifestly it is only the 'parable' which rescues the crowd from oblivion because parable and crowd belong together. If we have once understood Mark here then a serious literal interpretation of what he has to say has a comic effect. The crowd has heard nothing of his conversation with the representatives of the law and is then given the opportunity of hearing a parable which relates to something they have

---

[12] This seems to have struck Matthew as he represents the words about imitating Jesus in suffering (16.24) as addressed explicitly to the disciples.

[13] B. Weiss, in loc. Although Weiss has an explanation for the speaking to the people he nevertheless notes that the unmotivated appearance of the people is striking. 'The reason Mark introduces the *ochlos* ['crowd'] can ... only (!) lie in the fact that according to the apostolic source these sayings were addressed to the crowd (*ochlos*)...'

[14] See also 7.33.

not heard, and with the parable alone they must rest content, for its interpretation and significance are again not something for them!

Thirdly a word about the passage with the story of the Gerasene demoniac, in 5.19, 20. The request of the man who is healed to be allowed to accompany Jesus is rejected by Jesus. He merely enjoins him to tell his own people what the Lord has done for him.

This passage previously seemed to us an exception from Jesus' usual practice, and this is how it is mostly understood. The idea is that Jesus could have wished his deed to be proclaimed in a heathen region in a way in which he did not wish it to be among the Jews.[15] This explanation is entirely comprehensible but nevertheless gives the impression of being a *pis aller* ['stopgap']. What was to prevent Jesus' reputation spreading from this region into purely Jewish districts? This question would have to be put from the angle of the usual view of the prohibitions. From our standpoint the question obtrudes itself whether this contradiction to what Jesus does in other circumstances is not far too harsh. Why does not the evangelist even make it explicitly clear in the text, that here we are dealing with a Gentile region?

Might we not suppose the seeming deviation from the other prohibitions to be in reality a parallel? Jesus says, 'Go home to your friends and tell (*apaggeilon*) them how much the Lord has done for you, and how he has had mercy on you.' In his home and family knowledge of the benefaction is effectively guarded. But the Gerasene now does something different: he does the same as the leper and the deaf mute (145, 7.36, cf. 7.14). 'And he went away and began to proclaim in the Decapolis how much Jesus had done for him; and all men marvelled'. (Here it is Jesus, not 'the Lord'!) The two sentences naturally are not formally contrasted. And just because we have so often found the 'house' a place of secrecy, it need not always have this sense.

[15] e.g., Ritschl, *Theol. Jahrbücher,* 1851, p.514, Holtzmann, HC, p.8. B. Weiss, *Das Markusevangelium*, p.181, rightly says, 'Here too Jesus is not concerned about the broadcasting of his miracles of healing, which according to 1.44 he does not wish'. But the continuation is perhaps more in accord with the modern taste for edification than with that of Mark: he 'only wishes to establish the accomplished healing as a blessing for the family of the person healed'.

When all is said, even a narrator who speaks without reticence of the broadcasting of Jesus' deeds could himself have placed in his mouth an invitation to proclaim the miracle if he was motivated in a particular way; for instance, if he wished to refer to a first sermon among the Gentiles.[16] But Jesus does not after all say that the demoniac may go 'to his house' and broadcast what had been done at home. Thus to my mind the similarity to other passages where we have *oikos* ['house'],[17] the undeniable material contrast between Jesus' command and the way in which the healed man behaves, and the agreement into which this passage then enters with the prohibition, are strong supports for the proposed interpretation. That Jesus refuses the man's request will then have to be understood in accordance with this. He does not want to take him along with him for fear he might be betrayed by him. There will be some sense in this feature and it stands in contrast to the instruction to go into the house. What is communicated to those in the house no more excludes the idea of secrecy than does the mention of *mallon* ['more and more'] in 7.36.

Finally we may once again mention the particularly characteristic passage in 7.24f.: 'And from there he arose and went away to the region of Tyre and Sidon. And he entered a house,[18] and would not have anyone know it; yet he could not be hid. But immediately a woman, whose little daughter was possessed by an unclean spirit, heard of him, and came and fell down at his feet ...' Although it might seem that Jesus enters the house for other reasons[19] and *then* wishes to conceal his presence there, nonetheless it is the house itself that is thought of as a hiding-place. One might then ask why a special place of con-

---

[16] Cf. Volkmar, p.310.

[17] Specifically with 8.26: 'he sent him to his house'.

[18] It would not be so completely impossible for the variant reading *eis tēn oikian* ['into the house'] attested for D and Origen to be original here. The article could easily have seemed inappropriate. 7.17 and 9.28 have similar oscillations in the manuscripts between *oikos* anarthrous and with the article. Moreover 'the house' is not to be strongly emphasised. In these instances Mark is not thinking, say, of a particular house; he is mentioning the house by way of contrast to the road, as B. Weiss rightly says on 9.33, or just to what is 'outside', in general.

[19] B. Weiss in Meyer: in order to shelter there.

cealment is still necessary in an unknown land. But it would then be pointed out by knowledgeable people that according to 3.8 Jesus was known to many of the inhabitants of Tyre and Sidon. It may, however, be asked what the use of such a hiding-place would be if Jesus really wants to remain hidden at all and yet cannot always remain there, or why he hides here[20] when otherwise he does not hide. Moreover anyone can perceive the faulty tie-up between the region of Tyre and 'a' house. In short, in this description of the situation Mark is approximating to the style of the fairy-tale. One could tell of a disguised Spanish prince in this manner, and of his journey into French territory: there he went into a house because he did not wish to be recognised, but nonetheless it was learned that he was there and even a poor woman heard it and sought him out.[21]

In accordance with what we have suggested, the much lauded concreteness of Mark will also perhaps have to be assessed differently from usual.[22] First of all it turns out that many features reckoned as concrete motivations are in reality *motifs* connected with the Markan point of view, and perhaps similar things may be discerned in other points too. Many interesting observations remain to be made in Mark. Precisely where the material I have treated is under debate we are struck by a strong lack of concreteness, even if not always so great as 7.24. It is not as if the other Synoptists were any more concrete in the parallel passages. The distinction lies rather here: through the plasticity of his remarks Mark stimulates the demand for concreteness more strongly and yet leaves it unsatisfied. A brief hasty word of Jesus' or someone else's and a short remark on the impression it made;

---

[20] B. Weiss in Meyer answers that he wanted to dedicate himself to the training of the weak disciples, and it is for this reason he is supposed to have come to this region at all. Why then does the text tell us nothing of this main idea? The journey into the region of Tyre is manifestly told simply on account of the story of the Syro-Phoenician woman for apart from this his stay in this Gentile district is a vacuum. Already by 7.31 Jesus is again transferred to the Sea of Galilee.

[21] On the passage in 10.47f, which does not fit this context well, cf. Excursus VI.

[22] J. Weiss, *Reich Gottes*, pp.38f, is—to my great pleasure—certainly more sceptical than most, and this applies with reference to Mark's chronology.

quick sudden changes of location throughout and within individual scenes and manifold changes in the environment of Jesus;
the people or the disciples' psychological condition for now appearing and now withdrawing. The psychological and other
motivations which would be the pre-condition for giving palpa-
ble shape to the events are lacking. But it is not because they
might be freely supplied that they are lacking, but because they
were not thought of at all. Thus the appearance of Jesus and of
the other persons in the drama frequently gives the impression of
something hasty, shadowy, almost phantasmal. Naturally not for
this reason alone. If an exhaustive description were merited it
would specifically be necessary to show how the superhuman
features of Jesus contribute to this impression.

But the Gospel does also really contain much that is concrete. Yet here the entire character of the writing warns us not
to regard concreteness too quickly and incautiously as a characteristic of historicity. It may well be that Mark can prove itself
the oldest Gospel in relation to the others even as a result of its
greater concreteness. But this relative judgement is of little significance for an absolute evaluation of Mark. A document can
have a strongly secondary and indeed even quite apocryphal
character and yet display a great deal of concreteness. It is always
a question of what form this concreteness takes.

The view of the literary nature of Mark's Gospel which I have
in several respects contrasted with the usual critical treatment of
the document corresponds to an extent with the view taken in
relation to another document, namely the Gospel of John, by
scientific criticism itself—I mean by unprejudiced scientific criticism. It is worth while mentioning this because it shows that
here there is no unbridgeable gap in exegetical and critical
method and because it is possible to learn something from the
Gospel of John for our study of Mark.

When John makes Jesus say in 7.34, 'you will seek me and
you will not find me: where I am you cannot come', and then
makes the Jews ask, 'Where does this man intend to go, that we
shall not find him? Does he intend to go to the Dispersion
among the Greeks and teach the Greeks?', although Jesus has
already declared that he will go to him who sent him, a great

many people will regard it here as a coarse lack of taste to represent by psychological means what is not capable of representation. If the disciples of John are jealous of Jesus' successes although they themselves declare they have heard their master's testimony about Jesus, which makes such jealousy impossible (3.26), this is quietly accepted as something which is not at all striking in the Johannine context. When the evangelist tells us 'some of them wanted to arrest him, but no one laid hands on him' (7.44, cf. 7.30, 8.20) everybody knows that such an absolutely unconcrete feature is not to be made comprehensible by a consideration of the situation but has light cast on it from the thoughts of the evangelist, according to which Jesus is, on the one hand, constantly surrounded by mortal hostility but, on the other hand, is protected until his 'hour is come', in accordance with divine decree. And once having recognised the nature of the Gospel of John, who would be in a position to try to point to even just a mediocre amount of progress in the disputations of Jesus, where there is in fact no progress made at all? Who fails to see that John is not concerned with thinking of the natural consequences of his ideas? To be sure, much remains more difficult to understand than it ought to be and therefore the accent still does not always sufficiently fall, as it should if justice is to be done to the author, on what he is trying to say through these peculiar historical forms. But in principle this is where the right answer is to be found.

From such peculiarities we can, however, really learn something of relevance for the study of Mark. I am naturally not thinking of eliminating the difference between him and John. It is undoubtedly a very great one. The 'pale cast of thought' which we find in the Fourth Gospel is not exhibited by Mark. He is not concerned with a developed dogma nor does he indulge as John does in polemics and apologetics. His naïvety is of a completely different sort: so far as the real background for the history of Jesus is concerned, e.g. localities, his relationship to the tradition is essentially different from that of John.

However, the relationship in principle is far greater than is commonly supposed, simply because Mark too is already very far removed from the actual life of Jesus and is dominated by views of a dogmatic kind. If we look at Mark through a large magnifying-glass, it may well be that we find a type of authorship such as is exhibited in John.

The second reading deals with the central subject of Wrede's book, namely, the 'Messianic Secret'. For Wrede this term covers a cluster of phenomena found in the Gospel of Mark: the fact that Jesus commands that his identity as Messiah not be made known, the fact that he apparently conceals his teaching by speaking in parables, and the fact that on other occasions he simply keeps his teaching secret. Wrede begins by rejecting several interpretations of these phenomena. The first interpretation rejected is the idea that Mark is interested in the idea of a secret teaching as such (an idea found in some non-canonical Gospels). Nor is he convinced of the idea that the basis of these phenomena is the fact that Jesus spoke in parables. Next Wrede asks whether Mark's depiction might be rooted in a Jewish idea that the Messiah might exist on earth in a hidden form. This idea, too, he rejects. Wrede's own interpretation is that these phenomena reflect the early Christian conviction that Jesus became Messiah only at the resurrection. (Although Wrede doubts whether Jesus claimed the Messianic dignity for himself, in this work he is interested only in the development of the early Christian beliefs.) As the early Christians narrate the life of Jesus, his Messianic status is increasingly attributed to him even before his Resurrection. Wrede argues that, to ease the tension between the earlier and the later view, the idea emerged that Jesus had always been the messiah (at least since his baptism), but that he had deliberately kept his identity hidden. It is this idea which finds expression in the Gospel of Mark.

The Concealment of the Messiahship up to the Resurrection

From the start I wish to reject an idea which might perhaps manifest itself in our examination of this topic.

We have encountered the idea of a secret teaching in a variety of forms. And with some propriety everything might come under this heading in so far as it may be possible to reckon as the sum and substance of Christian teaching a messiahship or sonship of God on the part of Jesus which is hidden from the people, as someone like Mark conceives it. Ideas would therefore suggest themselves such as are evoked by the concept of 'secret teaching' in the history of dogma. Again and again this predicate has served the purpose of legitimising a particular teaching as the true one. No reflection is necessary in order to see that such a tendency (*Tendenz*) cannot be the starting-point of our idea. Where the title 'secret teaching' implies an authentication, it is usually concerned with the recommendation of a new teaching *alongside* a well-known and recognised one. In the instance of Mark no public teaching with a different content stands alongside the secret teaching. This is enough in itself to make us reject the idea.

But where then are we to begin with an attempt at an explanation? We have found the idea of the secret, or more plainly of *keeping* the secret, in several forms. Here we may distinguish three principal notions:

Jesus conceals his nature or his messiahship.
He conceals his teaching by talking in parables.
He keeps his teaching secret (without closer definition).

My assumption is that these notions belong together. This being so, we must ask before we go any further what is the basic one towards which the real explanation must be directed.

Here it seems clear to me that the notion of *secret teaching* in the indefinite sense cannot be regarded as the starting point of the whole process. In Mark at all events it recedes very much into the background, apart from the special idea about the mysterious prophecy of the future destiny of Jesus, from which it will hardly be thought proper to derive everything else. But above all it is hard to understand how from this starting-point the specific idea of the secret of the person of Jesus should have arisen. If on the contrary this idea is the prior element, then it is easy to proceed to the idea of secret teaching as soon as teaching is regarded as a function of the messiah too.

But it is nevertheless worth considering whether the theory of the *parables* is not the basis for the whole view. The advantage in this explanation would lie in the fact that we would immediately have a concrete motive for the formation of the idea. The notion that Jesus had taught in parables was a datum of the tradition; that he chose the language of parables in order to conceal his ideas was almost *necessitated* in consequence of the meaning of the word *parabolē* ['parable'].

Starting from the ready-made theory of parables we would then be obliged to imagine something like the following sequence of ideas. Jesus kept aloof from the people by dint of obscure discourse. In this respect he naturally did not make an exception of the main subject of the messiahship. Thus he concealed from the people the fact that he was the messiah. He therefore forbade discussion of this as soon as he was designated messiah.

No credence will be given by anyone to this train of thought, nor is this only because there is nothing intrinsically necessary about it. In the instance of Mark the theory of parables may be thought of as in a sense a *concomitant* of the individual parables, but the idea of veiled discourse is in no way detached from the concrete forms of the parables. Are we then to assume that its detachment was accomplished long before Mark and that in him there is represented the original theory in its first shape alongside the completely transformed idea? Such developments are indeed by no means impossible. However there must be better reasons than what we have here if we are to reckon with them, and here certainly it is a far cry to the concrete form the idea eventually assumed in Mark. (The prohibitions must be regarded as the chief point for him.) There is one thing to add to this.

If our view is correct[23], the idea of the moment of the resurrection is *essential* for the prohibitions. The significance of this moment cannot be grasped on the basis of the parable theory.

Accordingly I regard Jesus' *messianic self-concealment* in the most direct and strict sense of the word as the real subject with which we have to deal.

In this connection we may find it supposed that the explanation is to be found in a messianic idea in Judaism.

---

[23] What was said on pp.62f. also supports these considerations.

There is also a Jewish background for the idea that the messiah will exist for a period in concealment, and not merely in
heaven, which here would indeed mean nothing, but on earth.
Do we have here the predecessor of the Christian idea we find
in Mark? Even if the ideas were not wholly identical it might
well be important that Judaism had created such a way of looking at the matter. The growth of an idea becomes more easily
comprehensible if there is already extant a form into which its
content can be fitted.

The hidden Messiah in Judaism

The idea[24] is clearly expressed in Justin. Trypho the Jew says in
the Dialogue, ch. 8:

> But even if the Christ has already been born and lives somewhere
> (*kai esti pou*) he is unknown, and does not even know himself. Nor
> does he have any sort of power until Elias has come, and anointed
> him[25] and revealed him to everybody.

Similarly in ch. 110 Justin cites as a Jewish idea the notion
that even if the messiah had come nobody would know who he
is but that they would rather learn this only when he is made
manifest and appears in glory, *hotan emphanēs kai endoxos genētai*.

In Justin this view runs counter to the Christian assertion that
the messiah had already come. Judaism can concede the possibility that he has already been born but it does not attach the
importance to this which the Christians do. Indeed it really attaches no importance to it at all, for it cannot make anything of
this empty possibility. But the fulfilment of the hope begins only
with the moment when he appears in splendour and sovereign
power, or upon the arrival of Elijah, who is the sign of his own
coming.

---

[24] Cf. for what follows Gfrörer, *Jahrhundert des Heils* II, pp.223ff., Lücke on
Jn 7.27, Schürer, *Gesch. des jüd. Volkes*[3] II, pp.531f. ([2]II pp.447f.), Dalman. I
pp.247, 107.
[25] Cf. *Dialogue* ch. 49 where the Jew says *ek de tou mēde Hēlian elēluthenai
oude touton* (Jesus) *apophainomai einai* ['from the fact that Elijah has not come, I
conclude that this one (Jesus) is not (the Messiah)'].

A related idea is presupposed by the Gospel of John when in 7.27 the Jews say 'When the Christ appears no-one will know where he comes from'. The hiddenness of his origin appears as a characteristic of the messiah. Also related is the rabbinic *theologoumenon* that the messiah after he has been born is again removed from the scene before finally appearing as messiah.[26]

We do not know how old the idea attested by Justin is. We must not forget that the very existence of a Christian belief in the messiah will have very strongly activated Jewish scholarship and speculation about the messiah. This warns us not to place such ideas back in the pre-Christian era without further investigation. But it may be that this particular idea was already in existence when Mark wrote. It may also be that it was known fairly widely in Christian circles before Mark, however much it may look rather like a piece of learned pedantry than like a *popular* Jewish view. I myself cannot believe in any connection with the Christian idea of the hidden messiah among these presuppositions. For this view differs too much from the Christian idea.

For a start, it is a hazardous approach to expect another form of the Christian counterpart, namely a concealment only prior to the baptism by John, the Elijah who belongs to the messiah Jesus. Nevertheless the idea of the anointing and proclamation by Elijah need not be reckoned absolutely as a necessary feature of the Jewish view. This could have existed even apart from that idea. But the decisive factor is that the hiddenness signifies something completely different in each context. In Mark the messiah intentionally veils the dignity of which he is aware and also veils his activity which corresponds to this dignity. In Justin we have to do only with a contentless 'thereness' of the messiah prior to his appearing. He is unknown and this means merely that he is in the first instance only 'a man from among men'[27] of whom nothing is known. Characteristically it is added that not even he himself knows of his destiny. In other words this idea is nothing more than the shadow of the more important notion of an incalculable and sudden appearing of the messiah in glory; and it is certainly not improbable that it arose only because this

[26] See Dalman in loc.
[27] Dial. ch. 49.

sudden appearance was on the one hand an established idea and on the other hand the messianic dogma had come into fashion that the messiah would be born in Bethlehem as a child.[28] The idea then would represent a connection and balance between the two notions. I am unable to see how the Markan approach is in any sense to be explained on this basis.

Contrariwise we now have a Christian approach the near relationship of which to ours can hardly be denied. This is the idea that *Jesus becomes messiah only with the Resurrection.*

The comparison presses itself upon us for the very reason that the resurrection in both cases is the decisive item. But in these circumstances negative consideration of the earthly life of Jesus is closely related to this. On the one hand the conclusion must be formed that Jesus during his earthly activity was as yet not the messiah but on the other hand we have it that he did not wish to be the messiah as yet and did not as yet count as such. In the light of this the Resurrection is in the one instance the revelation, and in the other the realisation, of the messiahship. The impression that these ideas belong together is a strong one from the start.

The point demands exhaustive consideration. Let us for the sake of argument simply designate the idea that Jesus *becomes* messiah only after his earthly life[29] by the expression 'future messiahship'.

The secret and the future messiah

In his sermon at Pentecost in Acts 2.36 Peter says that God has *made* the Jesus whom the Jews crucified *both Lord and Christ.* In this it is implied that this has been done through his being raised from the dead. This saying quite by itself would prove that there

---

[28] See Schürer, in loc.

[29] It is a merit of Johannes Weiss to have championed particularly forcefully this view of the messiahship. See *Nachfolge Christi* pp.59ff., *Predigt vom Reiche Gottes*, pp.158f., and also the *Kommentar zu Lukas*, pp.637f. (on Lk 22.66ff.). Cf. further Brandt, *Die evangelische Geschichte und der Ursprung des Christentums*, p.478 (note), Dalman I p.259, also Wellhausen, *Israelit. u. jüd. Geschichte*, 1st ed., p.318. 4th ed. (1901) p.391, Holtzmann, *NT Theol.* I p.361, Jülicher, *Gleichnisreden* II, p.473.

was in primitive Christianity a view in accordance with which Jesus was not the messiah in his earthly life. I shall avoid the expression 'was not *fully* the messiah'. In his earthly life, to be sure, Jesus lacks only one thing in order to be the messiah: namely the sovereign dignity and power. But this one thing is the *whole* thing. It is precisely what makes the concept of messiah what it is, as Christianity received it from Judaism. The Resurrection showed that Jesus from now on had attained to this dignity and power, and did not merely show it, but put it into effect. From now on therefore the messiah can be expected. He exists and therefore he can come.

It has rightly been pointed out that Paul gives evidence of having an analogous view. Jesus is 'designated Son of God in power' (Ro. 1.4) 'by his resurrection from the dead'. It is all one whether Paul was able to call the earthly Jesus too 'Son of God'. If he did, this would only derive from the fact that in his pre-mundane existence he already possessed the sonship, the *einai isa theō* ['being equal to God' cf. Phil 2:6]. In reality the one who became man has already shed the existence which characterises the Son of God.[30] And thus according to Paul too he *becomes* something, as a result of the resurrection, which as a man he in no sense was. The well-known passage in the letter to the Philippians, 2.6ff., says this plainly too. The human existence in which Jesus is devoid and empty of all dignity and lordship that was his due is removed as a result of his exaltation, and thereby he receives the name above all names, that of 'Lord', but with it naturally also the substance, which is lordship over everyone and everything.

The way the New Testament speaks of his future appearance is also significant. We do not hear of his coming again, but simply of his coming. In all the eschatological discourses of the Gospel nothing is said differently of the Christ than what is said of the expected kingdom. The term is *erchesthai* ['to come'].[31] Further, *parousia* does not mean 'return' but always 'arrival'. The

---

[30] Sonship in the true sense depends for the Christians too on their abandonment of their carnal life (Ro. 8.23). Only thereby are they conformed to the 'image of the Son', that is, to his mode of being (8.29).

[31] Lk 17.30 *apokaluptesthai* ['to be revealed'].

wrong translation[32] should be strictly avoided, in order not to eliminate an important peculiarity of New Testament language. The entire usage manifestly rests upon the idea that the 'return' is the first and only messianic appearance. Jesus has been there but the messiah is yet to come. But this is not to say that he only *becomes* messiah when he arrives. He has been messiah since the resurrection.

It is useful to remember the alteration introduced in the subsequent period. Justin already distinguishes everywhere between a *prōtē* ['first'] and a *deutera parousia* ['second coming'] of Christ. The one is *adoxos* ['without glory'] but the other is *endoxos* ['in glory'].[33] It is the double coming which is a distinctively Christian doctrine over against Judaism. It too is of course already found in Scripture. The two goats in Lev. 16 are the type of the two *parousiai* ['comings'], Dial. ch. 40. But even already in Ignatius the new linguistic usage is observable, and by the phrase *parousia tou sotēros* ['coming of the saviour'] his appearance in the flesh is understood.[34] [35]

These alterations in terminology are characteristic. However the matter is not always entirely covered by terminology. The terminology is to an extent secondary; the substance is what matters. But this is already fully there, for example, in the Gospel of John. Jesus is manifestly already the messiah in his historical life. Whatever the future coming of Christ may mean,[36] the fact that he *has* come, appearing in the flesh, does not fall behind this in importance. The verdict that he *was* the messiah is precisely as necessary as the other, that he *has* revealed God and his truth and *has* accomplished everything necessary for salvation.

The development in the view of the messiah Jesus which we here perceive, is very easily comprehensible.

---

[32] This has also been the cause of trouble with the *parousia* of the Antichrist in 2 Thess. 2.8f.

[33] Dial. ch. 49.

[34] Ad Philad. 9, See also the Preaching of Peter (cf. Preuschen, *Antilegomena*, p.54, fragment 9).

[35] Justin uses alongside *parousia* also *epiphaneia* ['appearance'] (Apol. 1.44) or *phanerōsis tou Christou* ['manifestation of the Christ'] in this way. Moreover the transformation in usage is already to be seen in the writings of the N.T., cf. e.g. *epiphaneia* in 2 Tim 1.10.

[36] 1 Jn 2.28, *parousia*.

The view that Jesus only becomes messiah after his death is assuredly not merely an old one, but the oldest of which we have any knowledge. Had the earthly life of Jesus been looked upon from the start as the actual life of the messiah, it would have been only with difficulty that, by way of supplement to this, the idea could have been hit upon of regarding the resurrection as the formal beginning of the messiahship and the appearance in glory as the *single* coming of the messiah.

We may add here another consideration. Who was able to find the essence of the messiahship realised even only partially in the earthly life of Jesus, according to Jewish ideas? These Jewish ideas were, after all, hardly capable of being stretched to the point where an itinerant teacher and healer whose life gave no signs of lordship and glory could be regarded as the real messiah. The most that is conceivable is that the activity or personality of Jesus might already have awakened during his lifetime the question or presentiment, the hope or perhaps the belief that he had been chosen by God to be the messiah. But once again this would simply be as much as to say that as yet he was not messiah. Those who regard Peter's confession as a historical fact must draw the same conclusion from this too. For at all events it proves that despite all the preceding miraculous activity the people until then found nothing in Jesus which was a compelling indication of his messiahship, and even for the disciples, despite all their veneration for their master, the same thing must have held good for a very long time.

This oldest view of the messiahship of Jesus underwent more and more change as time went on. The decisive factor in this is not that the earthly Jesus was *called* messiah or that it was said that God *had sent* the messiah. This would still be capable of being taken to mean that he whom we can now expect as messiah was there. But the whole thing is rather a question of the facts of Jesus' past life gaining a new emphasis and a different aspect.

Here the clearest example is the death of Jesus, an event which originally must have represented the sharpest contrast to every hope focused on Jesus. Those who regarded this death as a saving death thereby recognised that what was past and had happened did not merely provide an earnest for future happenings: but really had already produced something of substance. Despite

what was said above, this is already true of Paul. To be sure it is
not right to say that in Paul yearning for the future came to take
second place to the perception of an already experienced salvation and we should not say that he emphasises faith more than
he does hope.[37] For there are other reasons for the emphasis on
faith, and it can be shown that all the pronouncements of Paul
on an already accomplished salvation do contain within them an
allusion to the future. But this much is correct, that however
much in his case too all thoughts are pressing towards the end,
his hope is based just as much on what God *has* done in Christ,
and on that past fact that he *has* died.

But alongside his death much else in the earthly life of Jesus
became significant and necessary and indispensable, whether it
was only an accretion that went along with reminiscence or was
already originally contained within that reminiscence. It is not
merely the endowment of Jesus with the Holy Spirit and his
supernatural birth which belong here but in the last resort the
miracles too,[38] as the signs and testimonies of his power and
glory, together with everything which proved that prophecy had
been fulfilled in him. For the mere fact that a feature of his life,
even a subordinate one, had been prophesied, transformed its
quality.

Parallel to some extent with this growing significance of the
life of Jesus there went an occlusion of the first hope. Belief in a
directly imminent *parousia*, though not indeed in the *parousia*
itself, recedes into the background.

Thus the verdict that Jesus *was* the messiah more and more
gained a content of its own and an independent significance.
There arose a new and *specifically Christian* concept of the messiah which cannot be sufficiently definitely distinguished from
the older one. It is a concept of a very complex kind. To a great
extent it came into existence as a result of the fact that a plethora
of new predicates became attached to the inherited concept of
the messiah, as a result of which even the old predicates took on

[37] Thus Wellhausen. *Israel u. jüd. Gesch.*[1] p.319. The fourth edition adds
love to faith.
[38] Even if already in Jesus' lifetime they might be supposed to have awakened thoughts about his messianic destiny, these were nevertheless evaluated
messianically in another sense, later.

a new look; or else it came into existence because anything essential known about the life of *Jesus*, or regarded as known about it, was attached to the concept of the messiah itself.

At all events the dating of the messiahship from the Resurrection is not an idea of Jesus' but one of the community. Experience of the appearances of the Risen One is presupposed in this. This can be denied only by those who think it possible for Jesus to have prophesied his immediate resurrection.

It seems equally clear to me, that Jesus cannot have spoken of his coming as messiah in the way in which the Synoptics report it. The pronouncements about the *parousia* regarding the Son of man, which privately some would frequently like to get rid of and others would just as frequently play as a trump card, do after all quite plainly presuppose the *Christian* idea of the messiah. Any Jew could to be sure speak of the coming of the messiah. But there is a big difference if third parties so speak or if Jesus himself is the speaker. The 'coming' is after all a coming on earth. But Jesus is speaking on the earth. Consequently the death which removes him from the earth is included in these pronouncements. The evangelists did not think about this. They gave those sayings from their own standpoint after the death of Jesus. Otherwise they, or at least Mark, would presumably have all the more insisted, on the strength of them, that the disciples did not understand Jesus. But here we come across an insurmountable difficulty. It does not come under discussion here at all whether Jesus reckoned with the *possibility* or *probability* of his death. The person who spoke thus was someone for whom death was neither the one thing nor the other but was in the normal course. It did not even require to be mentioned any longer when it was under discussion. If Jesus is to be reckoned as having spoken in this way, then he must have presupposed even for his hearers that they were so familiar with the idea that they would fill in the missing link without more ado. In the presence of his judges, a threat by Jesus to come on the clouds of heaven might yet seem comprehensible if his execution was a foregone conclusion. But the evangelists make Jesus speak in this way in other circumstances too. Mark does so immediately after Peter's confession and despite the rejection of the idea of suffering on the part of the disciples, 8.38, and Matthew does so even in the discourse on the commissioning of the disciples in 10.23.[39]

Jesus' belief in a future exaltation and a coming crowning with messianic glory is not as yet demonstrated to be impossible by this. It might be said that he did expect them on earth, say in the form of a transformation,[40] perhaps also that he later modified this expectation in accordance with the historical circumstances, by reckoning with the possibility of death prior to exaltation.[41] The evangelists of course know nothing of either of these points of view if we restrict ourselves to their actual words.

An essential difficulty for the supposition that Jesus gave himself out as messiah lies in the fact that we cannot easily indicate what he meant by it. If the idea of a messianic proclamation in the political, patriotic and revolutionary sense is excluded, what then is the significance of the messianic claim? It is characteristic of the way things stand that Wellhausen should have answered this question as follows:[42] Jesus rejected all Jewish ideas of the messiah. He directed men's hopes and longings to 'another ideal' and one of a higher order. Only in this sense can he have called himself messiah, that they were to await nobody else. He was not the one they wanted, but he was the true one whom they *ought* to want. I must admit that I cannot conceive of this at all. A Jewish man living and working amidst his people substitutes for the firmly established messianic concept something which removes from it all its proper characteristics and privately transforms a theocratic, eschatological idea into a spiritual and religious one such as was known to no Jew?

---

[39] The character of the pronouncements on the *parousia* and also that of the prophecies of suffering throws light in passing on the term *ho huios tou anthrōpou* ['the Son of Man'] which does indeed play a special part in both of them.

[40] Weizsäcker, *Apostal. Zeitalter*, p.14.

[41] Wernle, *Die Anfänge unserer Religion*, p.33.

[42] Wellhausen, *Israel. u. jüd. Gesch.*[1] p.315. The fourth edition on p.387 adds the following quotation: 'If (as we really must, when all is said) we give the word the meaning in which it was generally understood, then Jesus was not the messiah nor did he wish to be him.' But this means dismissing the possibility that he called himself messiah and, as is previously stated, gave himself out as such to the disciples.

But now the simple, clear supposition may be thought help-ful here, that Jesus considered and designated himself messiah purely 'in the proleptic sense'. In this way, continuity with the Jewish idea, that is, with the only one then extant, is guaranteed, a spiritualisation of the then current ideas by Jesus seems at the same time not to be excluded, and account is taken of the fact that all the prophetic power of his preaching and all the moral greatness of his appearance and all his healing activity were yet not enough to make his appearance a messianic one.

The confidence with which this view is presented[43] is not however entirely comprehensible to me. The difficulty is simply shunted on to another line, the psychological one.

A willing and acting messiah, a pretender seeking to call the masses to a movement against foreign overlordship, might be able to be certain that God would at the right hour place the crown itself on his head. How can we imagine such a certainty in the instance of Jesus, when he carefully avoids every such ef-fect on the masses? It is not that God is to give him blessing and support in general, but a quite definite and unique honour and dignity. How can he know this, that is to say, how can he be-lieve it firmly and with assurance?[44] How, if he does no more than hope, can he have made an *explicit* messianic claim?[45] And this he would no doubt in some sense have had to do if he is supposed to have pronounced his confession before the high priest and received the sentence of death as messiah. Nor is the matter made any easier by the idea that Peter in his confession and the high priest in his interrogation must have understood the messiahship 'proleptically' too.[46] Now, it is said that the yardstick of contemporary psychology is no criterion for a re-ligious personality like Jesus, and we know little about how sin-gular convictions arise in the minds of the greatest figures in the

[43] Cf. J. Weiss and Dalman.

[44] Brandt p.476ff. says that Jesus' destiny as messiah can never have become a complete certainty. But some uncertainty in relation to this assurance also seems to shine through J. Weiss' psychological explanations (*Reich Gottes*, p.156).

[45] This is also against Brandt.

[46] J Weiss, Dalman.

history of religion regarding their own vocation. And in the case of Jesus we can not forget his 'consciousness of Sonship'.

I am not going to pursue that at this juncture any further. We cannot decide here almost in passing, as it were, whether Jesus really considered himself to be the messiah. For this yet other quite different standpoints are relevant. It was my intention in these remarks to raise a question and thereby to indicate why I am not here attributing the view to Jesus himself.

At all events the view of the evangelists is more easily discernible for us at this point too. What attitude do they take in the development we have touched on a ove? My answer is that here it is certainly not as yet definitively rounded off, but that it is already tending towards such a definitive conclusion. That is to say that while they certainly have nothing as yet to tell us about a double coming, and the future appearance of the messiah is everywhere the object of their thoughts, none the less the entire life of Jesus is regarded as an emanation as well as a proof of his messiahship, *according to the circumstances.* The suffering and dying is a fixed and necessary predicate of the Son of man—*dei ton huion tou anthrōpou pathein* ['it is necessary that the Son of Man should suffer']. The receiving of the Spirit or the miraculous birth in the later Gospels *makes* him messiah.[47] The healings, the victories over the realm of the demons and other wonders of a yet higher order are messianic deeds. And even in the preaching, in the *euaggelizesthai,* just as in these, we see the fulfilment of what scripture promises for the messianic era, Mt 11.5, Lk 4.18f. The forgiveness of sins together with the lordship over the sabbath is a prerogative of the Son of man, Mk 2.10, 28. The Baptist is the prophesied forerunner of the messiah. In short it is the life of the messiah which is narrated.[48]

---

[47] Wellhausen, *Israel. u. jüd. Gesch.*[4] p.391, thinks that the beginning of the messiahship was pushed back from the Resurrection first of all to the Transfiguration, then to the Baptism and finally to the birth of Jesus. In my view the Transfiguration was never considered in this light.

[48] In this connection the *logia* ['sayings'] which in very similar form speak of the purpose, or of definite signs, of the 'coming' of Jesus merit special attention: Mk 2.17, 10.45 (cf. 1.24, 28), Mt 5.17 (*ouk ēlthon katalusai* ['I have not come to abolish...']), 10.34, 11.19, 18.11, Lk 12.49, 19.10, also 9.56 in T.R. and the Gospel of the Ebionites (*ēlthon katalusai tas thusias* ['I came to abolish

Here we compare the oldest Christian witness, viz. Paul.
How does it happen that for him Jesus' earthly life means nothing apart from death and resurrection? and that he values it only
as a slave's existence, Phil.2, and as an emptying of a heavenly
mode of being? Why does the messianic material of our Gospels
leave no trace in him? Did it perhaps not yet exist in its main
outlines?

But as we have said the development in the Synoptic Gospels
is not yet rounded off, and just for this reason the question can
arise here whether our interpretation does not still need supplementation. The demons, Peter and the voices from heaven say
that Jesus is the Christ or the Son of God. Does the messianic
predicate here have a future ring about it—'thou art the one for
whom the messianic glory is prepared'?

The expressions themselves do leave the possibility open.
Nor would a real contradiction necessarily enter into Mark's
ideas so far as this interpretation is concerned. A proleptic sense
for the messianic title would naturally look rather different in the
instance of an evangelist who is already aware of an actually
messianic earthly life of Jesus than it would in the mouth of Jesus
or those who lived along with him, where the messiahship
would be understood only in the sense of faith or of expectation.
But why should there be a contradiction in having Mark think
of the miracles and teaching, the suffering and the dying, as attributes and conditions of the messiahship and yet dating the
reception of the actual dignity and power and of the appropriate
mode of being from a later moment? It could only be supposed
that he had grasped the original concept of the anointed in the
sense of the Lord and Sovereign in all its clarity. The miracles
could also very easily be thus represented as disclosing the messiahship and even the descent of the Spirit could hold the
meaning which we have assumed for it. It would be necessary to
say that the *pneuma* ['Spirit'] creates the precondition for Jesus to
act as befits the messiah, equips him with the power of working
miracles and thus in fact makes out of a mere man something
new and higher, but does not as yet effect the realisation of the
messiahship. The appearance as Lord and King is still missing

the sacrifices']). Cf. Jn 5.43, 9.39, 12.46, 16.28, 18.37 etc. Is it here a question
of retrospective consideration of the life of Jesus?

and thus the title too could be related to the later moment. Jesus' baptism would then in the case of Mark be the beginning of the messiahship in so far as his *nature* is concerned, but the resurrection would be its beginning in so far as a definitive dignity is at issue.

In favour of this proleptic approach to the messianic confessions and testimonies may be cited the story of the Transfiguration. If the Transfiguration is really a prefiguring of what is to come, a glimmer of the coming glory in the earthly life of Jesus, then the testimony from on high would naturally take on an especially pregnant significance, if it also alluded directly to the Resurrection by the predicate 'Son of God'. It might further appear meaningful that the secret of which disclosure was forbidden did not simply lie beyond human discernment so far as its supernatural content is concerned, but also related to the future. Secret knowledge and knowledge about the future have indeed a natural relationship. Thus the point would arise, that what only comes into being as a result of the Resurrection also remains concealed till then. Such considerations could tell in favour of the idea. But they do not amount to proofs and for the present I cannot convince myself of the rightness of this exposition. Above all, in the Baptism, the idea that the predicate 'Son of God' is understood proleptically is decidedly remote. The content of the idea already seems to be realised here just because Jesus has become the bearer of the Spirit. Why then are the pronouncements of the demons supposed to have the subordinate futuristic meaning?

Moreover it is not very important how Mark the individual author meant the messianic title in this respect. The view we have discussed would indeed bring particularly close to each other the two ideas of the future and the concealed messiah. The second would in this instance simply include the first. But if this is left out of consideration nothing is altered in the connection of the ideas themselves.

How then is this connection to be defined? And how are we to conceive of the emergence of the idea of the hidden messiahship? With this we finally reach the main question.

The first supposition which struck me when I considered the problem was to the effect that there might be an apologetic tendency at work. Either the observation would have been made in the community itself that testimonies for the messiahship of Jesus were lacking in his earthly life, or it would have been pointed out in hostile quarters that he simply had not been known at all as messiah and had not declared himself as such. To this the answer would then have been given that Jesus of course was the messiah but that he himself commanded silence about it for the time being, so that it was no wonder that nobody knew him as such. This explanation would consequently have the value of direct testimony.

I quickly abandoned this supposition. The way in which Mark describes the concealed messiahship of Jesus at no point awakens the impression that in this we are dealing with an apologetic evasion. Now it is of course true that the original motive could already have become unclear in Mark. Once there, the idea could have developed further independently. However the supposition is also intrinsically improbable.

In the community itself there can hardly have been this sort of reflection about deficiencies in the transmission of material regarding Jesus' life. Observations about 'the' tradition could at all events only be made when this was available in finished form, that is, as writings. But there is also little to be said for the idea that this was the sort of objection made by opponents. A Christian pronouncement challenging attack is not here in question. But neither are we concerned with a point at which Christian belief in the messiah was particularly vulnerable. Jesus had been demonstrated to be messiah by the Resurrection. For his period on earth his (real) messiahship was not even at first asserted. What then was the point of such an attack?

Or was it simply necessary to give another sense to the apologetic meaning of the idea, in order to hold on to it itself? In the concealing of the messiahship up to the Resurrection is concealed Jesus' prior knowledge. Would this be the salient point? 'Jesus very probably knew in advance that the Resurrection would bring him the messianic dignity; he only concealed it during his lifetime.'? This is even less conceivable. This motive would rather have found expression in direct prophecies by Jesus. The secrecy would have been merely an evasion.

No, the less a special motivation for Jesus is assumed if he does so conceal himself, the less does the whole idea look like a *Tendenz*. This is not unimportant and it is to be kept in mind for what follows.

Certain it is, that the messiahship beginning with the Resurrection does not demand the idea of the concealed messiahship. It does not necessarily exclude the possibility that Jesus called himself messiah on earth, but still less does it exclude the possibility that the earthly Jesus simply was not thought of as messiah. As against this the secret messiah in my opinion presupposes the future messiah and thereby shows itself to be the later view.

Thus if the secret messiahship really is an idea of the community which arose after the life of Jesus I cannot see how it should have arisen if everyone already knew and reported that Jesus had openly given himself out as messiah on earth. Traditions can assuredly be corrected and in the process even be transformed into their opposite but in such cases a particular motive is usually at work. But what would have prompted making the messiahship of Jesus a matter for secrecy in contradiction to the original idea, in other words simply denying in retrospect Jesus' messianic claims on earth?

Let us try to picture this supposition. The explanation could probably be sought only in the idea that Jesus really revealed himself to the disciples alone. They received from him secret disclosures and thus to them too only the main thing was known, namely the messiahship. Accordingly it was withheld from the people. It would amount to the *indirect* self-disclosure of this idea; and it would then have to have attained an independent significance.

This development has little to be said for it. Let us suppose that the starting point, this dogmatic separation of the disciples and the people, is established. Let us also leave out of account that Mark, where he speaks about the concealment of the messiahship, certainly does not put the contrast between the disciples and the people all that prominently in the foreground. But it remains incomprehensible how *if it actually existed* the conviction should have been so lightly set aside or disregarded that Jesus came forward publicly with the messianic claim. It would not be immaterial that he already wished in his lifetime to be what the Resurrection showed him to be. Furthermore it is again important (cf. p.213 above) that the secret is supposed to be preserved until the Resurrection. In accordance with the supposition under discussion, which emphasises the concealment of the messiahship *from the people*, the meaning would have to be that Jesus as a result of the resurrection would now become manifest *to the people*. This idea is not found and assuredly this is not by accident. In itself it is inept; no early Christian thought[49] that the resurrection would bring a special revelation to the people. Thus if the resurrection is regarded as the terminus of the secret this tells against all the deductions we have taken into account. For the resurrection forms the terminus not because of the crowd but because now we have the event which is decisive for Jesus' messianic being itself.

Thus hardly any possibility remains other than the suggestion that the idea of the secret arose at a time when as yet there was no knowledge of any messianic claim on the part of Jesus on earth; which is as much as to say at a time when the resurrection was regarded as the beginning of the messiahship.

At that time, to be sure, the title messiah must really still have had a futuristic sense—reckoned from the life of Jesus onwards. Otherwise the secret messiahship could not have developed out of the future messiahship, which is in fact what happened. It did not merely arise *after* the future messiahship but out of it.

Naturally this would occur only once the original idea was already materially losing ground, that is, when already in the life of Jesus hints about his future standing, and characteristics and utterances about his messiahship were being found. For this is a further necessary presupposition which follows directly from the idea of the secret itself. The concealment includes the idea that there was something to conceal.

The carrying back of the messiahship into the life of Jesus was a very natural process, but Jesus himself must have awaited the moment of glorification. He must have lived for it. In his activity too he must already have betrayed something of his

---

[49] Acts 10.40ff. says that God through the resurrection made Jesus manifest 'not to all the people' but 'to us who were chosen by God as witnesses'.

coming greatness and thus in a certain sense have been the messiah. This above all was precisely the light in which his life had to be regarded if the experience of the resurrection really was the focal point of the ideas, and this it was. His previous life was only worthy of the Easter morning if the splendour of this day itself shone back upon it. But it was still plainly known that he had only later become the messiah. Hence if in contemplating his life one wished to say that he *was* the messiah there was just as much motivation for going back on this in part. But the tension between the two ideas was eased when it was asserted that he really was messiah already on earth and naturally also knew this but did not as yet say so and did not yet wish to be it; and even if his activities were entirely adapted to the awakening of belief in his messiahship nevertheless he did everything he could not to betray it for only the future was to be the bringer of revelation.

In this it may have been important that the resurrection was not regarded merely as God's establishment of his dignity but at the same time as the public intimation of this. It was the *phanerōsis* ['manifestation'] of *doxa* ['glory'] (Jn 21.1, 14; Mk 16, 14). The *revelation* was then axiomatically preceded by the secret or concealment. But nothing certain can be said about this. However it will at all events be noted that the idea of secrecy and secret knowledge played a role in religion at that time in the most varied connections. It is doubly easy to understand how the idea we are discussing came to be formed in such a period.

To my mind this is the origin of the idea which we have shown to be present in Mark. It is, so to speak, a transitional idea and *it can be characterised as the after-effect of the view that the resurrection is the beginning of the messiahship at a time when the life of Jesus was already being filled materially with messianic content.* Or else it proceeded from the impulse to make the earthly life of Jesus messianic, but one inhibited by the older view, which was still potent.

Perhaps a difficulty will be found in the fact that Mark does not content himself with suggesting that Jesus kept quiet about his dignity, but rather reports that he diligently and strictly forbade talking about it, and expressly took steps to prevent its disclosure.

However, even if one believed that Jesus did not wish that disclosure, there is nothing odd about this powerful expression of the idea. Moreover, in the idea of *mustērion* ['mystery'] there usually lies the stimulation to discover the mystery. It may have been the original idea that Jesus was not known as messiah, and only the later idea that he *wanted* to be unknown.

What I have just been saying should be regarded as a tentative solution. I am not asserting that I have provided a proof to remove every obscurity. It may perhaps be reckoned that this whole field of ideas is illuminated too little by written sources for us to make any completely certain progress. Can we after all say no more than that we are making an overall survey of the possible modes of explanation? I do not underestimate the aptness of this question; but I do believe that my attempt has a good solid basis in the strong similarity of the two ideas that we have compared.

If my deductions are correct, then they are significant for the assessment of Jesus' historical life itself. If our view could only arise where nothing is known of an open messianic claim on Jesus' part, then we would seem to have in it *a positive historical testimony for the idea that Jesus actually did not give himself out as messiah*. But this question cannot be fully worked out here.

4

The Kingdom of God

Albrecht Ritschl and Johannes Weiss

From the time of Reimarus, much of the debate surrounding
the historical Jesus has focused on the meaning of the phrase
'the kingdom of God', which all commentators believe to
have been central to Jesus' teaching. To understand the dimensions of this debate, it is helpful to return to the figure of
Albrecht Ritschl, a much neglected thinker in our own time
but perhaps the most important figure in the world of nineteenth-century theology. Ritschl was not only influential in
his own right, but he also ranks as the founder of a 'school',
whose influence (whether directly or by way of reaction) can
be traced as late as the work of Rudolf Bultmann (1884-
1976) and Karl Barth (1886-1968). Ritschl recognized the
centrality of 'the kingdom of God' in Jesus' teaching and
wished to give this concept a central place in his own theological system. Yet his understanding of what Jesus intended
by that term would be soon overturned by the work of his
own son-in-law, Johannes Weiss (1863-1914) and that of Albert Schweitzer (1875-1965). It may be noted that this famous discussion has taken on a new relevance today, with
the re-emergence of a loosely 'Ritschlean' understanding of
'the kingdom of God' among those scholars who see Jesus,
not as an apocalyptic prophet, but as a teacher of ethical wisdom. In this context, it is particularly important that the
nineteenth-century debate not be forgotten.

Albrecht Ritschl (1822-89)

Albrecht Ritschl was born in Berlin, where his father was a pastor and a supporter of the state-supported union of the Lutheran and the Calvinist branches of German Protestantism. When Albrecht was six years old, his family moved to the town of Stettin (now Szczecin, on the border of Poland and Germany), where his father had been appointed 'bishop'. In 1839 he began theological studies in Bonn, where he was not only shaped by the scriptural and supernaturalistic piety of the theological faculty of that time, but also came into contact with the work of David Friedrich Strauss. From 1841-43 Ritschl studied in Halle, where he began to be influenced by the 'Hegelian' school of theologians, most famously Ferdinand Christian Baur (1792-1860) from Tübingen. Worried by his son's turn towards such radical thinkers, Ritschl's father insisted he spend some time in Heidelberg, before allowing him to study in Tübingen, which he did from 1845-46. Under Baur's influence, Ritschl completed and published a dissertation on *Marcion's Gospel and the Canonical Gospel of Luke*, and in 1846 he began his teaching career in Bonn, where he soon produced a study entitled *The Emergence of the Early-Catholic Church* (1850). By this time Ritschl had broken with the Tübingen school, and his formerly warm relationship with Baur turned into conflict. Ritschl's interests now moved increasingly towards the development of a systematic theology, one firmly grounded in the theology of the sixteenth-century reformers and less shaped by what he saw as the *a priori* philosophical convictions of the Tübingen theologians. In 1864 he received a chair in dogmatic theology at Göttingen, where he remained until his death. It was during these years that Ritschl produced his major, three volume work, *The Christian Doctrine of Justification and Reconciliation* (1871-74). In 1875 he published a summary of his theology, intended (but never used) as a school text and entitled *Instruction in the Christian Religion* (the German title of which calls to mind John Calvin's great work, the *Institutes*). The last decade of Ritschl's scholarly career was dedicated to a major study of Pietism, also issued in three volumes (1880-86), a movement which he himself found distasteful but whose historical importance he recognized.

The following extract comes from Ritschl's 1875 work, *Instruction in the Christian Religion*. This concise summary of Christian doctrine is divided into four parts, dealing with 'the kingdom of God', 'reconciliation', 'the Christian life' and 'public worship' respectively. Our extract embraces the first of those four topics, its initial position in the work indicating its centrality within Ritschl's system. In the introduction to the *Instruction*, Ritschl argues that a right understanding of Christian doctrine must pay attention both to the person of Christ and to the life of the Church, a double perspective reflected also in paragraph 25 (below). This makes it clear that what Ritschl is engaged in here is nothing less than a systematic exposition of Christian theology. It is not 'merely' a work of historical reconstruction. For Ritschl believed that any depiction of Jesus which relied on historical reconstruction alone and which did not take into account his impact on believers would be radically incomplete. (In this sense he anticipates the objections to the quest which would later be put forward by Martin Kähler [1835-1912] as well as Karl Barth and Rudolf Bultmann.) Nonetheless, Ritschl also insists that this theological reflection on Jesus' message of 'the kingdom of God' must be based on what he calls the 'historically certified characteristics' of Jesus' active life. Thus Ritschl's discussion of 'the kingdom of God' assumes a certain historical grounding in Jesus' own teaching (a grounding spelt out more fully in volume 2 of his *Justification and Reconciliation*), even if it goes well beyond what the historian alone would feel able to affirm. It is this historical grounding of Ritschl's theology (and not necessarily his theological conclusions) which his later critics would call into question.

For Ritschl, then, what is 'the kingdom of God'? Ritschl insists that it is more than an inward union between Christ and believers (as defined by the sixteenth-century reformers), and it is certainly not to be narrowly identified with the institution of the Church (as in traditional Roman Catholicism). Rather it is the moral ideal of the religious fellowship founded by Jesus, an ideal which is both a gift from God (through the redemption wrought by Christ) and a task laid upon his followers. Thus the kingdom of God (as Ritschl writes elsewhere) may be identified with 'the organisation of humanity through action inspired by love'. The love which constitutes this ethical ideal is in principle universal, and thus goes beyond the natural bonds of human affection or the minimal demands of justice. The Christian meaning of the phrase also transcends the religious and political hopes for Israel implicit in the Old Testament conceptions of God's rule over the nations. The special vocation of Jesus was to bring in this kingdom, which he made a reality through his obedience to God. Thus goal of Jesus' life was identical with that of God himself; in this sense he may be understood as the revelation and indeed incarnation of God.

It may be noted that the following extract makes references to paragraphs within Ritschl's *Instruction* which are not reproduced here. To follow up these references, the reader is encouraged to turn to the full text translated and reproduced in Philip Hefner's edition, from which this extract is taken.

Instruction in the Christian Religion

Reprinted from *Three Essays* Albrecht Ritschl (1972), copyright ©Philip Hefner. Used by permission of Philip Hefner.

I. The Doctrine of the Kingdom of God

5. The kingdom of God is the divinely ordained highest good[1] of the community[2] founded through God's revelation in

---

[1] Rom. 14:16-18. The kingdom of God is the divinely ordained end of the preaching of Christ, extending the invitation to a change of heart and to faith (Mark 1:15), and forming the principle subject of prayer to God (Luke 11:2; Matt. 6:10). The value of the highest good is especially set forth in the parable of the wedding feast (Matt. 22:2-14; 8:11; Luke 14:16-24; 13:29). In John the promise of eternal life has the same significance.

[2] Christ in his office of revealer actualizes the kingdom of God (Matt. 12:28); in order to assure its task for men, he calls the twelve disciples so that they may be with him (Mark 3: 14; Luke 12:32), may learn the mysteries of the kingdom (Mark 4:11), and enter into the same fellowship with God which he himself maintained (John 17:19-23); in accordance with this purpose he

Christ; but it is the highest good only in the sense that it forms at the same time the ethical ideal for whose attainment[3] the members of the community bind themselves to each other through a definite type of reciprocal action.[4] This meaning of the concept 'kingdom of God' becomes clear through the imperative which is simultaneously expressed in it.

6. The righteous conduct through which the members of Christ's community share in effecting the kingdom of God finds its universal law and its personal motive in love to God and to one's neighbor.[5] This love receives its impulse from the love of God revealed in Jesus Christ (pars. 13, 22). The broadening of the concept of neighbor to include men as men, i.e., as ethical persons, opposes the kingdom of God to the narrower ethical communities (par. 8) which are limited by men's natural endowment [Ausstattung] and by the natural restrictions on their common activities.[6] The law of love appears in contrast to the

distinguishes them (the sons of God) as a special religious community, distinct from the Israelite community of the servants of God (Matt 17:24-27).

[3] The parables (Mark 4) which set forth the mysteries of the kingdom in figures of the growth of grain, etc., always signify by 'fruit' a human product, springing out of an individual activity called forth by the divine 'seed', i.e., by the impulse of the divine word of revelation. The parable of the laborers in the vineyard has the same meaning (Matt. 20).

[4] Fruit is the figure for a good deed or for righteous conduct (Matt. 7:16, 20; 13:33; James 3:18; Phil. 1:11). The kingdom of God consists in the exercise of righteousness, in the peace produced by it among all its members, and in the joy of blessedness proceeding from the Holy Spirit (Matt. 6:33; Rom. 14:17, 18). As to peace, compare Mark 9:50; Rom. 12:18; 14:19; 2 Cor. 13:11; 1 Thess. 5:13; Heb. 12:14. As to joy and blessedness, compare Gal. 5:22; James 1:25; and Luther's Small Catechism, II, 2: 'That I might live under him in his kingdom and serve him in everlasting righteousness, innocence, and blessedness.'

[5] The law which Christ points out in the two chief commandments of the Mosaic law (Mark 12:28-33) has reference to the conduct suitable to the kingdom of God. Love to God has no sphere of activity outside of love to one's brother (1 John 4:19-21; 5:1-3).

[6] One's neighbor is no longer one's relative or compatriot alone, but possibly also the benevolent citizen of a hostile people (Luke 10:29-37), thus love of one's enemy in its generally permissible manifestations is included in the Christian love which embraces all mankind (Matt. 5:43-48; Rom. 12:14, 20, 21). This special command does not mean that we shall support an enemy in what he is doing against us, but we shall have regard for his dignity as a human being. The ordinary duty, of course, is love of the brethren (1 Pet. 1:22; 3:8; 1

arrangement of human society based merely upon private right,[7] and it goes beyond the principle of personal regard for others set forth in the Mosaic decalogue.[8]

7. The Christian concept of God's kingly authority—to which the kingdom of God corresponds as the union of subjects bound together by righteous conduct—arose out of similarly expressed thoughts in the religion of Israel, thoughts which in turn indicate its original purpose.[9] These thoughts are, in their historical development, elevated by the prophets to the expectation that through God's supernatural judgment his dominion will be realized in the righteousness of a morally purified Jewish people and will be recognized even by the heathen.[10] This idea is to be distinguished from the heathen designation of their gods as kings, partly because of the background of the free creation of the world by God, and partly because of the humane content of

Thess. 4:9; Rom. 12:10; Heb. 13:1), to whom one is also bound to extend forgiveness (Luke 11:4; 17:3, 4); but since the Christian community is the special body in which the members of different peoples are bound together into a moral fellowship whose principle is brotherly love, the circle of the kingdom of God is in this latter command also extended to include all men (Gal.3:28; 5:6; 1 Cor. 7:19; Col. 3:10-11).

[7] The surrender of private rights which follows from the law of love is the rule in intercourse with the brethren (Matt. 5:23-24, 38-42; the evil doer referred to in 5:39 must also be understood to be a brother).

[8] The Mosaic decalogue, except in the command to honor one's parents prescribes negative regard for the personal rights of everyone, in the sense of not inflicting injury (Exod. 20:12-17). This negative care for the rights of others is always the presupposition of the positive regard which finds its completion in the love of others (Rom. 12:10); this love manifests itself in the positive demand for the good of all, therefore in the exercise of public spirit (Rom. 12:16-17; 15:7; Phil. 2:2-4; 2 Cor. 13:11, 1 Thess. 5:11, Heb. 10:24; 1 Pet. 3:8). Thus the 'royal law of love' includes in itself the decalogue and has a broader reach than its prohibitions (James 2:8-9; Rom. 13:8-10).

[9] The one and only God who created the world and therefore is the king of all nations (Jer. 10:10-16; Ps. 47; 97; 103:19-22) will especially lead his chosen people as their king, on condition that they by obedience keep his covenant (Exod. 19:5-6; Judg. 8:23; Isa. 33:22). As their ruler God administers justice among all peoples (Ps. 9:7-8; 1 Sam. 2:2-10, Isa. 3:13), but especially among the chosen people, partly as their leader in war, maintaining their cause against other peoples (Exod. 7:4; Ps. 7:6-13; 76:4-9, 99:1-5) and partly procuring justice for righteous individuals against their insolent oppressors (Ps. 35; 37; 50).

[10] Isa. 2:2-4; Mic. 4:1-4; Jer. 3:14-18; 4:1-2; Isa. 42:1-6; 51:4-6; 56:6-8.

the corresponding law (par. 6, n. 13); for these reasons it engenders the expectation of the religious and moral unification of the nations. The Christian meaning of this thought goes beyond its Old Testament form, in that the ethical intention of the dominion of God is freed from adulteration by the political and ceremonial conditions under which the Old Testament idea and the Jewish hope labored.[11]

8. The kingdom of God which thus (pars. 5-7) presents the spiritual and ethical task of mankind as it is gathered in the Christian community is *supernatural*, insofar as in it the ethical forms of society are surpassed (such as marriage, family, vocation, private and public justice, or the state), which are conditioned by the natural endowment of man (differences in sex, birth, class, nationality) and therefore also offer occasions for self-seeking. The kingdom of God is *supramundane*, even as it now exists in the world as the present product of action motivated by love, insofar as we understand as 'mundane' the nexus of all natural, naturally conditioned and organized existence. And the kingdom of God is at the same time the highest good of those who are united in it, to the degree that it offers the solution to the question propounded or implied in all religions: How can man, recognizing himself as a part of the world and at the same time capable of a spiritual personality, attain to that dominion over the world, as opposed to limitation by it, which this capability gives him the right to claim? The supernatural and supramundane kingdom of God continues to exist as the highest good of its members even when the present mundane conditions of spiritual life are changed (par. 76).

9. Although actions prompted by love and charitable human organisations are empirically perceptible as such, the motive of love which inspires them is in no case completely open to the observation of others. Therefore, the presence of the kingdom of God within the Christian community is always invisible and a matter of religious faith.[12] Especially must it be noted that the real continuance of the kingdom of God is not identical with the

[11] Mark 10:42-45; 12:13-17; 2:27-28 (Compare with Isa. 56:2-5); Matt. 17:24-27.
[12] Luke 17:20-21; Heb. 11:1.

continuance of the Christian community, as the latter is visible as the church in public worship.[13]

10. The equality of all men as such, regardless of differences of nation or rank (par. 6, n. 11), and the duty of universal brotherly love are recognized even in classical paganism. Greek poets recognize the equality of slave and freeman.[14] Stoic philosophers witness to the brotherhood of all men, and from this conception of human nature derive the virtues which are to lead to the establishment of the most comprehensive human fellowship[15] and

---

[13] The name of the community of believers (church, *ekklesia*, Heb. *Kahal*) as a result of this harmony with Old Testament use of terms, refers directly to the visible liturgy (sacrifice, prayer) (par. 81). But this religious community must at the same time unite itself to the kingdom of God by the mutual exercise of love. By virtue of the different nature of these two activities and the different conditions under which they arise, it follows that they are never exercised to an equal extent during the historical existence of the community. The community of believers must fulfill its mission in these two relations in such a way that the two lines of their activity shall stand in reciprocal relation to one another, but it is a mistake so to identify the two as to use the same name interchangeably for them both. For the actions by which the community becomes a church are not those by which it unites itself to the kingdom of God, and vice versa. And it is particularly misleading to claim, as the Roman Catholic church does for itself, designation as the kingdom of God because of a certain juridical form [*rechtliche Verfassung*].

[14] Menander: 'The slave becomes base, when he learns merely to bend himself to every service; give freedom of word to the slave and he will surely become the best of the good' (*Ex incertis comoediis*, 254). 'Serve in a free spirit and you are not a slave' (ibid., 255). Philemon: 'Even he who is a slave, madam, is still none the less human, since he is truly a human being' (ibid., 29). 'Though one be a slave, he is yet of the same flesh; for nature never created a slave, it is only fortune that has thrust the body into servitude' (ibid., 84).

[15] Antiochus of Askalon, in Cicero's *De finibus bonorum et malorum*, V. 23:65 [trans. H. Rackham, Loeb Classical Library (New York: Macmillan, 1914), pp. 467-69]: 'But in the whole moral sphere of which we are speaking there is nothing more glorious nor of wider range than the solidarity of mankind, that species of alliance and partnership of interests and that actual affection which exists between man and man, which, coming into existence immediately upon our birth, owing to the fact that children are loved by their parents and the family as a whole, is bound together by the ties of marriage and parenthood, gradually spreads its influence beyond the home, first by blood relationships, then by connections through marriage, later by friendships, afterwards by the bonds of neighborhood, then to fellow citizens and political allies and friends, and lastly by embracing the whole of the human race. This sentiment, assigning each his own and maintaining with generosity and equity

all of this apart from any thought of God. Nevertheless, it is a fact that the transformation of human society in accordance with these views was a development of Christianity, not Stoicism. Two reasons account for this: *First*, a diametrically opposite conclusion from that of the Stoics may as easily be drawn from their conception of the nature of man, depending upon the empirical view which informs this conception. *Second*, a knowledge of universal ethical precepts, as such, is never sufficient to call forth and organize the activity that is appropriate to those precepts. This activity follows only when a special, indeed a religious, motive or ground of obligation is linked with knowledge of the universal precept. Accordingly, the principles common to some degree to both Stoicism and Christianity became fruitful only upon the soil of the latter where they were taken up into the underlying principle of obligation of that particular religious community. The highest criterion for those obligations is the thought of a supramundane, supernatural God.[16] Accordingly, the exercise of one's humanness is all the more reliably connected with the thought of a supernatural God rather than a fluctuating concept of human nature when the union of men, *qua* men, at which it aims, bears in itself the stamp of the supernatural and supramundane (par. 8).

11. The complete name of God which corresponds to the Christian revelation is 'The God and Father of our Lord Jesus Christ'.[17] This name includes the fact, already recognized to some extent in the religions of all civilized nations [*Culturrelig-ionen*], that God is a spiritual person. It includes also the characteristics brought out first in the religion of the Old Testament, that God is the only being of his kind,[18] that he is not encum-

---

that human solidarity and alliance of which I speak, is termed justice.' Compare the collection in Schmidt, *Die bürgerliche Gesellschaft in der altrömischen Welt*, 306. Seneca expresses himself similarly.

[16] Concerning a standard of this relation which comes closer to us, cf. par. 19.

[17] 2 Cor. 1:3; 11:31; Rom. 15:6; Col. 1:3; Eph. 1:3; 1 Pet. 1:3.

[18] 1 Sam. 2:2; Isa. 45:18, 21-22; Exod. 20:2-3. The Old Testament conception of the gods of the heathen is accordingly either that they are nothing or vanity (Lev. 19:4; 2 Kings 17:15; Jer.2:5; 8:19) or, insofar as their existence is granted, that they are subordinate organs of the government of the only God (Deut. 4:19; 10:17; Ps. 95:3; 96:4; 1 Cor. 8:5-6). As the only God, the true

bered with nature and thus did not come into existence with the world like the many heathen divinities; that rather, he is the creator of the universe who, as the will that determines himself and all things for himself,[19] in particular designs a community of men for religious communion with himself and ethical communion with one another.

12.[20] Indirectly included in the complete Christian name of God (par. 1), 'The God and Father of our Lord Jesus Christ', is also that he is the Father of all, of whatever nationality, who are united in the community of the Lord Jesus Christ. Therefore in the abbreviated name, 'God our Father',[21] the thought is expressed that the one God directs his special purpose to this community, whose highest good and common imperative is the kingdom of God (par. 5). Now, however, the complete name of God means that he has assumed this special relationship to this particular community only because he is already and first of all the Father of Jesus Christ, who is recognized as Lord by his community. In this capacity, however, Christ stands nearer to God, nearer than any other, because he shares in God's attributes

God is the Holy One (1 Sam. 2:2), who is unattainable by the way of natural knowledge, exalted above all sense perception, unimpeachable.

[19] Gen. 1; Isa. 45:12; Matt. 11:25. That God as the absolutely free will determines himself and as the creator determines all that together makes the world is united into the statement that God is the end of the universe, or that the course of the world ministers to his glory (1 Cor. 8:6; Rom. 11:36; Eph. 4:6). The conception of the creation of the world by God lies entirely outside of all observation and ordinary experience and therefore outside of the realm of scientific knowledge, which is limited by these. Thus, even though we are able to obtain from experience a clear idea of natural causes and effects, the creation of the world by God cannot rightly be thought of as analogous to these forms of knowledge. It can only be analogous to the original force of our will as it is directed toward a goal and comprehended in such a way that the world as a whole, and not just its individual parts, is compared to God.

[20] Scientific observation of nature is directed toward the causal relationship of things. Since it regards organic beings (plants, animals) with reference to the end which they have in themselves, it denies itself the occasion to recognize them as necessarily existing for the sake of man. Such a relationship is apprehended everywhere only by the religious judgment; thus in the Old Testament everything is subservient to the world supremacy of the people of Israel.

[21] In the majority of the inscriptions of the New Testament epistles. As the end of creation (Col. 1:6; Eph. 1:10), Christ is also the central reason [*Mittelgrund*] for creation from the standpoint of the divine purpose (1 Cor. 8:6).

of being the end of creation[22] and recognizes himself as set apart from the world in his position of sonship to God the Father.[23] The key to the relationship between God the Father and the Son of God is found in the declaration that God is love.[24]

13. In the complete name of God the fact that God is the Father of human beings is connected with Jesus Christ insofar as he is recognized as the Lord of a particular fellowship (par. 12). Through Christ's mediation this community of human beings is also designated as the object of divine love.[25] Such a relation would be inconceivable if God's purpose were merely the maintenance of the natural existence of the human race. In this case men would not be of like nature with God (par. 12, n. 30). The concept of God as love corresponds to that idea of mankind which sees man destined for the kingdom of God and for the activity directed toward this kingdom, i.e., the mutual union of man through action springing from love (par. 6).[26] This destiny, however, is realized by men only in their union with the community of their lord Jesus Christ.

---

[22] As Lord over all he is the one 'to whom every knee shall bow', that is, he receives divine worship (Phil. 2:9-11). But note that God the Father is placed over him (1 Cor. 3:23, 8:6).

[23] Matt. 11:27. That God alone knows the Son signifies that he is set apart from all the world. God's knowledge of him, however, includes in itself a productive voluntary purpose (1 Pet. 1:20; Rom. 8:29). Thus Jesus, knowing his peculiar existence to be grounded in the love of his Father (John 10:17, 15:10), places this relation above the coherence and existence of the world (John 17:24).

[24] 1 John 4:8, 16. Love is the *constant* purpose to further another spiritual being of *like* nature with oneself in the attainment of his authentic destiny [*Bestimmung*], and in such a way that the one who loves in so doing pursues his *own* proper end [*Selbstzweck*]. This appropriation of the life-purpose of another is not a weakening negation but a strengthening affirmation of one's own purpose. Thus if God is revealed as love in that he directs his purpose toward Jesus Christ his Son, the love of *God* will be revealed in proportion as this purpose encompasses even the world of which this Son is Lord, and causes it to be recognized as the means to the end, this end being Christ as the head of the community.

[25] 2 Cor. 13:11, 13; Rom. 5:5-8; 8:39; 2 Thess. 2:16; 1 John 4:9-10; Heb. 12:6.

[26] In the love shown by Christians to their brothers the love of God is perfected (1 John 2:5; 4:12), i.e., it finds its complete revelation.

14. The correlation between the concept of God as love and the kingdom of God as the final purpose of the world is confirmed by the statement that God's decision to establish the community of the kingdom of God was decreed before the foundation of the world.[27] The eternity of God which this implies is not sufficiently contained in the affirmation that his existence reaches out beyond that of the world without beginning or end and that God therefore has a measure of time different from that of man.[28] Rather, we recognize God's eternity in the fact that amid all the changes of things, which also indicate variation in his working, he himself remains the same and maintains the same purpose and plan by which he creates and directs the world.[29]

15. The religious acknowledgment of the omnipotence and omnipresence of God, implied in the creation and preservation of the world by God's will,[30] does not undertake to explain the continuance of natural things in whole or in part,[31] but rather always seeks to emphasize that God's care and gracious presence are certain for the pious man, because the world-creating and world-preserving will of God has the well-being of man as its purpose. Therefore, the thought of the omnipotence of God

---

[27] Eph. 1:4-6. 'God has chosen us (the Christian community) in Christ (as Lord of the same) before the foundation of the world, that we might be holy and without blame before him; having in love predestined us to the adoption of children through Jesus Christ to himself, according to the good pleasure of his will, to the praise of the glory of his grace.'

[28] Ps. 90:2, 4.

[29] Ps. 102:25-27.

[30] Ps. 24:1-2; 115:3; 135:6; 139:7-12

[31] This is the application given to these divine attributes in the theological doctrine that God as the first cause is present in all mediate causes. This doctrine consists, nevertheless, of a confused mixture of religious and scientific observation. The idea of God is not at the disposal of a scientific explanation of nature, and any such explanation would indeed offend against the content of the idea of God, if it should make him, under the concept of causation, similar to the natural causes which are intelligible by observation. The religious view of nature, however, does not limit itself to the explanation of natural phenomena as such, but subordinates their existence for the sake of man to the will of God (cf. n.20, above), which is entirely different in kind from natural causes.

finds its consistent fulfilment in the thought of his wisdom, omniscience, and disposition to meet the needs of men.[32]

16. The first perception to arise out of the thought of the omnipotence of God is the insignificance of man. However, inasmuch as the same thought is also the foundation of our impression of God's constant readiness to help (goodness, grace, pity),[33] omnipotence receives the peculiar stamp of *righteousness* in the particular revelation of the old and new covenants. By 'righteousness' the Old Testament signifies the consistency of God's providence [*Leitung zum Heil*], validated on the one hand in the existence of pious and upright adherents to the old covenant,[34] and undertaken on the other hand for the community whose salvation would bring God's government to completion.[35] Insofar as the righteousness of God achieves his dominion in accordance with its dominant purpose of salvation, in spite of all the difficulties which proceed from the Israelites themselves, it is *faithfulness*.[36] Thus in the New Testament also the righteousness of God is recognized as the criterion of the special actions by which the community of Christ is brought into existence and led on to perfection;[37] such righteousness cannot therefore be distinguished from the grace of God.

17. The religious view of the world is based on the fact that all natural occurrences stand at God's disposal when he wishes to help men (par. 15). Accordingly, remarkable natural occurrences with which the experience of the special help of God is connected,[38] are regarded as miracles, and thus as special tokens[39] of his gracious readiness to help believers. Therefore, the conception of miracles stands in a necessary correlation to a special be-

---

[32] Ps. 139 (as a whole, culminating in verses 23, 24); 33:13-19; 104; Job 5:8-27; 11:7-20, 36, 37.

[33] Ps. 145:8-9; Exod. 34:6; Ps. 103:8; Acts 14:15-17; James 5:11; Rom. 2:4; 2 Cor. 1:3.

[34] Ps. 35:23-28; 31:2, 8; 48:10-12; 65:6; 143:11-12; 51:16.

[35] Isa. 45:21; 46:13; 51:5-6; 56:1.

[36] Hos. 2:18-21; Zech. 8:8; Ps. 143:1.

[37] 1 John 1:9; Ps. 51:14; Rom. 3:25-26; John 17:25, 26; Heb. 6:10 (1 Cor. 1:8, 9; 1 Thess. 5:23-24).

[38] Ps. 105; 107; 71:16-21; 86:8-17; 89:5-14; 98:1-3; 145:3-7; Job 5:8-11.

[39] Miracles and signs, Ps. 135:8, 9; Exod. 3:12, 13:9.

lief in the providence of God and is quite impossible apart from such a relationship.[40]

18. God administers the government of the world—and adjusting of the relation between man and the world—by means of retribution. This legal conception is employed in Christianity, as in all religions, because several of its characteristics correspond to the relations which are recognized in every religious view of the world. For law as well as religion has to do with regulating the *position* of the individual *vis-à-vis the world* in accordance with his social or moral worth, and has to do further with the fact that this position is assigned or recognized by an external will (of society, or the state, or God). Thus the concept of divine reward and punishment is also employed in Christianity.[41] The analogy with law extends also to the fact that as the exercise of the right of punishment in the state is only a means of upholding the public well-being, so also the divine punishments which are visited upon godless and persistently rebellious men are always subordinate to the purpose of perfecting the salvation of the righteous and maintaining their cause in the world. But in his purpose these dispensations of God are never a matter of equivalents. On the contrary, there is in this divine administration of justice, *first of all*, no admission of human right over against

---

[40] Mark 5:34; 10:52; 6:5-6. We shift completely the religious conception of miracle when we begin by measuring it against the background of the scientific acceptance of the orderly coherence of all natural events. Since this scientific concept lies outside the horizon of the men of the Old and New Testaments, a miracle never signifies to them an occurrence contrary to nature nor a disruption of the laws of nature by divine arbitrariness. Hence the belief in miracle in the sense referred to above, as a gracious providence of God, is perfectly consistent with the probability of the coherence of the whole world in accordance with natural law. If, nevertheless, certain accounts of miracles in the Bible appear to be contrary to these laws, it is neither the duty of science to explain this appearance nor to confirm it as a fact, nor is it the duty of religion to recognize these narrated events as divine operations contrary to the laws of nature. Neither ought one base his religious faith in God and Christ upon a preceding judgment of this kind (John 4:48, Mark 5:11-12; 1 Cor. 1:22), especially since every experience of miracle presupposes faith. Beginning, however, with faith, everyone will meet the miraculous in his own experience; in view of this, it is entirely unnecessary to ponder over the miracles which others have experienced.

[41] Matt. 5:12, 6:1, 2; 1 Cor. 3:8; 2 Thess. 1:8, 9; Heb. 10:29.

God,[42] *secondly*, no equality between reward and worthiness on the one hand, and punishment and unworthiness on the other,[43] and, *thirdly*, no immediate congruence between misfortune and guilt or prosperity and goodness in individual cases, as might have been expected from the divine power. Any such congruence is referred rather to the future, particularly to the final judgment and the future life.[44] Therefore, the familiar conclusion drawn by the pre-Christian manner of judgment, i.e., that great misfortune was evidence of great guilt, is especially invalidated,[45] and the probability is introduced that a high degree of worldly misfortune may exist precisely in connection with religious and moral worthiness.[46] Finally, a point of view is introduced that substitutes an organic relation of cause and result[47] for

[42] Job 41:3; Rom. 11:35. In general, the view of human life set forth in the biblical writings moves within the limits set by the covenant grace of God. When, therefore, the righteousness of God is appealed to for the reward of righteous men (Ps. 7:8-10; 17:3; 58:11; 139:23, 2 Thess. 1:5-7), the mutual legal relation thereby indicated is only apparent. For the righteousness of God signifies in these cases also only the consistent completion of the salvation of the righteous (par. 16), which, however, has the appearance of reward because it deals in these cases with a condition of innocence and righteousness that is already present in men. Properly, the recompense of the righteous is the work of the grace of God (Ps. 62:12); that of the wicked is their exclusion from (his grace =) righteousness (Ps. 69:24-28). Reward and punishment are not coordinated as expressions of the righteousness of God, but only as visible acts of his exercise of justice, i.e., of his government of the world (Ps. 94: 1, 2; 58: 10, 11).

[43] Exod. 34:7; Mark 4:12; 10:29, 30. The divine punishment in its common Old Testament representation as the wrath of God, because of the nature of the emotion involved in the term wrath, excludes the idea of an exact weighing of the amount of the punishment.

[44] The poets of the Old Testament find themselves completely disappointed in their natural expectation that the good would be prosperous and the wicked unhappy. They must content themselves with praying to God for the righting of the wrong condition of affairs in the future. Thus the establishment of the right order awaits the future judgment of God in the Old as well as in the New Testament.

[45] Eliphaz draws this conclusion in the book of Job (4:7, 22:4-11), on the other hand, consider Job's assurance of his integrity (6:28-30, 23:10-12). As against this combination compare John 9: 1-3; Luke 13: 1-5.

[46] Matt. 5:11; Mark 8:34, 45; Phil. 1:28. Cf. par. 32.

[47] The scheme of retribution in the final judgment (Rom. 2:6-12; 2 Cor. 5:10; 2 Thess. 1:6, 7; Eph. 6:8) is surpassed by the analogy of the seed and the harvest (Gal. 6:7-8). The final result in the case of the good as in that of the

the mechanical relation between reward (punishment) and worthiness (unworthiness) which is recognized in human law. That such a principle as this is operative in all cases can, in truth, be discerned only at the end of time. In the course of history clear examples of this principle are surrounded and obscured by manifold instances of exactly opposite nature. But the Christian faith does not allow itself to be confused as to the consistent direction of the world by God through the apparently purposeless complications of the present and the suffering of the righteous in consequence of the guilt of the unrighteous,[48] because the regular experience of an exact and immediate connection between happiness and worthiness would endanger the freedom and dignity of the moral disposition.

19. The imperative of the moral association of all men as men could become effective as a practical principle only insofar as it grew out of the religious motive of the specifically Christian community (par. 10). Moreover, since that imperative raises itself above all naturally conditioned moral motives, its authority in the Christian community finds its necessary criterion in the idea of a supernatural God developed in paragraphs 11-18. Moreover, the peculiar fact of such a community, which sets itself to the realization of this universal task as the thrust of the kingdom of God, is not a natural given but is comprehensible in its distinctive nature only as the work of Christ's own establishment (par. 13). Therefore, in order for us to understand and rightly participate in the existence of this community, it is necessary to acknowledge and understand the permanent relation which exists between the community of the kingdom of God and its founder Jesus Christ.[49]

---

evil is but the appropriate legitimate effect of the power of the good or the evil will. By comparison, the transitory temporal experiences of a contrary nature are not worthy of consideration.

[48] Rom. 11:33-36. From par. 13 there follows the universal law of the divine government, maintained everywhere in the Old as well as in the New Testament, that all punishment or destruction of the wicked by God serves as a means to the complete salvation of the righteous. It is not, however, a means to the end of God's own glory or righteousness, as is set forth in Luther's and Calvin's doctrine of predestination.

[49] In all folk religions the person of the founder, even when known (Zoroaster, Moses), is a matter of indifference, because the religious community,

20. The historical connection of Christianity with the religion of the Old Testament (par. 7) makes it natural that Jesus
should in general represent himself as a prophet sent by God
who was ordained in God's decree concerning the world and
mankind.[50] However, he sets himself above all the preceding
prophets of the Old Testament by making himself known as the
Son of God and the promised king of David's race (Christ the
anointed),[51] who need not first prepare the way for the kingdom
of God but effects *the* work of God,[52] i.e., himself exercises immediate divine rulership over the new community of the sons of
God, and establishes it for the future (par. 5, n. 7). The prophetic vocation of Jesus is not annulled by his claim to messianic
dignity, but only modified by it, since he exercises his right as
lord only through his morally effective teaching and by his
readiness to engage in the action of servant—not by the com-
pulsion of legal judgment.[53]

21. In the moral world all personal authority is conditioned
by the nature of one's vocation and by the connection between
one's fitness for his particular vocation and his faithful exercise of
it. Accordingly, the permanent significance of Jesus Christ for his
community is based, *first*, on the fact that he was the only one
qualified for his special vocation—bringing in the kingdom of
God;[54] that he devoted himself to the exercise of this highest

consisting of the whole race or people, is determined by nature. On the other
hand, in universal religions (Buddhism, Christianity, Islam), allegiance to the
founder, or worship of him, is prescribed, because only through the founder
does the corresponding community exist as it is, and only by allegiance to him
can it be preserved. In these cases the difference in the estimation of Moham-
med and Christ is to be explained by the difference in the nature of the two
religions.

[50] Mark 6:4; 9:37; John 4:34; 5:23, 24; 6:44. It comes also under the prophetic conception (Exod. 33:11; Num. 12:8) that Jesus speaks what he hears
from God (John 8:26, 40; 15:15) and has seen of him (John 6:46; 8:38).

[51] Mark 12:1-9; 8:29; 14:61-62; John 4:25-26.

[52] John 4:34; 17:4.

[53] John 18:36; Mark 10:42-45.

[54] The fitness of Jesus finds expression in his assertion of the mutual knowledge existing between himself and God as his Father (Matt. 11:27; John 10:15;
compare Luke 2:49). He does not know God as his Father without being
himself conscious that he is *the* one called of God to found the kingdom of
God in a new religious community. This conviction vouches also for all the
other sides of his spiritual endowment for this vocation, because all the char-

conceivable vocation in the preaching of the truth and in loving action without break or deviation;[55] and that, in particular, as a proof of his steadfastness[56] he freely accepted in willing patience[57] the wrongs brought upon him by the opposition of the leaders of the nation of Israel and the fickleness of the people, all of which were so many temptations to draw back from his vocation.

22. *Second*, the imperative of Jesus Christ's vocation, or the final purpose of his life, namely, the kingdom of God, is the very purpose of God in the world, as Jesus himself recognized.[58] The solidarity between Christ and God, which Jesus accordingly claims for himself,[59] has reference to the whole range of his activity in his vocation and consists therefore in the reciprocal relation between God's love and Jesus' vocational obedience.[60] Since he is the first to actualize in his own personal life the final purpose of the kingdom of God, Jesus is therefore unique, for should any other fulfill the same task as perfectly as he, he would be unlike him because of his dependence upon Jesus. Therefore, as the prototype of the humanity to be united into the kingdom of God, he is the original object of God's love (par. 12), so that the love of God for the members of his kingdom is also mediated only through him (par. 13). Therefore, when this person is valued at his whole worth, this person who was active in his

---

acteristics of his life witness to his perfect spiritual soundness, and there is not the least trace in him of fanaticism or self-deception.

[55] The sinlessness of Jesus (John 8:36; 1 Pet. 2:21; 1 John 3:5; 2 Cor. 5:21; Heb. 4:15) is only the negative expression for the constancy of his disposition and conduct of his vocation (obedience, Phil. 2:8; Heb. 5:8) or for the positive righteousness in which he differs from all other men (1 Pet. 3:18).

[56] Heb. 2: 18; 4: 15; Mark 14: 33-36; 1:13.

[57] The principle of Matt. 11:28-30. The two Greek words *praüs kai tapeinos* ('gentle and lowly') point to the use of one Hebrew or Aramaic word, *anav*, which indicates the regular characteristics of the righteous in their suffering under the persecution of the godless (Pss. 9:12; 10:12-17; 25:9; 37:11; 69:32). The addition of *te kardia* ('in heart') denotes that Jesus in his righteousness is ready to endure all the undeserved sufferings which follow from the reaction against his activity in his vocation. Thereby, however, he makes a distinction in kind between himself and the righteous of the Old Testament, who always seek to be delivered from their undeserved suffering.

[58] John 4:34.

[59] John 10:28-30, 38; 14:10; 17:21-23.

[60] John 15:9, 10; 17:24, 26; 10:17; 12:49, 50.

peculiar vocation, whose constant motive is recognizable as unselfish love to man, then we see in Jesus the complete revelation
of God as love, grace and faithfulness.[61]

23. In every religion, not only is some sort of communion
with God (or the gods) sought after and attained, but there is
also a search at the same time for such a position of the individual vis-a-vis the world as will correspond with the idea of God
which guides that religion. Hence, *third*, Jesus Christ's prerogative, that the rulership of the world is delivered over to him,[62]
corresponds to the solidarity of Jesus with the supramundane
God in the realization of the supramundane (par. 8) kingdom of
God, which as the final purpose of God is also the final purpose
of the world. The significance of this attribute is not secured if
we suppose that Jesus did not exercise it, but allowed it to remain inactive in his public historical life. Moreover, he did not
merely exercise it indirectly, as if by his deeds and his words and
his patience in suffering he prepared the way for the kingdom of
God in his community, so that his dominion over the world
would be established only in the world-historical progress of that
community. Rather, he exercised this dominion directly, not
only in the independence of his action from the standard of religion peculiar to his people,[63] but also in his very readiness to
suffer everything even unto death for the sake of his vocation.[64]
For through this suffering he transformed the world's opposition
to his life purpose into a means of his glorification, i.e., into the
certainty of overcoming the world by the very fact of this mo-
mentary subjection to its power and assuring the supramundane
continuance of his life.[65] Accordingly, his resurrection through
the power of God is the consistent fulfilment, corresponding to
the worth of his person, of the revelation effected through him

---

[61] John 1:14; Exod. 34:6, 7; compare par. 16.

[62] Matt. 11:27.

[63] Matt. 17:24-27; 8:11, 12; Mark 12:9.

[64] Matt. 11:28-30. Compare n.57, above.

[65] John 71:1, 4, 5; 16:16, 33. Accordingly, the view of Jesus' life given by
Paul in Phil. 2:6-8 is not complete. The path of obedience even to death is for
Jesus only apparently a degradation beneath his dignity. It is in truth the form
of his self-exaltation above the world and above its usual standards (Mark
10:42-45). That is to say, one *becomes* great through degradation in service only
because one *is* already great in unselfish obedience (Phil. 2:1-5).

which is final in respect to both the actual will of God and the destiny of man.

24. In Christ's vocational activity, directed to the divine purpose of the kingdom of God, the same acts of love and patience are both manifestations of the grace and faithfulness which are essential to God himself and proofs of his dominion over the world.[66] These relations, which are necessary to the full appreciation of Jesus and are evident in his life, are referred to in the confession of the Godhood of Christ which the Christian community has made from the beginning. That is to say, this attribute of Godhood cannot be maintained unless the same activities in which Jesus Christ proves himself man are thought of as being simultaneously and in the same way also distinctive predicates of God and the peculiar means of his revelation through Christ. If the grace and faithfulness and dominion over the world, which are evident both in Christ's active life and in his patience in suffering, are also the essential attributes of God and decisive for the Christian religion, then the right appreciation of the completeness of the revelation of God through Christ is assured by the predicate of his Godhood, in accordance with which Christians are to trust in him and to worship him even as they do God the Father.[67]

25. The estimate of Christ set forth in paragraphs 20-24 is intentionally directed with the greatest possible exactness to the

---

[66] In apostolic usage, the Old Testament name of God, 'Lord', is applied only to the risen Christ, exalted to the right hand of God (Phil. 2:9-11). Yet this conception can only be understood on the condition that this attribute is discernible also as an actual characteristic in the historical life of Christ (par. 23). But this dominion of Christ over the world has no other sphere of activity save such as is maintained through the power of a will concentrated upon God's supramundane purpose of love. Also the apostles regard Christ as creator only in this respect, that because he comprises typically in himself the goal of the world, i.e., the kingdom of God and the glory of God, he furnishes in the divine creative will the means for the creation of the world (Col. 1:15-18; 1 Cor. 8:6; Heb. 1:1-3). This line of thought, however, leads over into the territory of theology proper and has no direct and practical significance for religious belief in Jesus Christ.

[67] Melanchthon, Loci (1535, CR [*Corpus Reformatorum*] XXI, 366): 'The scriptures teach us the divinity of the son not only speculatively, but practically, i.e., they command us to pray to Christ and to trust in Christ, for thus is the honor and divinity truly accorded to him.'

historically certified characteristics of his active life, but at the same time it is undertaken from the standpoint of the community of the kingdom of God founded by him. These two criteria, historical and religious, for the understanding of his person should coincide[68] inasmuch as Christ's purpose was directed at founding the community in which he was to be acknowledged in religious faith as the Son of God. And if this purpose is in any measure historically realized, it follows that the perfect historical estimate of Christ is possible only for his religious community and that this estimate will be religiously correct in proportion as his community remains faithful to its historically unquestionable task. Accordingly, it is essential to the continuance of the Christian community as such, that it should keep alive within itself the memory of the finished life-work of Christ[69] and that accordingly the personal impulses of its founder should be ceaselessly operative in like efforts on the part of the members of his community.[70] In the fulfilment of these conditions we see the visible side of the mystery of Christ's exaltation to the right hand of God, which is acknowledged by his community[71] as a guarantee that the purpose of his life was not frustrated but rather fully accomplished in his death.[72]

[68] There is a complete misconception of the problem, and the understanding desired is rendered impossible, if the principle is followed that historical knowledge of Christ is possible only insofar as one is divested of religious devotion to him.

[69] Accordingly, his death will be regarded, not as a just punishment for blasphemy as his enemies intended it, nor as the result of fanatic daring, but as the completion of the work of his vocation, which he accepted with dutiful determination because he recognized in it God's purpose for him. This significance of the death of Christ, set forth by the apostles, marks also the right and complete understanding of Christ's obedience in life, as it was completed in his death. (Cf. n. 110, below [not reproduced here].)

[70] Gal. 2:20; 3:27; Rom. 6:5, 11; 8:2, 10; 12:4, 5; 1 Cor. 12:12.

[71] Rom. 10:9; 1 Cor. 15:3-20; 1 Pet. 1:3; 3:21, 22; Heb. 13:20, 21.

[72] Mark 14:62; John 10:17, 18; 17:4, 5.

Johannes Weiss (1863-1914)

There is much that is attractive in Albrecht Ritschl's theological vision. By defining 'the kingdom of God' as he did Ritschl succeeded in connecting Christian theology with the ethical concern which thinkers since Kant had seen as the core of religion. By directing attention to the believer's moral relationship to Christ, Ritschl also avoided some of the ambiguities inherent in Schleiermacher's grounding of religion in a particular form of experience. Yet insofar as this theology claimed to be based on a historically defensible reconstruction of Jesus' intentions, it was open to historical objections. It fell to Ritschl's son-in-law, Johannes Weiss, who had cared for the aging theologian in his retirement, to articulate those objections.

Born in Kiel (North of Hamburg, on the Baltic Sea), Johannes Weiss was the son of a noted conservative New Testament scholar, Bernhard Weiss (1827-1918). Having been educated at the Universities of Marburg, Berlin, Göttingen, and Breslau (the Polish Wroclaw), the young Johannes Weiss took up a teaching position at Göttingen in 1888, where he married the daughter of his teacher, Albrecht Ritschl. It was here, too, that Weiss became associated with those scholars known as the 'history of religions school' (including Ernst Troeltsch and William Wrede). During his time at Göttingen he wrote his most famous work, a short essay entitled *Jesus' Proclamation of the Kingdom of God* (published in 1892). Weiss was called to a professorial chair at the University of Marburg in 1895, and in 1908 he moved to the University of Heidelberg, where he remained until his death.

The following extracts are taken from *Jesus' Proclamation of the Kingdom of God*. Weiss begins his work by noting that theologians of his time had rightly begun to centre their theology on the idea of 'the kingdom of God'—an idea central to Jesus' own teaching—rather than on the Pauline concept of 'justification by faith'. Yet he argues that this very fact had made necessary a closer historical investigation of what Jesus meant by the kingdom of God. After a careful discussion of the sources, Weiss describes the reported sayings of Jesus on repentance and the kingdom. He argues that for Jesus himself that kingdom was something still to be realized, although there was a sense in which the power of Satan was already being destroyed through his work as healer and exorcist. In our first reading Weiss continues this discussion, arguing that Jesus did not think of himself as the 'founder' of God's kingdom, certainly not in the sense in which Ritschlean theology had used this term. Even if his ministry witnesses to the power of God over Satan, this is a fact which as yet lies outside of history. For Jesus the establishment of God's kingdom as a historical reality still lies in the future.

Jesus' Proclamation of the Kingdom of God

[Chapter] 5

The recent dogmatic interpretation of the concept βασιλεία τοῦ θεοῦ ['Kingdom of God'] speaks unhesitatingly of Jesus as the 'Founder' and 'Establisher' of the Kingdom of God, without bothering to inquire whether this use of the term reflects Jesus' understanding or ours instead. Though in retrospect *we* certainly can say as a judgment of faith that Jesus established the Kingdom of God within his church, it is just as certain that such a conception or expression is far-removed from the sphere of Jesus' ideas.

Aside from Matt. 16:17f., there is no reliably attested saying of Jesus in which he designates himself as founder of God's Kingdom. He is the sower, who scatters the seed of the Word in men's hearts, but all this is only preparatory, for he never says that it is his task ἀποκαθιστάναι τὴν βασιλεῖαν τῷ 'Ισραήλ ['to restore the Kingdom to Israel' cf. Acts 1:6]. Such an idea is altogether impossible from the standpoint of Jesus' outlook as a whole, as we shall see when we attempt to answer the more far-reaching question: What role did Jesus assign to himself with respect to the establishment of the Kingdom of God, and within that Kingdom? Only in one respect is Jesus more important than the sower or a mere preparer: he prepares the way for the Kingdom of God in that he is successfully engaged in driving the present imperious Ruler of αἰὼν οὗτος ['this age'], Satan, from his position of lordship. Indeed, according to Luke 10:18ff., the real, superhistorical basis for all the success of Jesus and his disciples is the fact that Satan has fallen. Previously he had held a position in heaven as one among the other angels of God; indeed, the present world had been handed over to him by God (Luke 4:6) for him to rule and enslave. Now he has fallen from heaven, and thereby the backbone of his dominion is broken. Thus it is to be understood that his agents, the demons, also are no longer in a position to offer any resistance to the powerful command of Jesus or even to the mere naming of his feared name.

Jesus was convinced (ἐθεώρουν ['I watched (sc. Satan fall from heaven)' cf. Luke 10:18]), whether in a vision of the sort that he had experienced at his baptism and temptation, or in some moment of inner assurance, that such was the case. Usually this ἐθεώρουν is presumed to have taken place sometime during the absence of the seventy (Luke 10:1-16),[1] but this interpretation is arbitrary since Jesus' own earlier success presupposes the fall of Satan (Luke 11:21f.). It is necessary, then, to look for some earlier occasion. The 'victory over the strong one' has been regarded quite correctly by many as an allusion to the temptation. However one may interpret this, the substance of the reports in the Gospels must somehow or other be derived from sayings of Jesus to the effect that at the beginning of his activity he had overcome Satan, so that the δύναμις ['power'] of the Adversary is under control and can no longer harm him or his followers (Luke 10:17ff.; 22:31f.). How we ourselves are to think of this struggle can only be conjectured—what alone matters is the result of the struggle as it later lived on in Jesus' consciousness. There can be no objection to speaking of Jesus as 'Founder of the Kingdom of God' if one is willing to think of it in these terms just described—that is, if one keeps in view the destruction of the kingdom of Satan (1 John 3:8). I imagine, however, that most people will neither be satisfied with this more negative description of the concept, nor want to understand it in this completely supranaturalistic way of looking at things, which is mythological from our standpoint.

---

[1] E.g., Wendt, *Lehre Jesu*, 2: 301f.

In the following chapters Weiss argues that, rather than understanding himself as the 'founder' of God's kingdom, Jesus thought of his role as that of its proclaimer. In other words, Jesus did not think of his own (present) role as properly messianic, but merely preparatory. It is true that the 'Son of Man' has a crucial role to play in the establishment of God's kingdom, but this is a role Jesus would have only after his exaltation by God. In the meantime even Jesus cannot *bring about* God's kingdom, the inauguration of which is entirely in God's hands. Even at the Last Supper, Weiss continues, Jesus thought of that kingdom as yet to be realized. Apparently he had originally believed that the kingdom would be established during his lifetime, but by the end of his ministry Jesus had come to the realization that the end had been postponed. For the kingdom of God could not be established until the guilt of God's people had been removed, and Jesus had come to the shocking conclusion that his own death would be a ransom for a people 'otherwise destined to destruction'. Yet this death was also something transitory, for it would be followed by his exaltation by God and return in glory. It is only then, in God's good time, that the promised kingdom would be established, after the transformation of the present order of the world and the judgement of human beings.

In the extract which follows, Weiss looks more closely at the question of what Jesus meant by the phrase 'kingdom of God'.

[Chapter] 11
The Meaning of Salvation in the Kingdom of God

We now ask: If Jesus proclaimed the Kingdom of God without generally defining this conception more closely for his hearers, what did he understand the impending but still future Kingdom of God to mean? And what did he wish his hearers to understand by it? It is generally conceded that Jesus adopted this concept primarily and predominantly in the sense in which it was understood by his contemporaries and without correcting it. Certainly this is true. But what was this sense? Wellhausen[2] ex-

---

[2] Julius Wellhausen, *Die Pharisäer und Sadducäer. Eine Untersuchung zur inneren jüdischen Geschichte* (Greifswald: L. Bamberg, 1874), pp.23ff.

pressed the prevailing viewpoint when he said that the *Malkuth* ['Kingdom'] is always to be conceived antithetically: the Kingdom *of God* in opposition to another βασιλεία. But this tells us little, so long as we do not know what, for Jesus, it was opposed to. It has already been shown that in an important passage, Matt. 12:28, the βασιλεία τοῦ θεοῦ is set over against that of Satan. The question arises whether this is only a passing thought or whether it is fundamental to Jesus' way of thinking. Few passages yield any direct evidence. But if in Matt. 12:45 Jesus is describing his experience with this generation, and in this connection uses the idea of demon exorcism; if we note how the demons regard him as the one who has come to destroy them; and if originally all the afflictions which Jesus healed were traced, ultimately, to the influence of Satan (Matt. 8:16-17; Luke 13:16); then we realize that Jesus conceived of his work as a struggle against Satan,[3] and the opposition between God and mammon as really between God and Satan, i.e., between the Kingdom of God and Satan.[4] This opposition also determines the meaning of the salvation brought by the Kingdom of God. As we have seen already, if the Rule of God primarily brings release from all affliction of body and soul (from all *tristitia* ['sadness'] *Assumption of Moses,* 10:2), then the evil spirits to whom the people have been subjected must give way, for they have lost their power (Luke 10:18).

The deliverance of the people from their enemies and oppressors belongs in this context. There are no direct sayings of Jesus in which the Roman rule is represented as Satan's work,[5] except perhaps Luke 4:6. Yet there can be no doubt that in the βασιλεία τοῦ θεοῦ this was to be a matter of foremost importance. Some may think that the earthly-political character of the idea must be denied in view of the story about tribute money. But what was expressed here in principle, was shown in practice in John 6:15, and finally emerges clearly in the reprimand of Matt. 11:11f., is nothing more than the self-evident consequence of what has previously been stated. How can one expect even the slightest inclination on Jesus' part towards any kind of revo-

---

[3] Cf. John 8:32, 43f.; 12:31; 1 John 3:8.

[4] Issel, *Lehre vom Reiche Gottes,* pp.41ff., thinks similarly on this point.

[5] Luke 22:25 expresses only great disdain.

lutionary act? By force and insurrection men might establish a Davidic monarchy, perhaps even as glorious a kingdom as David's had been; but God will establish the Kingdom of God without human hands, horse, or rider, with only his angels and celestial powers. To hope for the Kingdom of God in the transcendental sense that Jesus understood it and to undertake revolution are as different as fire and water.

Josephus noted as a characteristic of Pharisaic piety that they would rather let themselves be killed than join with the cunning power-politics of the Sadducees. A person of Jesus' markedly religious temperament would necessarily have agreed with them completely. This is not to say that he did not believe in any kind of political restoration; but that only God should bring it about. But when he promises the πραεῖς ['meek'] (Matt. 5:5) that they were to inherit the land of promise, as before him the Psalmist (37:11) and *Enoch* (5:7) had promised they would, this meant that there at last they were to be masters, where now they are still servants. He promises those who yearn for righteousness a complete deliverance from their oppressors and the full restoration of their rights. And, finally, the formula 'to possess the Kingdom of God', or 'to enter the Kingdom of God' means nothing but this: In this Kingdom, the land of promise, risen anew in more beautiful splendor, will be possessed and ruled by them. This is how the Jewish Christian psalms in the first two chapters of Luke understand it, especially that of Zechariah, in Luke 1:68f., 71-75.

By way of counter-evidence, someone might point to the sayings regarding the worthlessness of earthly goods, the danger of riches to the soul, and so forth. But these are only intended as warnings for the time of preparation, admonitions to detach one's self completely from αἰὼν οὗτος ['this age'] in order to be the more fully prepared for the αἰὼν μέλλων ['coming age']. This devaluation of the goods of this αἰών ['age'], therefore, proves nothing about the so-called earthly or outward splendor of the future age, because all these valuable things will be present there in a completely different, pure, unworldly, and spiritual condition. They will still be there in the new world, but all that clings to things of flesh and blood, and sin and impurity, will have dropped away. And then, certainly, the θησαυροί ['treasures'] (Matt. 6:19f.) will be opened, the joys of the great messianic banquet, exaltation and power, sitting on the throne and judging even this is meant concretely and literally—all these things will be refined and transfigured by the heavenly δόξα ['glory'] of God, in whose light all things will shine in splendor. But these 'external-political goods'—which are usually mentioned with a shrug of the shoulders and without understanding—are by no means absent from Jesus' picture of the future. And who would really wish to venture that these are only fantasies which have nothing to do with serious thought? To do so, in other words, would be to fail to recognize one of the important characteristics in the portrait of our Lord which makes him tower over prophets, apocalyptists and his contemporaries, namely, that in these things which concern the 'color' of the messianic salvation, Jesus was so sparing and, as it were, so conventional. His greatness consisted in the fact that he followed the traditional scheme, but with modesty, reserve and sobriety. He did not allow himself or his disciples to revel in these prospects. He kept his eye all the more seriously on that which according to his entire religious and ethical sensibility was most crucial: what was genuinely religious in the Kingdom of God, and ethical preparation for its coming.

> In the following sections of his study Weiss examines more closely Jesus' ethical teaching, noting that the righteousness for which Jesus called was not a state to be achieved *within* the Kingdom of God (as an ethical ideal); rather it was the condition of repentance necessary if that Kingdom was to be received. Jesus' ethical teaching, too, can only be understood in light of his expectation of the imminent establishment of God's rule on earth. His radical demands stem from the conviction that 'the things of this world, however high and godly they may be in themselves, have lost all value now that the world is ripe for destruction'. Weiss also clarifies the distinction between Jesus and John the Baptist. While both proclaim the imminence of God's Kingdom, Jesus is also convinced of his own messianic identity. However, that identity goes far beyond the common hope for a king in the line of David; it is as the 'Son of Man' found in Daniel and *Enoch*, a heavenly figure, established by divine and not by human action, that Jesus will enter into his messianic dignity. He

gradually becomes aware that this exaltation is destined to occur only after his death. Thus Jesus' messianic claim, too, can only be understood in the light of his 'thoroughly transcendental and apocalyptic' expectations.

The last section of the study offers a summary of Weiss's findings, reproduced below. It is worth noting in this context that Weiss makes a clear distinction between Jesus' understanding of the Kingdom of God and that ethical understanding which had been prevalent in nineteenth-century theology. Yet he also insists that the ethical sense of the phrase is the only one which we can adopt today. The world of Jewish apocalyptic is so foreign to our own that we are obliged to reinterpret Jesus' language. In doing so, however, we should be aware that we are departing from that meaning which Jesus himself intended.

Let me now summarize once more the principal results of our study:

1) Jesus' activity is governed by the strong and unwavering feeling that the messianic time is imminent. Indeed, he even had moments of prophetic vision when he perceived the opposing kingdom of Satan as already overcome and broken. At such moments as these he declared with daring faith that the Kingdom of God had actually already dawned.

2) In general, however, the actualization of the Kingdom of God has yet to take place. In particular, Jesus recognized no preliminary actualization of the rule of God in the form of the new piety of his circle of disciples, as if there were somehow two stages, a preliminary one, and the Kingdom of Completion. In fact, Jesus made no such distinction. The disciples were to pray for the coming of the Kingdom, but men could do nothing to establish it.

3) Not even Jesus can bring, establish, or found the Kingdom of God; only God can do so. God himself must take control. In the meantime, Jesus can only battle against the devil with the power imparted to him by the divine Spirit, and gather a band of followers who, with a new righteousness, with repentance, humility and renunciation, await the Kingdom of God.

4) The messianic consciousness of Jesus consists of the certainty that when God has established the Kingdom, judgment and rule will be transferred to him. God will raise him to the office of 'Son of man' (John 3:14), to which he is entitled (John 5:27), and will *make* him Lord and Messiah (Acts 2:36).

5) Although Jesus initially hoped to live to see the establishment of the Kingdom, he gradually became certain that before this could happen, he must cross death's threshold, and make his contribution to the establishment of the Kingdom in Israel by his death. After that, he will return upon the clouds of heaven at the establishment of the Kingdom, and do so within the lifetime of the generation which had rejected him.

Jesus does not fix the time when this will take place more exactly, since the coming of the Kingdom cannot be determined in advance by observation of signs or calculation.

6) But when it comes, God will destroy this old world which is ruled and spoiled by the devil, and create a new world. Even mankind is to participate in this transformation and become like the angels.

7) At the same time, the Judgment will take place, not only over those who are still alive at the coming of the Son of man, but also over those who will then be raised from the dead, good and evil, Jews and Gentiles alike.

8) The land of Palestine will arise in a new and glorious splendor, forming the center of the new Kingdom. Alien peoples will no longer rule over it, but will come to acknowledge God as Lord. There will be neither sadness nor sin; instead those who are in God's Kingdom shall behold the living God, and serve him in eternal righteousness, innocence, and bliss.

9) Jesus and his faithful ones will rule over this newborn people of the twelve tribes, which will include even the Gentiles.

10) The rule of God is not suspended by the rule of the Messiah, but thereby actualized, whether it be that they reign together side by side, or that Jesus reigns under the higher sovereignty of God.

The results just summarized present peculiar difficulties for systematic and practical theology. Jesus' idea of the Kingdom of God appears to be inextricably involved with a number of es-

chatological-apocalyptical views which systematic theology has
been accustomed to take over without critical examination. But
now it is necessary to inquire whether it is really possible for
theology to employ the idea of the Kingdom of God in the
manner in which it has recently been considered appropriate.
The question arises whether it is not thereby divested of its essential traits and, finally, so modified that only the name still remains the same. Thus, for example, Jesus' consciousness of the
nearness of the Kingdom is a feature that cannot be disposed of.
Protestant theology, however, generally regards its task to be
that of framing a unified Christian view of the world and life,
which is supposed to be authoritative both for the individual and
for all people for a long time to come. It would, therefore, at
least have to mitigate the ardent eschatological tone of Jesus'
proclamation. Thus it is explained first, that although the Kingdom
of God has secondary significance for us as the 'heavenly Kingdom of Completion', we should think of it primarily as the invisible community of men who venture to honor God as their
King and Father and seek to obtain the effectiveness and extension of his rule among themselves and others by fulfilment of his
will.

A new point of view concerning both the ideas of Jesus and
dogmatics has recently been attempted: specifically by J. Kaftan,
who in his volume on *Das Wesen der christlichen Religion* [*The
Essence of the Christian Religion*][6] represents the Kingdom of God
even in Jesus' preaching less as a 'community of men' than as the
highest 'religious good'. Kaftan stresses, quite correctly, against
Reischle among others, that the dominant idea in Jesus' proclamation is 'not that of a Kingdom of ethical righteousness in the
world, but that of a superworldly, transcendent Kingdom of
Blessedness'. With this Kaftan contrasts the Kingdom of God as
'supreme ethical ideal'; as such it is 'inner worldly and its actualization a matter involving human initiative [*Selbsttätigkeit*]'. After
all that we have previously said, we can recognize that this conception is incorrect. The actualization of the Kingdom of God is
not a matter for human initiative, but entirely a matter of God's
initiative. The only thing man can do about it is to perform the

---

[6] 2nd ed., pp.236ff.

conditions required by God. The Kingdom of God, in Jesus'
view, is never an ethical ideal, but is *nothing other than the highest
religious Good*, a Good which God grants on certain conditions.
This does not imply a pharisaic conception of reward, but naturally only a person who is entirely detached from αἰὼν οὗτος
['this age'] can really possess and enjoy this Good in the Kingdom of God. Otherwise he lacks completely the proper spiritual
disposition; hence, participation in this Kingdom corresponds
only to that which is spiritually possible. This interpretation of
the Kingdom of God as an innerworldly ethical ideal is a vestige
of the Kantian idea and does not hold up before a more precise
historical examination.

But modern notions easily creep in, even with the formula
'the Kingdom of God is "highest Good"'. On this point even
Baldensperger[7] showed his bondage to the older dogmatic-
exegetical method. He says,

> ... the term Kingdom of God also designated that which Jesus, for
> his part, possessed already, what he felt in his own soul. His God-
> consciousness was so vivid that it awakened and confirmed his con-
> viction that he lived in this Kingdom, or bore it in himself.

The linguistic form of this thesis alone (what does it mean:
'to bear a Kingdom in oneself'?) can teach us that an undissolved
dogmatic residue, something surprising in the case of Baldensperger, is present here. He obviously means the principal bless-
ings which will be imparted to men in the messianic Kingdom—God's nearness and being completely a child of God—
which Jesus already fully possessed. But this highest Good is certainly never connected with the expression 'Kingdom of God'.
The Kingdom of God as Jesus thought of it is never something
subjective, inward, or spiritual, but is always the objective messianic Kingdom, which usually is pictured as a territory into
which one enters, or as a land in which one has a share, or as a
treasure which comes down from heaven.[8]

---

[7] Baldensperger, *Das Selbstbewusstsein Jesu*, pp.132ff.

[8] According to Baldensperger, what is basically new in the preaching of
Jesus is the shift from the category of *place* to that of *quality*. But this distinction
is inadequate, because both are always *present*, side by side, in the idea of the
Kingdom of God: the picture of a place and the Good, which includes many
goods of a religious kind. The parables of the treasure and the pearl are as op-

One must say, therefore, that the idea of the highest Good, which Kaftan has described with such eloquent words as the basic idea of Christianity, may not, strictly speaking, be tied to Jesus' idea of the Kingdom of God, for the latter signifies a still future and objective Good. Moreover, Jesus does not use the term 'Kingdom of God' to refer to the 'supreme ethical ideal', for the 'righteousness' which he demanded is nothing but the condition for the future enjoyment of that objective Good.

For Jesus, the highest, present, personal Good is, instead, the consciousness of the love and care of the heavenly Father, *of being a child of God [die Gotteskindschaft]*. He himself lived in the enjoyment of this love, with a certainty and freshness which we cannot imitate, and also invited and instructed his disciples to lay hold of this highest Good in thankfulness and joy. The supreme ethical ideal is to serve God the Father with surrender of the whole heart, and to become free from the world. The highest proofs of this *freedom from the world* are the *love of one's enemy*, and *the sacrifice of one's life* for the sake of God. It is now possible indeed to embrace both of these sides of the Christian life under the inclusive category 'Kingdom of God'. This, then, would signify the invisible community established by Jesus and comprised of men who call upon God as Father and honor him as King. But then one will have to say more exactly, that *in the Kingdom of God* we have the highest Good, that of being children of God, and we earnestly endeavor to obtain the highest ethical ideal, that of perfectly fulfilling God's will. If one would like a *shorter* formulation, one might say (corresponding to the meaning of the word βασιλεία) the *Rule* of God is the highest religious Good and the supreme ethical ideal.

But this conception of ours of the βασιλεία τοῦ θεοῦ parts company with Jesus' at the most decisive point. We do not mean the religious side of this concept antithetically, as the counterpart to αἰὼν οὗτος, but merely thetically: it expresses our belief that God the Creator maintains his control *over this world*, and governs it for the spiritual benefit of his children. Its ethical side is thoroughly unbiblical and un-Jewish, inasmuch as the notion of an 'actualization of the Rule of God' by human ethical

posed to the meaning of a present spiritual Good as they could be, for they teach that one must make sacrifice in order to reach a *still distant* Good.

activity is completely contrary to the transcendentalism of Jesus'
idea. Under these circumstances, one will perhaps judge the
connection of the modern dogmatic idea with the words of Jesus
to be a purely external one. This is, in fact, the case. That which
is universally valid in Jesus' preaching, which should form the
kernel of our systematic theology is not his idea of the Kingdom
of God, but that of the religious and ethical fellowship of the
children of God. This is not to say that one ought no longer to
use the concept 'Kingdom of God' in the current manner. On the
contrary, it seems to me, as a matter of fact, that it should be the
proper watchword of modern theology. Only the admission
must be demanded that we use it in a different sense from Jesus'.

The real difference between our modern Protestant world-
view and that of primitive Christianity is, therefore, that we do
not share the eschatological attitude, namely, that τὸ σχῆμα τοῦ
κόσμου παράγει ['the form of this world is passing away' cf. 1
Cor 7:31]. We no longer pray, 'May grace come and the world
pass away' [cf. *Didache* 10:6], but we pass our lives in the joyful
confidence that *this* world will evermore become the showplace
of the people of God. But another attitude has silently come
among us in place of the strictly eschatological one and where it
is not present, preaching and instruction should do all they can
to awaken it. The world will further endure, but we, as individuals, will soon leave it. Thereby, we will at least approximate
Jesus' attitude in a different sense, if we make the basis of our life
the precept spoken by a wise man of our day: 'Live as if you
were dying'. We do not await a Kingdom of God which is to
come down from heaven to earth and abolish this world, but we
do hope to be gathered with the church of Jesus Christ into the
heavenly βασιλεία. In this sense we, too, can feel and say, as
did the Christians of old: 'Thy Kingdom come!'[9]

---

[9] We would give attention here once more (see above, p.97) to the fact
that this transformation of the idea of the Kingdom of God is perhaps already
very ancient. As early as in the Jewish-Christian source of Luke, which contains the parable of poor Lazarus, the episode of the thief on the cross and perhaps also the saying in Acts 14:22, the idea seems to be present that when the
faithful and righteous die, they are directly transported into the messianic
Kingdom, which is in Paradise or Heaven. To be sure, the idea of the return of
the Son of man was also retained along with this.

5

Consistent Eschatology

Albert Schweitzer (1875–1965)

If William Wrede's approach could be characterized as a consistently sceptical attitude towards the historical value of the Gospels, Albert Schweitzer's approach was consistently apocalyptic (or, in his terms, consistently 'eschatological'). While Wrede regarded even the earliest of the Gospels as already shaped by early Christian belief, Schweitzer believed that the story of Jesus as found in the Gospels is quite comprehensible, provided that the apocalyptic context of Jesus' thought is taken into account. In this sense Schweitzer picked up, developed, and popularized the work already done by Johannes Weiss. Indeed Schweitzer's work would come to so overshadow that of his predecessor that Weiss's contribution is today sometimes overlooked (a state of affairs which Schweitzer himself would have been keen to avoid).

Born in the village of Kaysersberg in Alsace, the young Albert Schweitzer was brought up in the nearby town of Günsbach, where his father worked as the Lutheran pastor. After attending the *Gymnasium* (academic high school) in Mulhouse, he began his advanced studies at the University in Strasbourg, studying also in Paris and Berlin, before completing a Licentiate in Philosophy (on the work of Immanuel Kant) and in Theology (on the New Testament accounts of the Last Supper). His most prominent teacher during this period was the New Testament scholar H.J. Holtzmann (1832–1910), who in 1863 had produced a ground-breaking study of the synoptic gospels. In 1901 Schweitzer published his first major work on the historical Jesus, entitled *The Last Supper in Connection with the Life of Jesus and the History of Early Christi-*

anity, the second part of which (issued separately) was headed *The Secret of the Messiahship and Passion—A Sketch of the Life of Jesus*. (It is this second part which was translated by Walter Lowrie and published in English, in 1914, under the new title *The Mystery of the Kingdom of God*.) Schweitzer's next major work was a survey of the existing literature on the historical figure of Jesus, published in 1906 as *From Reimarus to Wrede: A History of the Life-of-Jesus Research* (translated into English by W. Montgomery under the more memorable title *The Quest of the Historical Jesus*). Although Schweitzer later extended his research into the world of Jewish apocalyptic to produce two books on the theology of the apostle Paul, it is his first two works on Jesus, which have exercised the greatest influence on New Testament studies. In 1913, having added a medical qualification to his already impressive qualifications in music, philosophy and theology, Schweitzer left his native land to work as a doctor among the peoples of the Gabon district of French Equatorial Africa, a work which he continued (with some interruptions) until his death in 1965. While Schweitzer was widely regarded as a living saint during his lifetime, being awarded a Nobel Peace Prize in 1952, his work as a medical missionary has recently become controversial. However, that controversy need not detain us, for it is Schweitzer's scholarly work which is of significance here.

The reader may be surprised that the following extract does not come from Schweitzer's most famous work, *The Quest of the Historical Jesus*. However, that work is essentially a survey of the scholarship, in which Schweitzer outlines his own position only in a final chapter, while dealing simultaneously with the views of William Wrede. A clearer presentation of Schweitzer's eschatological view is to be found in his earlier work, *The Mystery of the Kingdom of God*. Indeed it is this work to which Schweitzer makes reference when he summarizes his position in *The Quest*. Translated by Walter Lowrie and published in 1914, *The Mystery of the Kingdom of God* is the second part of Schweitzer's 1901 study, originally published (as noted above) under the title *The Secret of the Messiahship and Passion—A Sketch of the Life of Jesus*. In the first chapter of the work, Schweitzer outlines the depiction of

Jesus' ministry which characterized what he called the 'modern-historical' (as opposed to the older, dogmatic) theology of the nineteenth century. According to this view, Jesus saw his sacrificial death as the supreme exemplification of the ethical ideal of service represented by the concept of the 'Kingdom of God'. During his ministry in Galilee Jesus had proclaimed this ideal, which had at first met with acceptance. But these happy beginnings were soon overshadowed by the opposition which came from Jerusalem. In the light of this opposition Jesus at first withdrew from public proclamation, and then determined to carry his message into the very heart of the Jewish world, even if this meant facing death. Schweitzer argues against each aspect of this depiction, before offering his own, 'eschatological-historical' reconstruction, in the chapter reproduced below.

The Mystery of the Kingdom of God

Reprinted from *The Mystery of the Kingdom of God: The Secret of Jesus' Messiahship and Passion* (1925), copyright ©Rhena Schweitzer Miller. Used by permission of Rhena Schweitzer Miller.

Chapter II: The 'Development' of Jesus

1. The Kingdom of God as an Ethical and as an Eschatological Fact

The concurrence in Jesus of an ethical with an eschatological line of thought has always constituted one of the most difficult problems of New Testament study. How can two such different views of the world, in part diametrically opposed to one another, be united in *one* process of thought?

The attempt has been made to evade the problem, with the just feeling that the two views cannot be united. Critical spirits like T. Colani (*Jesus-Christ et les croyance messianique de son temps.* 1864, pp.94ff., 169ff.) and G. Volkmar (*Die Evangelien.* 1870, pp.530ff.) went to the length of eliminating altogether eschatology from the field of Jesus' thought. All expressions of that sort were accordingly to be charged to the account of the eschatological expectation of a later time. This procedure is frustrated

by the stubbornness of the texts: the eschatological sayings belong precisely to the best attested passages. The excision of them
is an act of violence.

No more successful has been the attempt to evade the problem by *sublimating* the eschatology, as though Jesus had translated
the realistic conceptions of his time into spiritual terms by using
them in a figurative sense. The work of Eric Haupt (*Die eschatologischen Aussagen Jesu in den synoptischen Evangelien*, 1895) is
based upon this thought. But there is nothing to justify us in
assuming that Jesus attached to his word a non-natural sense,
whereas his hearers, in accordance with the prevailing view,
must have understood them realistically. Not only are we at a
loss for a rational explanation of such a method on Jesus' part,
but he himself gives not the slightest hint of it.

So the problem remains as urgent as ever, how the juxtaposition of two discordant views of the world is to be explained.
The sole solution seems to lie in the assumption of a gradual
development. Jesus may have entertained at first a purely ethical
view, looking for the realisation of the Kingdom of God
through the spread and perfection of the moral-religious society
which he was undertaking to establish. When, however, the
opposition of the world put the organic completion of the
Kingdom in doubt, the eschatological conception forced itself
upon him. By the course of events he was brought to the pass
where the fulfilment of the religious-ethical ideal, which hitherto he had regarded as the terminus of a continuous moral development, could be expected only as the result of a cosmic ca-
tastrophe in which God's omnipotence should bring to its conclusion the work which he had undertaken.

Thus a complete revolution is supposed to have occurred in
Jesus' thought. But the problem is veiled rather than solved by
disposing the terms of the contrast in chronological sequence.
The acceptance of the eschatological notion, if it is to be rendered intelligible in this fashion, signifies nothing less than a total
breach with the past, a break at which all development ceases.
For the eschatological thought, if it be taken seriously, abrogates
the ethical train of thought. It accepts no subordinate place. To
such a position of impotence it was brought for the first time in
Christian theology as the result of historical experience. Jesus,

however, must have thought either eschatologically or un-
eschatologically, but not both together—nor in such a wise that
the eschatological was superadded to supplement the unescha-
tological.

It has been proved that in the thought of the Passion it is
only the eschatological idea of the Kingdom of God which is in
view. It has been shown likewise that the assumption of a period
of illsuccess after the mission of the Twelve is without historical
justification. This, however, constitutes the indispensable pre-
sumption for every such development as has been assumed on
the part of Jesus. Therefore the eschatological notion cannot
have been forced upon Jesus by outward experiences, but it
must from the beginning, even in the first Galilean period, have
lain at the base of his preaching!

2. The Eschatological Character of the Charge to the Twelve

'The Kingdom of God is at hand' (Mt 10.7)—this word which
Jesus commissions his Disciples to proclaim is a summary expression of all his previous preaching. They are to carry it now
throughout the cities of Israel. The charge of Jesus to the
Twelve furnishes no means of determining in what sense this
proclamation is meant.

If the common conception is right about the significance of
this mission of the Twelve, the words with which he dismisses
them present an extraordinary riddle. Full of hope and with the
joy of productive effort he goes about to extend the scope of his
activity for the founding of the Kingdom of God. The commission to the Twelve ought therefore to contain instruction about
the missionary propaganda they were to carry out in this sense.
One must hence expect that he would direct them how they
should preach about the new relation to God and the new morality of the Kingdom.

The commission, however, is anything but a summary of the
'teaching of Jesus'. It does not in the least contemplate instruction of a thoroughgoing kind, rather what is in question is a
flying proclamation throughout Israel. The one errand of the
Apostles as teachers is to cry out everywhere the warning of the

nearness of the Kingdom of God to the intent that all may be warned and given opportunity to repent. In this, however, no time is to be lost; therefore they are not to linger in a town where men are unsusceptible to their message, but to hasten on in order that they may pass through all the cities of Israel before the appearing of the Son of Man takes place. But 'the coming of the Son of Man' signifies—*the dawning of the Kingdom of God with power.*

"When they persecute you in this city flee unto another, for verily I say unto you, Ye shall not have gone through the cities of Israel till the Son of Man be come" (Mt 10.23). If one understands the commission to the Twelve as to suppose that Jesus would say through his Disciples that the time is now come for the realisation of the Kingdom by a new moral behaviour, that eschatological saying lies like an erratic boulder in the midst of a flowery meadow. If, however, one conceives of the embassage eschatologically, the saying acquires a great context: it is a rock in the midst of a wild mountain landscape. One cannot affirm of this saying that it has been interpolated here by a later age; rather with compelling force it fixes the presence of eschatological conceptions in the days of the mission of the Twelve.

The one and only article of instruction that is required is the call to repentance. Whosoever believes in the nearness of the Kingdom repents. Hence Jesus gives the Disciples authority over unclean spirits, to cast them out and to heal the sick (Mt 10.1). By these signs they are to perceive that the power of ungodliness is coming to an end and the morning glow of the Kingdom of God already dawns. That belongs to their errand as teachers, for whosoever fails to *believe* their signs, and thereupon brings forth no works of repentance unto the Kingdom of God,—that man is damned. Thus have Corazin, Bethsaida, and Capernaum come into condemnation. Faith and repentance were made easy for them by the signs and wonders with which they were favoured beyond others—and yet they did not come to themselves, as even pagan cities like Tyre and Sidon would have done (Mt 11.20-24). This saying addressed to the people shows what significance Jesus ascribed to the signs in view of the eschatological embassage.

Thus the Disciples were to preach *the Kingdom, Repentance, and the Judgement*. Inasmuch, however, as the event they proclaimed was so near that it might at any moment surprise them, they must be prepared for what precedes it, namely, for the final insurrection of the power of this world. How they are to comport themselves in the face of this emergency so as not to be confounded—here is the point upon which Jesus' parting words of instruction bear! In the general tumult of spirits all ties will be dissolved. Faction will divide even the family (Mt 10.34-36). Whosoever would be loyal to the Kingdom of God must be ready to tear from out his heart those who were dearest to him, to endure reproach, and to bear the cross (Mt 10.37, 38). The secular authority will bring upon them severe persecution (Mt 10.17, 31). Men will call them to account and subject them to torture in order to move them to denial of their cause. Brother shall deliver up brother to death, and the father his child; and children shall rise up against parents and cause them to be put to death. Only he who remains steadfast in the midst of this general tumult, and confesses Jesus before men, shall be saved in the Day of Judgment, when he intervenes with God in their behalf (Mt 10.32, 33).

In the commission to the Twelve Jesus imparts instruction about the woes of the approaching Kingdom. In the descriptive portions of it there may be much perhaps that betrays the colouring of a later time. By this concession, however, the character of the speech as a whole is not prejudiced. The question at issue is not about a course of conduct which they are to maintain *after his death*. For such instruction not a single historical word can be adduced. The woes precede the dawning of the Kingdom. Therefore the victorious proclamation of the nearness of the Kingdom must accommodate itself to the woes. Hence this juxtaposition of optimism and pessimism which the current interpretation finds so unaccountable. It is the sign manual of every eschatological *Weltanschauung* ['worldview'].

3. The New View

The idea of Passion is dominated *only* by the eschatological conception of the Kingdom. In the charge to the Twelve the question is only about the eschatological—not about the ethical-nearness of the Kingdom. From this it follows, for one thing, that Jesus' ministry counted *only* upon the eschatological realisation of the Kingdom. Then, however, it is evident that the relation of his ethical thoughts to the eschatological view can have suffered no alteration by reason of outward events but must have been the same from beginning to end.

> In the following chapters of *The Mystery of the Kingdom of God*, Schweitzer develops his 'eschatological' view. In chapter three he notes that Jesus' ethical teaching consisted of a proclamation of that repentance which was required of those who would be part of God's future Kingdom. Jesus' ethical teaching is therefore an 'interim-ethics', conditioned by the expectation of an imminent divine intervention, bringing human history to an end. Once that intervention has occurred, evil will have been overcome and the proclamation of an ethics will no longer be necessary. In chapter four Schweitzer discusses the interpretation of the phrase 'the secret of the Kingdom of God' (Mark 4:11), which he understands as a reference to Jesus' synthesis of Old Testament prophetic expectation and Jewish apocalyptic tradition. For Jesus went back to the prophetic idea that Israel's repentance would hasten the establishment of God's rule, but he recast that idea in the apocalyptic language of a cosmic catastrophe and transformation. This 'secret of the Kingdom of God' is taken up and developed during the last period of Jesus' ministry in 'the secret of the Passion' (which Schweitzer gradually unfolds in chapters five to nine). Here Schweitzer deals with Jesus' messianic consciousness, arguing that Jesus first became aware of his identity as the future Messiah at his baptism, although during this first part of his ministry he keeps this identity hidden, even from his own disciples. When Jesus spoke of the Messiah he did so in the third person, for the Messiah (the 'Son of Man') would be manifested only in the future, when God established his Kingdom. (It is in this sense that his messianic identity is—for the moment—a hidden matter or a 'secret'.) Thus the people came to regard him, not as the Messiah, but as Elijah (the Forerunner). Similarly,

the 'resurrection' of which Jesus spoke was the general resurrection which would inaugurate the messianic age and simultaneously the act whereby he would be revealed in
power as the 'Son of Man' spoken of by Daniel. What Judas
did was to betray this secret to the Jewish authorities, thus
bringing about Jesus' conviction and death. Jesus accepted
this fate because he had become convinced that the expected
afflictions of the end-times had become focused on himself.
God had imposed on the one destined to be the Son of Man
the afflictions which all of Israel must otherwise suffer, and
he is to bear these sufferings as a ransom for the guilt of the
nation.

In the last chapter of his book Schweitzer offers his own
summary of Jesus' ministry and death. It is this chapter which
is reproduced below.

Chapter X: Summary of the Life of Jesus

The 'Life of Jesus' is limited to the last months of his existence
on earth. At the season of the summer seed-sowing he began his
ministry and ended it upon the cross at Easter of the following
year.

His public ministry may be counted in weeks. The first period extends from seed time to harvest; the second comprises the
days of his appearance in Jerusalem. Autumn and winter he
spent in heathen territory alone with his Disciples.

Before him the Baptist had appeared and had borne emphatic
witness to the nearness of the Kingdom and the coming of the
mighty premessianic Forerunner, with whose appearance the
pouring out of the Holy Ghost should take place. According to
Joel, this among other miracles was the sign that the Day of
Judgment was imminent. John himself never imagined that he
was this Forerunner; nor did such a thought occur to the people,
for he had not ushered in the age of miracles. He is a prophet,—
that was the universal opinion.

About Jesus' earlier development we know nothing. All lies
in the dark. Only this is sure: at his baptism the secret of his existence was disclosed to him,—namely, that he was the one
whom God had destined to be the messiah. With this revelation

he was complete, and underwent no further development. For now he is assured that, until the near coming of the messianic age which was to reveal his glorious dignity, he has to labour for the Kingdom as the unrecognised and hidden Messiah, and must approve and purify himself together with his friends in the final Affliction.

The idea of suffering was thus included in his messianic consciousness, just as the notion of the pre-messianic Affliction was indissolubly connected with the expectation of the Kingdom. Earthly events could not influence Jesus' course. His secret raised him above the world, even though he still walked as a man among men.

His appearing and his proclamation have to do only with the near approach of the Kingdom. His preaching is that of John, only that he confirms it by signs. Although his secret controls all his preaching, yet no one may know of it, for he must remain unrecognised till the new aeon dawns.

Like his secret, so also is his whole ethical outlook ruled by the contrast of 'Now and Then'. It is a question of repentance unto the Kingdom, and the conquest of the righteousness which renders one fit for it,—for only the righteous inherit the Kingdom. This righteousness is higher than that of the Law, for he knows that the law and the Prophets prophesied until John,—with the Baptist, however, one finds oneself in the age of the Forerunner, immediately before the dawn of the Kingdom.

Therefore, as the future Messiah, he must preach and work that higher morality. The poor in spirit, the meek, those that endure suffering, those that hunger and thirst after righteousness, the merciful, the pure in heart, the peacemakers,—these all are blessed because by this mark they are destined for the Kingdom.

Behind this ethical preaching looms the secret of the Kingdom of God. That which, as performed by the individual, constitutes moral renewal in preparation for the Kingdom, signifies, as accomplished by the community, a fact through which the realisation of the Kingdom in a supernatural way will be hastened. Thus individual and social ethics blend in the great secret. As the plentiful harvest, by God's wonderful working, follows mysteriously upon the sowing, so comes also the Kingdom of

God, by reason of man's moral renewal, but substantially without his assistance.

The parable contains also the suggestion of a chronological coincidence. Jesus spoke at the season of seed-sowing and expected the Kingdom at the time of the harvest. Nature was God's clock. With the last seed-sowing he had set it for the last time.

The secret of the Kingdom of God is the transfiguration in celestial light of the ethics of the early prophets, according to which also the final state of glory will be brought about by God only on condition of the moral conversion of Israel. In sovereign style Jesus effects the synthesis of the apocalyptic of Daniel and the ethics of the Prophets. With him it is not a question of eschatological ethics, rather is his world view an ethical eschatology. As such it is modern.

The signs and wonders also come under a double point of view. For the people they are merely to confirm the preaching of the nearness of the Kingdom. Whosoever now does not believe that the time is so far advanced, he has no excuse. The signs and wonders condemn him, for they plainly attest that the power of ungodliness is coming to an end.

For Jesus, however, there lay behind this affirmation the secret of the Kingdom of God. When the Pharisees wished to ascribe these very signs to the power of Satan, he alluded to the secret by a parable. By his acts he binds the power of ungodliness, as one falls upon a strong man and renders him harmless before attempting to rob him of his possessions. Wherefore, in sending out his Apostles, he gives them, together with the charge to preach, authority over unclean spirits. They are to deal the last blow.

A third element in the preaching of the Kingdom was the intimation of the pre-messianic Affliction. The believers must be prepared to pass with him through that time of trial, in which they are to prove themselves the elect of the Kingdom by steadfast resistance to the last attack of the power of the world. This attack will concentrate about his person; therefore they must stand by him even unto death. Only life in God's Kingdom is real life. The Son of Man will judge them according as they have stood by him, Jesus, or no. Thus Jesus at the conclusion of the Beatitudes turns to his own Disciples with the words: 'Blessed are ye when men persecute you for my sake.' The charge to the Apostles turns into a consideration of the Affliction. The embassage to the Baptist about the imminence of the Kingdom concludes with the word: 'Blessed is he whosoever shall not be offended in me.' At Bethsaida, the morning after he had celebrated the Supper by the seashore, he adjured the multitude to stand by him, even when he shall become an object of shame and scorn in this sinful world,—their blessedness depends upon this.

This Affliction meant not only a probation but also an atonement. It is foreordained in the messianic drama, because God requires of the adherents of the Kingdom a satisfaction for their transgressions in this aeon. But he is almighty. In this omnipotence he determines the question of membership in the Kingdom and the place each shall occupy therein, without himself being bound by any determining cause whatsoever. So also in view of his omnipotence the necessity of the final Affliction is only relative. He can abrogate it. The last three petitions of the Lord's Prayer contemplate this possibility. After beseeching God that he would send the Kingdom, that his name might be blessed and his will be done on earth as it is in heaven, men beg him to forgive them the transgressions and spare them the Temptation, rescuing them directly from the power of evil.

This was the content of Jesus' preaching during the first period. He remained throughout this time on the northern shore of the lake. Chorazin, Bethsaida, and Capernaum were the principal centres of his activity. From thence he made an excursion across the lake to the region of the Ten Cities and a journey to Nazareth.

Precisely in the towns which were the scenes of his chief activity he encountered unbelief. The curse which he must utter over them is proof of it. The Pharisees, moreover, were hostile and sought to discredit him with the people, on account of his very miracles. In Nazareth he had experience of the fact that a prophet is without honour in his own country.

Thus the Galilean period was anything but a fortunate one. Such outward illsuccess, however, signified nothing for the coming of the Kingdom. The unbelieving cities merely brought down judgment upon themselves. Jesus had other mysterious indications for measuring the approach of the Kingdom. By these he recognised that the time was come. For this reason he sent forth the Apostles just as they were returning from Nazareth, *for it was harvest time.*

By means of their preaching and their signs the reputation of his mighty personality spread far and wide. Now begins the time of success! John in prison hears of it and sends his disciples to ask him if he is 'he that should come', for from his miracles he concluded that the time of the mighty Forerunner whom he had heralded had arrived.

Jesus performed signs, his Disciples had power over the spirits. When he spoke of the Judgment he laid stress upon the fact that the Son of Man stood in such solidarity with him that he would recognise only such as had stood by him, Jesus. The people therefore opined that he might be the one for whom all were looking, and the Baptist desired to have assurance on this point.

Jesus cannot tell him who he is. 'The time is far advanced'—that is the gist of his reply. After the departure of the messengers Jesus turned to the people and signified in mysterious terms that the time is indeed much further advanced than the Baptist dreamed in asking such a question. The era of the Forerunner had already begun with the appearance of the Baptist himself. From that time on the Kingdom of God is with violence compelled to draw near. He himself who asks the question is Elijah—if they could comprehend it. Men were not able to perceive that the man in prison was Elijah. When he began his preaching, they knew not the time. That was due not alone to the fact that John performed no miracles, but to the hardening of their hearts. They are unreasonable children that do not know what they want. Now there is one here who performs signs,—but even on his testimony they do not believe the nearness of the Kingdom. So the curse upon Chorazin and Bethsaida concludes the 'eulogy upon the Baptist'.

The sending of the Twelve was the last effort for bringing about the Kingdom. As they then returned, announced to him their success, and reported that they had power over the evil spirits, it signified to him, *all is ready.* So now he expects the dawn of the Kingdom in the most immediate future,—it had seemed to him, indeed, already doubtful whether the Twelve would return before this event. He had even said to them that the appearing of the Son of Man would overtake them before they had gone through the cities of Israel.

His work is done. Now he requires to collect himself and to be alone with his Disciples. They enter a boat and sail along the coast towards the north. But the multitude which had gathered about him at the preaching of the Disciples, in order to await the Kingdom with him, now follow after them along the shore and surprise them at their landing upon a lonely beach.

As it was evening the Disciples desired that he would send the people away to find food in the neighbouring hamlets. For him, however, the hour is too solemn to be profaned by an earthly meal. Before sending them away he bids them sit down and celebrates with them an anticipation of the messianic feast. To the community that was gathered about him to await the Kingdom, he, the Messiah to be, distributes hallowed food, mysteriously consecrating them thereby to be partakers of the heavenly banquet. As they did not know his secret, they understood as little as did his Disciples the significance of his act. They comprehended only that it meant something wonderfully solemn, and they questioned within themselves about it.

Thereupon he sent them away. He ordered the Disciples to skirt the coast to Bethsaida. For his part he betook himself to the mountain to pray and then followed along the shore on foot. As his figure appeared to them in the obscurity of the night they believed—under the impression of the Supper where he stood before them in mysterious majesty—that his supernatural apparition approached them over the turbulent waves through which they were toiling to the shore.

The morning after the Supper by the seashore he collected the people and the Disciples about him at Bethsaida and warned them to stand by him and not to deny him in the humiliation.

Six days later he goes with the Three to the mountain where he had prayed alone. There he is revealed to them as the Messiah. On the way home he forbade them to say anything about it until at the Resurrection he should be revealed in the glory of the Son of Man. They, however, still remark the failure of Elijah to appear, who yet must come before the Resurrection of the dead can take place. They were not present at the eulogy over the Baptist to hear the mysterious intimation he let fall. He must therefore make it clear to them now that the beheaded prisoner was Elijah. They should take no offence at his fate, for it was so ordained. He also who is to be Son of Man must suffer many things and be set at naught. So the Scripture will have it.

The Kingdom which Jesus expected so very soon failed to make its appearance. This first eschatological delay and postponement was momentous for the fate of the Gospel tradition, inasmuch as now all the events related to the mission of the Twelve became unintelligible, because all consciousness was lost of the fact that the most intense eschatological expectation then inspired Jesus and his following. Hence it is that precisely this period is confused and obscure in the accounts, and all the more so because several incidents remained enigmatical to those even who had a part in the experience. Thus the sacramental Supper by the seashore became in the tradition a 'miraculous feeding', in a sense totally different from that which Jesus had in mind.

Therewith, too, the motives of Jesus' disappearance became unintelligible. It seems to be a case of flight, while on the other hand the accounts give no hint how matters had come to such a pass. The key to the historical understanding of the life of Jesus lies in the perception of the two corresponding points at which the eschatological expectation culminated. During the days at Jerusalem there was a return of the enthusiasm which had already showed itself in the days at Bethsaida. Without this assumption we are left with a yawning gap in the Gospel tradition between the mission of the Twelve and the journey to Jerusalem. Historians find themselves compelled to invent a period of Galilean defeat in order to establish some connection between the recorded facts,—as if a section were missing in our Gospels. *That is the weak point of all the 'lives of Jesus'.*

By his retreat into the region of the Genesareth Jesus withdrew himself from the Pharisees and the people in order to be alone with his Disciples, as he had in vain tried to do since their return from their mission. He urgently needed such a retreat, for he had to come to an understanding about two messianic facts.

Why is the Baptist executed by the secular authority before the messianic time has dawned?

Why does the Kingdom fail to appear notwithstanding that the tokens of its dawning are present?

The secret is made known to him through the Scripture: God brings the Kingdom about *without the general Affliction*. He whom God has destined to reign in glory accomplishes it upon himself by being tried as a malefactor and condemned. Wherefore the others go free: he makes the atonement for them. What though they believe that God punishes him, though they become offended in him who preached unto them righteousness,—when after his Passion the glory dawns, then shall they see that he has suffered for them.

Thus Jesus read in the Prophet Isaiah what God had determined for him, the Elect. The end of the Baptist showed him in what form he was destined to suffer this condemnation: he must be put to death by the secular authority as a malefactor in the sight of all the people. Therefore he must make his way up to Jerusalem for the season when all Israel is gathered there.

As soon therefore as the time came for the Passover pilgrimage he set out with his Disciples. Before they left the north country he asked them whom the people took him to be. For reply they could only say that he was taken for Elijah. But Peter, mindful of the revelation on the mountain near Bethsaida, said: Thou art the Son of God. Whereupon Jesus informed them of his secret. Yes, he it is who shall be revealed as Son of Man at the Resurrection. But before that, it is decreed that he must be delivered to the high priests and elders to be condemned and put to death. God so wills it. For this cause they are going up to Jerusalem.

Peter resents this new disclosure, for in the revelation on the mountain there was nothing said to such an effect. He takes Jesus apart and appeals to him energetically. Whereupon he is sharply rebuked as one who gives ear to human considerations when God speaks.

This journey to Jerusalem was the funeral march to victory. Within the secret of the Passion lay concealed the secret of the Kingdom. They marched after him, and knew only that when all this was accomplished he would be Messiah. They were sorrowful for what must come to pass; they did not understand why it must be so, and they durst not ask him. But above all, their thoughts were occupied about the conditions that awaited them in the approaching Kingdom. When once he was Messiah, what would they then be? That occupied their minds, and about it they talked with one another. But he reproved them and explained why he must suffer. Only through humiliation and the meek sacrifice of service is one prepared to reign in the Kingdom of God. Therefore must he, who shall exercise supreme authority as Son of Man, make now an atonement for many by giving up his life in meek sacrifice.

With the arrival upon the Jewish territory begins the second period of Jesus' public ministry. He is again surrounded by the people. In Jericho a multitude gathers to see him pass through. By the healing of a blind beggar, the son of Timaeus, the people are convinced that he is the great Forerunner, just as they thought already in Galilee. The jubilant multitudes prepare for him a festal entry into Jerusalem. As the one who according to prophecy precedes the Messiah they acclaim him with *Hosanna*. *Hosanna in the highest*, however, is their acclaim of the Kingdom about to appear. Therewith the same situation is reached again as in the great days near Bethsaida: Jesus is thronged by the multitudes expectant of the Kingdom.

The instruction contained in the parables which were uttered at Jerusalem has to do with the nearness of the Kingdom. They are cries of warning, with a note of menace as well for those that harden their hearts against the message. What agitates men's minds is not the question, Is he the Messiah, or no? but, Is the Kingdom so near as he says, or no?

The Pharisees and Scribes knew not what hour had struck. They showed a complete lack of sensibility for the nearness of the Kingdom, for else they could not have propounded to him questions which in view of the advanced hour had lost all significance. What difference does it make now about the Roman tribute? What do the farfetched Sadduceean arguments amount to against the possibility of the resurrection of the dead? Soon, with the advent of the Kingdom, all earthly rule is done away, as well as the earthly human nature itself.

If only they understood the signs of the times! He proposes
to them two questions, which should cause them to ponder and
hence take note that the time they live in is pregnant with a
great secret which is not dreamed of in the learning of the
Scribes.

By what authority did the Baptist act? If they but knew that he
was the Forerunner, as Jesus had mysteriously suggested to the
people, then they must know too that the hour of the Kingdom
had struck.

*How is the Messiah at one time David's Son—that is, subordinate
to him; at another, David's Lord—that is, his superior?* If they could
explain that, then would they understand also how he who now
labours lowly and unknown in behalf of God's Kingdom shall be
revealed as Lord and Christ.

But as it is they do not even suspect that the messianic indications harbour *secrets*. With all their learning they are blind
leaders of the blind, who, instead of making the people receptive
for the Kingdom, harden their hearts, and instead of drawing out
from the Law the higher morality which renders men meet for
the Kingdom, labour against it with their petty outward precepts
and draw the people after them to perdition. Hence: Woe to the
Pharisees and scribes!

True, even among them are such as have kept an open eye.
The scribe who put to him the question about the great commandment and welcomed his reply is commended as 'having
understanding' and therefore 'not far from the Kingdom of
God',—for he shall belong to it when it appears.

But the mass of the Pharisees and scribes understand him so
little that they decree his death. They had no effective charge to
bring against his behaviour. A disrespectful word about the
Temple that was all. *Then Judas betrayed to them the secret.* Now
he was condemned.

In the neighbourhood of death Jesus draws himself up to the
same triumphant stature as in the days by the seaside,—for with
death comes the Kingdom. On that occasion he had celebrated
with the believers a mystic feast as an anticipation of the messianic banquet; so now he rises at the end of the last earthly supper and distributes to the Disciples hallowed food and drink,
intimating to them with a solemn voice that this is the last

earthly meal, for they are soon to be united at the banquet in the Father's Kingdom. Two corresponding parables suggest the secret of the Passion. For him, the bread and wine which he hands them at the Supper are his body and his blood, for by the sacrifice of himself unto death he ushers in the messianic feast. The parabolic saying remained obscure to the Disciples. It was also not intended for them, its purpose was not to explain anything to them,—*for it was an enigma-parable.*

Now, as the great hour approaches, he seeks again, as after the Supper by the seashore, a lonely spot where he may pray. He bears the Affliction for others. Therefore he can say to the Disciples beforehand that in the night they shall all be offended in him—and he does not need to condemn them, for the Scripture had so determined it. What endless peace lies in this word! Indeed, he comforts *them*: after the Resurrection he will gather them about him and go before them in messianic glory unto Galilee, retracing the same road along which they had followed him on his way to death.

It still remained, however, within the scope of God's omnipotence to eliminate the Affliction for him also. Wherefore, as once he prayed with the believers, 'And lead us not into the Temptation', so now he prays for himself, that God may permit the cup of suffering to pass his lips by. True, if it be God's will, he feels himself strong enough to drink it. He is sorrowful rather for the Three. The sons of Zebedee, to gain the seats upon the throne, have boasted that they can drink with him the cup of suffering and receive with him the baptism of suffering. Peter swore that he would stand by him even if he must die with him. He knows not what God has ordained for them,—whether he will lay upon them what they desire to undertake. Therefore he bids them remain near him. And while he prays God for himself he thinks of them and twice wakes them up, bidding them remain awake and beseech God that he may not lead them through the Temptation.

The third time he comes to them the betrayer with his band is near. The hour is come,—therefore he draws himself up to the full stature of his majesty. He is alone, his Disciples flee.

The hearing of witnesses is merely a pretence. After they have gone the High Priest puts directly the question about the

messiahship. 'I am', said Jesus, referring them at the same time to
the hour when he shall appear as Son of Man on the clouds of
heaven surrounded by the angels. Therefore he was found guilty
of blasphemy and condemned to death.

On the afternoon of the fourteenth of Nisan, as they ate the
Paschal lamb at even, he uttered a loud cry and died.

Albert Schweitzer and Liberal Theology

We have seen how Schweitzer outlined his 'consistently eschatological' (or 'apocalyptic') understanding of the life and
teaching of Jesus. In doing so, he made it clear to what extent Jesus inhabited a religious world very different from our
own. Thus Schweitzer joined Johannes Weiss in protesting
against the way in which liberal theologians had identified
our modern ideal of an ethical society with Jesus' proclamation of the Kingdom of God. Yet we would be left with a
one-sided view of Schweitzer's position if we were to leave
the matter there. For neither Weiss nor Schweitzer believed
the liberal theology to be entirely wrong. Liberal theology
was correct to seize upon Jesus' ethical teaching as the only
aspect of Jesus' message we can appropriate today. It was
wrong only in identifying that ethical teaching with what
Jesus intended by 'the Kingdom of God'. In his autobiography of 1931, Schweitzer develops these reflections in a most
interesting manner, and it is an extract from that work which
is reproduced below.

Schweitzer opens the door to a contemporary re-
appropriation of the message of Jesus by distinguishing between Jesus' 'religion of love' and the 'worldview' in which
that message was expressed. Our obligation as modern believers is to separate that message from the worldview in
which it is clothed, so that we can re-clothe it in the garb of
modern ideas. The problem with liberal theology was that it
did this in a covert manner, subtly reshaping Jesus' teaching
so that it could be made palatable to a modern audience.
Schweitzer insists that this is not acceptable: we now need
boldly to admit that religious truth varies from age to age, at
least with regard to its outward form. Schweitzer grounds

this attitude in the teaching of Jesus by noting that Jesus (un-like some of his contemporaries) was not interested in ex-pounding the apocalyptic worldview as such. Rather, he merely takes it for granted as the background to his message, which is one of repentance. Jesus is not interested in teaching about the Kingdom of God; his task is to prepare men and women to be worthy of it. We are therefore not being un-faithful to his purpose if we work our way through the his-torically-conditioned form of that message to discover that which is eternally true. Indeed even the apocalyptic form of Jesus' message can be seen to have a certain religious signifi-cance, for it reminds us that a certain spiritual freedom and detachment from the world is a necessary first step to Chris-tian engagement. In these ways we can come face to face with the historical Jesus and find in him one who continues to make a claim on our powers of decision. Whatever criti-cisms may be made of Schweitzer's life and work, there can be little doubt that he believed it to be a response to that ethical claim.

My Life and Thought: An Autobiography

Chapter VI
The Historical Jesus and the Christianity of Today

As my two books on the life of Jesus gradually became known, the question was put to me from all sides, what the eschatologi-cal Jesus, who lives expecting the end of the world and a super-natural Kingdom of God, can be to us. My own thoughts were continually busy with it while at work on my books. The satis-faction which I could not help feeling at having solved so many historical riddles about the existence of Jesus, was accompanied by the painful consciousness that this new knowledge in the realm of history would mean unrest and difficulty for Christian piety. I comforted myself, however, with words of S. Paul's which had been familiar to me from childhood: 'We can do nothing against the truth, but for the truth' (2 Cor. xiii. 8). Since the essential nature of the spiritual is truth, every new truth means ultimately something won. Truth is under all circumstances more valuable than non-truth, and this must apply to truth in the realm of history as to other kinds of truth. Even if it comes in a guise which piety finds strange and at first makes difficulties for her, the final result can never mean injury; it can only mean greater depth. Religion has, therefore, no reason for trying to avoid coming to terms with historical truth.

How strong would Christian truth now stand in the world of to-day, if its relation to the truth in history were in every respect what it should be! Instead of allowing this truth its rights, she treated it, whenever it caused her embarrassment, in various ways, conscious or unconscious, but always by either evading, or twisting, or suppressing it. Instead of admitting that new elements towards which she had to advance were new, and justifying them by present action, she proceeded with artificial and disputable arguments to force them back into the past. To-day the condition of Christianity is such that hard struggles are now required to make possible that coming to terms with historical truth which has been so often missed in the past.

In what a condition we find ourselves to-day merely because in the earliest Christian period writings were allowed to appear, bearing quite falsely the names of apostles, in order to give greater authority to the ideas put forth in them! They have been for generations of Christians a source of painful dissension. On one side stand those who in face of the abundance of material for judgement, cannot exclude the possibility of there being in the New Testament writings which, in spite of their valuable contents that we have learnt to love, are not authentic; on the other are those who, to save the reputation of the oldest Christian thought, try to show this to be not proven. And meanwhile, those on whom the whole guilt rests were scarcely conscious of doing anything wrong. They only followed the custom which was universal in antiquity and against which no further objection was raised, of maintaining that writings which were said to express the ideas of any particular person were really written by him.

Because, while I was busied with the history of earlier Christianity, I had so often to deal with the results of its sins against the truth in history, I have become a keen worker for honesty in our Christianity of to-day.

The ideal would be that Jesus should have preached religious truth in a form independent of any connexion with any particular period and such that it could be taken over simply and easily by each succeeding generation of men. That, however, He did not do, and there is no doubt a reason for it.

We have, therefore, to reconcile ourselves to the fact that His religion of love appeared as part of a world-view which expected a speedy end of the world. Clothed in the ideas in which He announced it, we cannot make it our own; we must re-clothe it in those of our modern world-view.

Hitherto we have been doing this ingenuously and covertly. In defiance of what the words of the text said we managed to interpret the teaching of Jesus as if it were in agreement with our own world-view. Now, however, it must be clear to us that we can only harmonize these two things by an act, for which we claim the right of necessity.

We are obliged, that is, to admit the evident fact that religious truth varies from age to age.

How is this to be understood? So far as its essential spiritual and ethical nature is concerned, Christianity's religious truth remains the same through the centuries. The variations belong only to the outward form which it assumes in the ideas belonging to different world-views. Thus the religion of love which Jesus taught, and which made its first appearance as an element in the late Jewish eschatological world-view enters later on into connexion with the late-Greek, the medieval, and the modern world-views. Nevertheless, it remains through the centuries what it is essentially. Whether it is worked out in terms of one *Weltanschauung* or another is only a matter of relative importance. What is decisive is the amount of influence over mankind won by the spiritual and ethical truth which it has held from the very first.

We of to-day do not, like those who were able to hear the preaching of Jesus, expect to see a Kingdom of God realizing itself in supernatural events. Our conviction is that it can only come into existence by the power of the spirit of Jesus working in our hearts and in the world. The one important thing is that we shall be as thoroughly dominated by the idea of the Kingdom, as Jesus required His followers to be.

The mighty thought underlying the Beatitudes of the Sermon on the Mount, that we come to know God and belong to Him through love, Jesus introduces into the late-Jewish, Messianic expectation, without being in any way concerned to spiritualize those realistic ideas of the Kingdom of God and of blessedness. But the spirituality which lies in this religion of love must gradually, like a refiner's fire, seize upon all ideas which come into communication with it. Thus it is the destiny of Christianity to develop through a constant process of spiritualization.

Jesus never undertakes to expound the late-Jewish dogmas of the Messiah and the Kingdom. His concern is, not how believers ought to picture things but that love, without which no one can belong to God, and attain to membership of the Kingdom, shall be powerful within it. The subject of all His preaching is love, and, more generally, the preparation of the heart for the Kingdom. The Messianic dogma remains in the background. If He did not happen to mention it now and then, one could forget that it is presupposed all through. That explains why it was possible to overlook for so long the fact that His religion of love was conditioned by Time.

The late-Jewish Messianic world-view is the crater from which bursts forth the flame of the eternal religion of love.

To let the historical Jesus Himself be the speaker when the Christian message is delivered to the men and women of our time does not mean that the preacher will expound again and again the meaning which the passage taken for his text had under the eschatological Messianic world-view. It suffices if they have come to accept as a matter of course the fact that Jesus lived in expectation of the end of the world and of a Kingdom of God which would be manifested supernaturally. But whoever preaches to them the Gospel of Jesus must settle for himself what the original meaning of His sayings was, and work his way up through the historical truth to the eternal. During this process he will again and again have opportunity to notice that it is with this new beginning that he first truly realizes all that Jesus has to say to us!

How many ministers of religion have confirmed my experience that the Jesus who is known historically although He speaks to us from another thought world than our own, makes preaching not harder but easier.

There is a deep significance in the fact that whenever we hear the sayings of Jesus we tread the ground of a world-view which is not ours. In our own world and life-affirming world-view Christianity is in constant danger of being externalized. The Gospel of Jesus which speaks to us out of an expectation of the end of the world leads us off the highway of busy service for the Kingdom of God on to the footpath of inwardness, and urges us, in spiritual freedom from the world to seek true strength for working in the spirit of the Kingdom of God. The essence of Christianity is world-affirmation which has gone through an experience of world negation. In the eschatological world-view of world-negation Jesus proclaims the ethic of active love!

Even if the historical Jesus has something strange about Him, yet His personality, as it really is, influences us much more strongly and immediately than when He approached us in dogma and in the results attained up to the present by research. In dogma His personality became less alive; recent research has been modernizing and belittling Him.

Anyone who ventures to look the historical Jesus straight in the face and to listen for what He may have to teach him in His powerful sayings, soon ceases to ask what this strange-seeming Jesus can still be to him. He learns to know Him as One who claims authority over him.

The true understanding of Jesus is the understanding of will acting on will. The true relation to Him is to be taken possession of by Him. Christian piety of any and every sort is valuable only so far as it means the surrender of our will to His.

Jesus does not require of men to-day that they be able to grasp either in speech or in thought Who He is. He did not think it necessary to give those who actually heard His sayings any insight into the secret of His personality, or to disclose to them the fact that He was that descendant of David who was one day to be revealed as the Messiah. The one thing He did require of them was that they should actively and passively prove themselves men who had been compelled by Him to rise from being as the world to being other than the world, and thereby partakers of His peace.

Because, while I was investigating and thinking about Jesus, all this became a certainty to me, I let my *Quest of the Historical Jesus* end with the words: 'As one unknown and nameless He comes to us, just as on the shore of the lake He approached those men who knew not who He was. His words are the same: "Follow thou Me!" and He puts us to the tasks which He has to carry out in our age. He commands. And to those who obey, be they wise or simple, He will reveal Himself through all that they are privileged to experience in His fellowship of peace and activity, of struggle and suffering, till they come to know, as an inexpressible secret, Who He is ...'

Many people are shocked on learning that the historical Jesus must be accepted as 'capable of error' because the supernatural Kingdom of God, the manifestation of which He announced as imminent, did not appear.

What can we do in face of what stands clearly recorded in the Gospels? Are we acting in the spirit of Jesus if we attempt with hazardous and sophisticated explanations to force the sayings into agreement with the dogmatic teaching of His absolute and universal incapability of error. He Himself never made any claim to such omniscience. Just as He pointed out to the young man who addressed Him as 'Good Master' (Mark x. 17f.) that God alone is good, so He would also have set His face against those who would have liked to attribute to Him a divine infallibility. Knowledge of spiritual truth is not called upon to prove its genuineness by showing further knowledge about the events of world-history and matters of ordinary life. Its province lies on a quite different level from the latter's, and it is quite independent of it.

The historical Jesus moves us deeply by His subordination to God. In this He stands out as greater than the Christ personality of dogma which, in compliance with the claims of Greek metaphysics, is conceived as omniscient and incapable of error.

The demonstration of the fact that the teaching of Jesus was conditioned by eschatology was at once a heavy blow for liberal Protestantism. For generations the latter had busied itself investigating the life of Jesus in the conviction that all progress in the knowledge of history could not but make more evident the undogmatic character of the religion of Jesus. At the close of the nineteenth century it seemed to see it finally proved that our religious thought could without further ado adopt as its own Jesus' religion of a Kingdom of God to be founded on earth. It was not long, however, before it had to admit that this description was true, only for the teaching of Jesus as it had been unconsciously modernized by itself, and not of the really historical teaching of Jesus. I myself have suffered in this matter, by having had to join in the work of destroying the portrait of Christ on which liberal Christianity based its appeal. At the same time I was convinced that this liberal Christianity was not reduced to living on an historical illusion, but could equally appeal to the Jesus of history, and further that it carried its justification in itself.

For even if that liberal Christianity has to give up identifying its belief with the teachings of Jesus in the way it used to think possible, it still has the spirit of Jesus not against it but on its side. Jesus no doubt fits His teaching into the late-Jewish Messianic dogma. But He does not think dogmatically. He formulates no doctrine. He is far from judging any man's belief by reference to any standard of dogmatic correctness. Nowhere does He demand of His hearers that they shall sacrifice thinking to believing. Quite the contrary! He bids them meditate upon religion. In the Sermon on the Mount He lets ethics, as the essence of religion, flood their hearts, leading them to judge the value of piety by what it makes of a man from the ethical point of view. Within the Messianic hopes which His hearers carry in their hearts, He kindles the fire of an ethical faith. Thus the Sermon on the Mount becomes the incontestable charter of liberal Christianity. The truth that the ethical is the essence of religion is firmly established on the authority of Jesus.

Further than this, the religion of love taught by Jesus has been freed from any dogmatism which clung to it, by the disappearance of the late-Jewish eschatological world-view. The mould in which the casting was made has been broken. We are now at liberty to let the religion of Jesus become a living force in our thought, as its purely spiritual and ethical nature demands. We know how much that is precious exists within the ecclesiastical Christianity which has been handed down in Greek dogmas and kept alive by the piety of so many centuries, and we hold fast to the Church with love, and reverence, and thankfulness. But we belong to her as men who appeal to the saying of S. Paul: 'Where the Spirit of the Lord is, there is liberty', and who believe that they serve Christianity better by the strength of their devotion to Jesus' religion of love than by acquiescence in all the articles of belief. If the Church has the spirit of Jesus, there is room in her for every form of Christian piety, even for that which claims unrestricted liberty.

I find it no light task to follow my vocation, to put pressure on the Christian Faith to reconcile itself in all sincerity with historical truth. But I have devoted myself to it with joy, because I am certain that truthfulness in all things belongs to the spirit of Jesus.

6

Rejection of the Quest

Martin Kähler (1835-1912)

As the gap between the historical Jesus and the Christ of faith widened—whether through radical scepticism or the realization that Jesus belonged to a world very different from our own—it was perhaps inevitable that a reaction would occur. That reaction was first manifest in the work of Martin Kähler, himself a prominent biblical theologian, but one who rejected the assumptions on which the quest of the historical Jesus had been based. Kähler's protest may be regarded as the beginning of a counter-movement which in the early twentieth century would find expression in the work of the 'dialectical theologians' and in particular that of Karl Barth and Rudolf Bultmann. Each of these may be regarded as articulating a deep unease which many within the churches felt with the results of the historical criticism of the Christian Scriptures. That unease continues until today, a fact which gives the work of these thinkers an ongoing significance.

Martin Kähler was born in 1835 in the town of Neuhausen (near Königsberg). His student career began with the study of jurisprudence, but a serious illness directed his mind towards theological matters, and he studied theology at Heidelberg, Tübingen and Halle. At Heidelberg he was particularly influenced by the theologian Richard Rothe (1799-1867), whose work forced the young Kähler to develop a strongly biblical doctrine of creation. At Tübingen he came into contact, not only with the radical criticism of the famous Ferdinand Christian Baur (1792-1860), but also with the so-called 'mediating' theologians, Friedrich August Gottreu Tholuck (1799-1877) and Julius Müller (1801-78), who tried

to defend the reliability of the biblical accounts without re-
sorting to theories of verbal inspiration. It was under
Tholuck's guidance that he undertook a dissertation on the
biblical idea of conscience. In 1860 Kähler began his teaching
career in Halle, spent three years in Bonn from 1864-67, and
then returned to Halle as Professor of Systematic Theology
where he remained until his death in 1912.

Kähler's major theological work was his one-volume
dogmatics, *The Science of Christian Doctrine* (published in
1883), which took as its organizing principle the great Reformation doctrine of justification. Yet the work for which he
is best remembered was an apparently minor essay first published in 1892 as *The So-Called Historical Jesus and the Historic,
Biblical Christ*, and originally written as an address for a conference of pastors. An expanded edition was published in
1896, with three additional essays developing Kähler's ideas
and responding to his critics. The English translation by Carl
E. Braaten (an extract from which is reproduced below) follows the 1956 German edition in including only the first two
of these essays. The extract reproduced below is the first essay
of 1892, and it is this discussion to which my remarks will be
devoted.

Kähler begins his essay with some introductory comments, in which he sets forth his central claim: the idea that
'the historical Jesus of modern authors conceals from us the
living Christ'. Kähler goes on to remark that the Jesus reconstructed by historical criticism of the Gospels is no less a human fabrication than the dogmatic Christ of Chalcedonian
Christology. He then sets out his own aim, which is both to
criticize the failings of the existing approach to the historical
Jesus question and to outline an alternative.

In the first section of his essay (reproduced below) Kähler
begins by outlining the impossibility of constructing a biography of Jesus from the Gospels we have before us. Kähler's
reasoning here has something in common with that of William Wrede: both argue that the Gospels are not adequate
sources for the task of biographical reconstruction. Kähler
brings forward several reasons for this claim. First of all, the
Gospel accounts exist in isolation: we have no independent

testimony for Jesus' life. Secondly, it is not at all clear that
they are eyewitness accounts. Thirdly, the Gospels deal with
only the very last part of Jesus' life. Finally, the Gospel tradition exists in two very different and apparently irreconcilable
forms (the Synoptic tradition and that of John's Gospel), a
fact which adds further weight to doubts about their reliability. A further difficulty arises from the fact that the Gospel
writers were not at all interested in a matter central to modern biographies, namely the development of Jesus' personality. It is true that one can draw conclusions in this regard by
way of the principle of analogy, but to employ this principle
implies immediately setting oneself in opposition to what the
Gospel writers wish to assert about Jesus. In other words, recourse to the principle of analogy means that the Gospel
claim that Jesus was unique—a personality without parallel
because of his very particular relationship to God—is excluded from the outset. It is true that historical research can
legitimately tell us something about the world in which Jesus
lived, but this is entirely inadequate for the construction of a
biography (in the modern sense). Under these conditions,
Kähler argues, any reconstruction of the historical Jesus will
be shaped by the theological assumptions of the interpreter.
Thus depictions of 'the historical Jesus' become ways of
making religious claims which are disguised as objective,
historical judgements.

More positively, Kähler argues that the focus of our attention should not be 'the historical Jesus' but 'the historic,
biblical Christ'. His reasoning here is theological rather than
simply historical: we approach the figure of Jesus because of
his religious significance as the incarnate Word of God. For
this reason, the Christian is interested, not in the ways in
which Jesus resembles us, but in the ways in which he is utterly different. Therefore our focus should be, not on the
historical details of Jesus' life, but on the way in which he
continues to encounter us in the Church's proclamation as
Saviour and Redeemer. In this light, historical details are
relatively insignificant, and it would (in any case) be a tragedy
if Christian faith were made to depend on the ever-changing
and uncertain results of historical science. In a way which is

perhaps paradoxical in the light of his earlier argument, Kähler illustrates what he means by 'the historic, biblical Christ' by way of an analogy. For he argues that a truly historic individual is one whose life produces a certain impact on later generations, and the truly historic aspect of his or her life is precisely this later influence. In the same way the historic Christ is not the figure behind the Gospels, but the figure of the apostolic proclamation, and therefore of the whole New Testament witness. This positive conclusion, Kähler notes, will not be shared by those who regard 'revelation' as merely a historically-conditioned state of human religious consciousness, but even those who have thus departed from the Christian tradition should recognize the force of his negative criticisms.

Before one grapples with Kähler's own presentation of his case, a word of warning may be in order. The reader should not be misled by Kähler's tendency to outline the position with which he is disagreeing, before taking issue with it. It is easy to be following a train of thought and to end up mistaking Kähler's position for that of his opponents. (German syntax allows an author to outline a position while distancing himself from it in a way which is difficult to reproduce in English.)

The So-Called Historical Jesus and the Historic, Biblical Christ

Against the Life-of-Jesus Movement

I regard the entire Life-of-Jesus movement as a blind alley. A blind alley usually has something alluring about it, or no one would enter it in the first place. It usually appears to be a section of the right road, or no one would hit upon it at all. In other words, we cannot reject this movement without understanding what is legitimate in it.

The Life-of-Jesus movement is completely in the right insofar as it sets the Bible against an abstract dogmatism. It becomes illegitimate as soon as it begins to rend and dissect the Bible without having acquired a clear understanding of the special nature of the problem and the peculiar significance of Scripture for such understanding. In other cases the problem is simply historical; here that is not so. The justification for the movement can be expressed in Luther's statement that we can never draw God's Son deep enough into our flesh, into our humanity.[1] Every truly evangelical movement shares this point of view in reflecting upon our Savior—ever since John 1 and I John 1:1ff were written. But Luther's statement makes sense only if Christ is more than a mere man. It has no meaning at all for those who wish to maintain and demonstrate that he is of no more importance to us than any other significant figure of the past. This was not Luther's view, nor can it be ours, so long as we agree with the apostle that 'if you confess with your lips that Jesus is Lord, you will be saved' (Rom. 10:9). If we believe with Christian dogmatics in the Christ who is more than a mere man in his essence, his mission, and his present function—i.e., if we believe in the supra-historical[2] Savior—then the historical Jesus acquires for us that incomparable worth that moves us to confess before the biblical picture of Jesus,

> My soul it shall refresh, my ear
> Can apprehend no tale more dear.

Every detail that we can learn about him becomes precious and meaningful for us. The tradition about him cannot be studied diligently and faithfully enough. Hence a person may immerse himself in Jesus' actions, trying to understand them and to trace them to their presuppositions. So he plumbs the depths of

---

[1] Cited in I.A. Dorner, *Entwicklungsgeschichte der Lehre von der Person Christi* (2nd ed.; Berlin: Gustav Schlawitz, 1853), Part II, p.544.

[2] This is a term coined to designate what, to be sure, would not even exist apart from history but whose significance is not exhausted in the historical effects of a particular link in the chain of history or in the beginnings of a new historical movement, because in the supra-historical what is universally valid is joined to the historical to become an effective presence. Cf. my *Die Wissenschaft der christlichen Lehre* (2nd rev. ed.; Leipzig: A. Deichert, 1893), par. 13. Cf. also pars. 8f., 365, 397, 404f.

Jesus' consciousness and development before his public ministry; he accompanies the boy Jesus through ravines and fields, from his mother's bosom to his father's workshop and into the synagogue and then he is most certainly heading up a blind alley!

For the cardinal virtue of genuine historical research is modesty. Modesty is born of knowledge, and he who knows the historical facts and sources acquires modesty in knowledge as well as in understanding. But such modesty is unpopular with many because their imaginations, sick of the field of speculation, have now projected themselves onto another field, onto the green pastures of alleged reality and into the business of historiography by conjecture or of so-called positive criticism. On this field people are running wild; they paint images with as much lust for novelty and as much self-confidence as was ever exhibited in the *a priori* metaphysics of the philosophers or the speculations of the theosophists, confident (with Richard Rothe) that pious thinking can dissect God as the anatomist can dissect a frog. As far as the efforts of positive criticism are concerned, I can very often recognize no difference between the 'positive' and the 'negative' theologians, to use the common labels.

To substantiate such a negative verdict some scientific assertions must now be made which at first sight may seem startling: we do not possess any sources for a 'Life of Jesus' which a historian can accept as reliable and adequate. I repeat: we have no sources for a biography of Jesus of Nazareth which measure up to the standards of contemporary historical science. A trustworthy picture of the Savior for believers is a very different thing, and of this more will be said later. Our sources, that is, the Gospels, exist in such isolation that without them we would know nothing at all about Jesus, although the time and setting of his life are otherwise entirely clear to historians. He could be taken for a product of the church's fantasy around the year A.D. 100. Furthermore, these sources cannot be traced with certainty to eyewitnesses. In addition to this, they tell us only about the shortest and last period of his life. And finally, these sources appear in two basic forms whose variations must—in view of the proximity of the alleged or probable time of origin of these forms—awaken seri-

ous doubts about the faithfulness of the recollections.[3] Consequently the 'unbiased' critic finds himself confronted by a vast
field strewn with the fragments of various traditions.[4] From these
fragments he is called upon to conjure up a new shape if his task
is to compose, according to modern requirements, a biography
of this figure who looms up out of the mist. Even the task of
establishing the external course of his life is fraught with serious
difficulties—leaving us often with mere probabilities.[5] The bi-

---

[3] This summary will scarcely meet with any serious objection. The exclu-
siveness with which we are referred to Christian sources must certainly arouse
suspicion outside the Christian circle of vision. The way that the Gospel materials would be handled if we possessed some other sources can be indicated, for
example, by the fate of the canonical Acts of the Apostles at the hands of current writers of 'histories of New Testament times'. In their preoccupation with
F.C. Baur and with Strauss's revised edition of his life of Jesus (*Das Leben Jesu
für das deutsche Volk*, 1864), people have almost forgotten the earlier edition of
Strauss's work, with its interpretation of Jesus' life in terms of myth. But already Strauss's idea is emerging again—very understandably.

The uniqueness of the sources must be evaluated, of course, in accordance
with one's view of their general nature. Above all, the relation between the
Fourth Gospel and the Synoptics is important for the question of the reliability
of the records. I must call attention especially to P. Ewald's work, *Das
Hauptproblem der Evangelienfrage* (Leipzig: J.C Hinrichs, 1890). His reference to
the unmistakable one-sidedness of the Synoptic reports (p.5, cf. pp.50ff) is
completely justified. The enigma cannot be solved by passing over the difficulty in silence. In any case, this insight prevents one from pursuing the con-
venient method of making a bias in favor of the Synoptics into a principle of
historical research, and of arbitrarily inserting either a few or many details from
the Fourth Gospel into the framework of the Synoptic narrative, or even of
borrowing the framework of the Fourth Gospel and then continuing from
there as if the presentation of the Synoptics were normative and adequate.
Obviously, this essay cannot furnish the specific proofs for these assertions.
However, this seems to me unnecessary, for the facts are clearly known and
beyond doubt to anyone who has had some kind of theological training. Differences exist only with respect to the evaluation and utilization of these facts.

[4] On the discourses of Jesus cf., e.g., E. Haupt, *Die eschatologischen Aussagen
Jesu in den synoptischen Evangelien* (Berlin: Reuther und Reichard, 1895), pp5f.

[5] We have in mind, for example, the question of the day of the month on
which the crucifixion occurred. But even apart from such secondary matters,
how meager the prospects of harmonizing just the passion narratives, even
when one puts the Fourth Gospel to one side. Of course, if a person assumes
the impartiality and objectivity of the records in general, then the questions are
not so painful. The materials agree on the whole. It is only the details that we
can no longer know. There are many times when historians must accept such
restrictions. However, here there is something special to bear in mind that

ographers, however, set themselves even more difficult tasks. Not all of them refrain from discussing certain questions which titillate one's curiosity but the answers to which still remain irrelevant to the main issue. To cite some examples, there are discussions about how handsome or homely Jesus was, or about his early life at home and at his work. Inquiries into his temperament or his individuality I would put into the same category. We could go on to mention others.

The biographers may refrain from such dubious inquiries, however. The more recent ones, for example, are strong on psychological analysis. They seek to show the variety and sequence of causes that would account for the life and ministry of Jesus. Does the true humanity of Jesus not demand that we understand how he grew, his gradual development as a religious genius, the breakthrough of his moral independence, the dawning and illumination of his messianic consciousness? The sources, however, contain nothing of all that, absolutely nothing! At best only the short story of the twelve-year-old Jesus can pass muster as a historical report; from the standpoint of literary criticism, however, it is sheer caprice to sever it from the infancy narrative of Luke's Gospel. And is there any section of this whole literature that has been treated with more suspicion than precisely this one?[6] To be

---

should make one especially cautious. The last week of Jesus' life is the period reported in greatest detail; yet, its actual course impressed itself upon the memory of the eyewitnesses so indefinitely that the later narrators took pains again and again to harmonize the various events and reports—but in vain—and almost each one did it differently from his predecessor. This hardly encourages us to assume such a reliability of the given materials that further conclusions can be drawn with confidence about matters which are not even recorded in the Gospels.

[6] I am, of course, not unaware that it is common for historians to demonstrate from the Gospels the development of Jesus' messianic consciousness during his public ministry. Yet it will surely be generally conceded that such a development is outside the purview of the sources themselves, or of those who reported in them. Therefore, here too the reconstructions are based on what the scholars profess to discover *behind* the sources. I cannot escape the notion, however, that historical research must adhere strictly to the sources. As soon as one disregards the task of evaluating the sources themselves and begins to appraise the materials without paying any attention to their origins and the question of their historicity, one moves merely in the realm of uncertain conjecture. Negative judgments bearing some degree of certainty may be possible; but regarding the actual course of events, one cannot be sure of anything.

able to say anything more about Jesus requires recourse to *a pos-teriori* conclusions, and to make them cogent calls for extreme caution in one's approach, thoroughly reliable evidence, and a careful appraisal of the significance of one's findings. If we follow this reliable procedure, we shall scarcely achieve lavish results. That this is especially true of the Gospel materials I shall now show through a critique of the current methods used in writing the biographies.

The New Testament presentations were not written for the purpose of describing how Jesus developed. They show him manifesting himself and playing an active role, but not making confessions about his inner life, certainly not unpremeditated ones, except perhaps for a few sighs and ejaculations (e.g., Mark 9:19; John 12:27; Mark 14:36; 15:34).[7] An unprejudiced reader or scholar will hardly deny this. Therefore, the Gospels do not invite the drawing of *a posteriori* conclusions concerning the exact nature of Jesus' earlier development. It is, of course, undeniable that the Old Testament and Hebrew thought-forms have conditioned Jesus' outlook on things.[8] Yet such obvious remarks gain us almost nothing. To assert anything more one must, in view of the silence of the sources, use as a means of research the principle of analogy with other human events—thus contradicting the whole tenor of the Gospel portrayals of Jesus.

Otherwise the flawless fiction of a novel would constitute a proof of the reality of its contents. It seems to me that in the work of the critics great unclarity reigns regarding the distinction between psychological (i.e., poetic) truth and the proper reproduction of reality in its often incomprehensible paradoxicality. Whereas present-day artists [*Künstler*] are trying to refrain from purely imaginative effort and pride themselves on faithful reproductions of reality, historians ['*die historische Kunst*' ('the historical art')] are pouring their energies into conjuring up before us a past reality from some 'psychological law' that seems to be valid for the moment.

[7] Matt. 11:25f., with its solemn cadence, does not bear the marks of a confession forced out half unwillingly. To me it seems to be a public prayer, like John 17, with conscious reference to the disciples (cf. John 11:41, 42). The other view is supported neither by what follows (verse 28f) nor by the context (Luke 10:17-23).

[8] Cf. my essay, *Jesus und das Alte Testament* (2nd ed.; Leipzig: A. Deichert, 1896).

First, there is the attempt to use psychology for the purpose of analyzing or supplementing data. Is such an attempt justified in this area? We will admit the validity of psychology only insofar as it rests demonstrably upon experience. A certain trustworthiness may be claimed for it where it deals with the *forms* of our inner experience, and undoubtedly they were the same for Jesus as for the rest of us. But here this is a matter of complete indifference. The dubious studies I have in mind always deal with the *content* of the inner life that developed and manifested itself in Jesus, and with the roots, the development, and the ramifications of his moral and religious consciousness (to use the going terms). Modern scientific psychology, however, no longer busies itself with the content of the inner life. That falls more in the province of other sciences. The poet, too, is accustomed to observe and depict that content. Where does the poet get his information? It is well known that in his poetry Goethe was describing mainly himself and his own experiences. He is such a great man because his observations 'penetrated into the depths of human existence'. Likewise, sensitive observers are generally impressive painters. Jeremias Gotthelf was as shunned in the region of Berne as Wildermuth was in Swabia—people were afraid of seeing an image of the haunted house in print. Here, too, the person who employs the principle of analogy will have to seek his materials in the manifoldness of reality. Therefore I ask once again, Is this method justified in writing about Jesus? Will anyone who has had the impression of being encountered by that unique sinless person, that unique Son of Adam endowed with a vigorous consciousness of God, still venture to use the principle of analogy here once he has thoroughly assessed the situation? We must not think that we can solve the problem with a pantograph, reproducing the general outlines of our own nature but with larger dimensions. The distinction between Jesus Christ and ourselves is not one of degree but of kind. We all know that poets create unreal and impossible figures insofar as they idealize them and cease to portray them with mixed qualities. Such idealization usually means simply the elimination of all the displeasing traits. We cannot, however, deal with Jesus merely by removing the blemishes from our own nature—that would merely leave us with a blank tablet. Sinlessness is not merely a negative concept. The inner development of a sinless person is as inconceivable to us as life on the Sandwich Islands is to a Laplander.[9] In the depths of our being we are different from him, so different in fact that we could become like him only through a new birth, a new creation. How then can we hope to analyze and explain Jesus' development, its stages and changes, in analogy with the common experience of humanity? Indeed, if we look deeper we encounter the objection, How could he have been sinless in the midst of a world, a family, and a people so full of offense? How could the boy Jesus develop in a pure and positive way when in his years of infancy, filial dependence, and immaturity he was surrounded by bad influences, and when his whole education, however well meant, must have been on the whole distorted? All this is a miracle which cannot be explained merely in terms of an innocent disposition. It is conceivable only because this infant entered upon his earthly existence with a prior endowment quite different from our own, because in all the forms and stages of his inner life an absolutely independent will was expressing itself, because God's grace and truth became incarnate in him. In view of this fact we would all do well to refrain from depicting his inner life by the principle of analogy.

There remains the historical analogy. Here one goes back to the conditions and the thought world of Jesus' environment and to the historical records and Jewish literature which still survive from that period. Perhaps an examination of the history of such attempts will place them in proper perspective. Long before Baur, Semler had discovered the Judaistic tendencies of the early Christian writers. Yet Semler's school exempted Jesus from any such attachment to Judaism. Was this mere prejudice or was it the result of observation, of a correct insight? David Strauss found Hellenistic influences in Jesus, or in any case something totally unrelated to late Judaism. If we compare the Jesus of our Gospels with Saul of Tarsus, we do in fact see a great difference between the disciple of the Pharisees and the Master. On the one hand we see the true Jew, so profoundly and indelibly influ-

---

[9] With good reason Dorner preferred the expression 'sinless perfection', although he too did not think of Jesus as fully developed right from the beginning.

enced by the cultural forces of his people and epoch; on the other hand we see the Son of Man, whose person and work convey the impression of one who lived, as it were, in the timeless age of the patriarchs. Thus a return to the first century does not appear to be very promising.

Obviously we would not deny that historical research can help to explain and clarify particular features of Jesus' actions and attitudes as well as many aspects of his teaching. Nor will I exaggerate the issue by casting doubt on the historian's capacity to trace the broad outlines of the historical institutions and forces which influenced the human development of our Lord. But it is common knowledge that all this is wholly insufficient for a biographical work in the modern sense. Such a work is never content with a modest retrospective analysis, for in reconstructing an obscure event in the past it also wishes to convince us that its *a posteriori* conclusions are accurate. The biographical method likes to treat that period in Jesus' life for which we have no sources[10] and in particular seeks to explain the course of his spiritual development during his public ministry. To accomplish that something other than cautious analysis is required. Some outside force must rework the fragments of the tradition. This force is nothing other than the theologian's imagination—an imagination that has been shaped and nourished by the analogy of his own life and of human life in general. If, in other areas, the historian's muse often paints pictures which lack every breath of the past and its distinctive characteristics, what will it make of this unique material? The Gospels confront each of us with an Either/Or. The question is whether the historian will humble himself before the unique sinless Person—the only proper attitude in the presence of the norm of all morality. What a difference it must make in a person's interpretation whether he confesses the sinlessness of the Redeemer whom he is portraying or whether he charges Jesus with a catalog of sins, whether, with Jesus, he reckons every sinner as lost or whether he regards the boundaries as so fluid that moral errors are viewed as exaggerated virtues![11]

[10] Bernard Weiss, however, does not do this.

[11] Thus Theodor Keim, *Geschichte Jesu* (3rd ed., 1873), p.372. Keim perceives a lack of harmony in the moral development of Jesus at several points.

It is plainly evident that the imagination which thus orders and shapes the Gospel materials is being guided by still another force, namely, by a preconceived view of religious and ethical matters. In other words, the biographer who portrays Jesus is always something of a dogmatician in the derogatory[12] sense of the word. At best he shares the point of view of the dogmatics of the Bible; most modern biographers, however, do so only to a very limited degree. Indeed, quite a few place themselves in conscious opposition to the 'primitive world-view of the New Testament'.

With this observation, however, we have made a very important discovery. There is no more effective method for securing the gradual triumph of a political party than to write a history of one's country like that of Macaulay. Stripped of its historical dress, the bare thesis of the 'historian' would arouse too many suspicions. Disguised as history, the historian's theory passes imperceptibly into our thought and convictions as an authentic piece of reality, as a law emanating therefrom. Thus Rotteck's 'history' of the world was in reality a party pamphlet, which, through its wide distribution, shaped the political thinking of large numbers of the German middle class. The same is true of dogmatics. Today everyone is on his guard when a dogma is frankly presented as such. But when Christology appears in the form of a 'Life of Jesus', there are not many who will perceive the stage manager behind the scenes, manipulating, according to his own dogmatic script, the fascinating spectacle of a colorful biography. Yet no one can detect the hidden dogmatician so well as a person who is himself a dogmatician, whose job it is to pursue consciously and intentionally the implications of basic ideas in all their specific nuances. Therefore, the dogmatician has the right to set up a warning sign before the

---

He noticed in Jesus the 'scars' of a person refined through conflict, which David Strauss was not able to discover, although Strauss maintained that it was necessary and therefore self-evident to assume 'individual perturbations and defects' in Jesus' development. Those who know the literature will recall the disgusting tirades of Renan, for example, in connection with the Gethsemane episode.

[12] Naturally those who think of themselves simply as historians and claim to be completely without bias will view the dogmatician in this way.

allegedly presuppositionless historical research that ceases to do real research and turns instead to a fanciful reshaping of the data.

We all enjoy it when a gifted writer interprets a significant figure or event of the past in a play or novel. By freeing his portrayal from the requirements of historical accuracy and by giving his imagination freer rein, he can sometimes better reveal the true character of the event or figure. In biblically oriented circles, however, epics about the Messiah and dramas about Christ have always been viewed with some uneasiness; and, for the most part, we certainly share these reservations and these qualms. How many authors of the 'Lives' blithely compose epics and dramas without being aware that this is what they are doing! And because this is done in prose, perhaps even from the pulpit, people think that this is merely a presentation of the historic, biblical picture of Christ. Far from it! What is usually happening is that the image of Jesus is being refracted through the spirit of these gentlemen themselves. This makes considerably more difference here than in any other field. For here we are dealing with the source from which the outpouring of the purifying Spirit is to proceed now as it has in the past. How can the Spirit perform his purifying work if he is not permitted to reach our ears and hearts without obstruction?

Let us take a good look at this matter. What is the Life-of-Jesus research really searching for? In going behind Jesus Christ as he is portrayed in the church's tradition—and this means also behind the New Testament picture of Christ—it wants to get at the *real* Jesus, as he actually existed in all those respects that all, or some, might consider important or indispensable, or often only desirable or titillating ('How interesting!').[13] Although the

---

[13] Even a serious theologian has been known to go astray by speculating on Mary's relation to Jesus on such a matter as his laundry! In the case of Schiller students try to conclude from his financial state of affairs at a given point in his life as ascertained from his notebooks—his incentives for public activity or his state of mind. If a theologian lacks a comparable basis for such imaginative additions to the tradition about Jesus, then these embellishments are merely a piece of phantasy, which is the exact counterpart, on another level, to the Moravians' playful intimacy with the Savior. This shows lack of taste even from the aesthetic point of view. For even the keenest aesthetic sensitivity can show a lack of delicacy in treating sacred subjects.

attempt to answer concerns such as these encounters the various kinds of difficulties we have pointed out, it is important that we capitalize on the opportunity they offer to seek out the legitimate element in such self-imposed quests. We shall find the answer when we succeed in isolating the real and ultimate reason behind the attempt—legitimate and indeed unavoidable as it is—to present the historic figure of Jesus, in its full reality, to our inner perception.

This brings us to the crux of the matter: *Why* do we seek to know the figure of Jesus? I rather think it is because we believe him when he says, 'He who has seen me has seen the Father' (John 14:9), because we see in him the revelation of the invisible God. Now if the Word became flesh in Jesus, which is the revelation, the flesh or the Word?[14] Which is the more important for us, that wherein Jesus is like us, or that wherein he was and is totally different from us? Is it not the latter, namely, that which he offers us, not from our own hearts, but from the heart of the living God? I do not want to be misunderstood. That he was like us is, of course, incomparably significant for us and is treasured by us; Scripture always emphasizes it, too, but hardly ever without adding expressions like 'without sin', 'by grace', 'in humility and perfect obedience', etc. (Heb. 4:15; 7:26, 27; II Cor. 8:9; Phil. 2:6ff.). How he was like us is self-evident. It is also fairly obvious why the evidence of his likeness to us is to be found on every page of the Gospels. And yet how we have to search to muster such a biblical proof from statements which deliberately emphasize that likeness. Does this not explain why we recognize the emphasis on Jesus' moral achievement [*die sittliche Arbeit*] as a distinguishing peculiarity of the Epistle to the Hebrews? (Cf. 2:17, 18; 4:15; 5:7ff., perhaps also 12:2, 3.)[15] If a person really asks himself what he is looking for when he reads the Gospels, he will admit to himself, 'I am not seeking someone

[14] The person well versed in Scripture will not answer that it is the flesh which reveals and the Word which is revealed, for precisely the Word itself is the revelation. Cf. the quotation from Luther, cited by Herrmann: 'We must let the humanity of Christ be a way, a sign, a work of God, through which we come to God' (*Erlanger Ausgabe*, 7,73).

[15] These are passages that emphasize how important his moral achievement is for us, but also that it is important only because it appears striking in the light of his *total* person.

like myself, but rather my opposite, my fulfilment, my Savior.'
When a person reflects on what he finds when reading the Gospels, he will say, 'No man has ever spoken or acted thus; never
has such a man existed.' He will not say that no one has ever
said the same things Jesus said. For Jesus repeated many things
which religious thinkers had written and said prior to him—
things which become different, however, when he says them.[16]
Nor will a reader of the Gospels maintain that everything Jesus
did was unique, for he stands surrounded by a cloud of
witnesses. And yet, there is something unique in the *way* he did
things, for there has never been a man like him.[17]

Why, in the final analysis, do we commune with the Jesus of our
Gospels? What does he offer us? 'In him we have redemption
through his blood, the forgiveness of our trespasses'[18] (Eph. 1:7).
Do I really need to know more of him than what Paul 'delivered to [the Corinthians] as of first importance, what [he] also
received, that Christ died for our sins in accordance with the
Scriptures, that he was buried, that he was raised on the third
day in accordance with the Scriptures, and that he appeared' (I
Cor. 15:3f)? This is the good news brought in the name of God
(I Cor. 15:12f.; Rom. 1:1f.; II Cor. 5:18f.; Gal. 1:6f.). This is
the witness and confession of faith which has overcome the
world (I John 5:4). If I have all this I do not need additional information on the precise details of Jesus' life and death.

Then why the Gospels? Why do we need that kind of
preaching the content of which is, so often, what Jesus did and
taught? We have redemption through *him*.[19] 'Who is to con-

---

[16] One might compare, for example, the Lord's Prayer with the Jewish
prayers which in fact bear a resemblance to it. (See August Tholuck, *Die Ber-
grede Christi*.) One also ought to note Jesus' use of Scripture. Cf. also the writing by Haupt cited earlier.

[17] On pp.53f [pp.223-24 above] we indicated in part what we mean by the
'uniqueness' of Jesus. More will be said about this subject toward the end of
our discussion.

[18] I adduce this quotation of course only to summarize the answer, not as
an adequate proof. That is hardly necessary; the New Testament and the cate-
chisms are clear enough in this respect.

[19] I place this emphasis on these words from Eph. 1:17 [*sic*, read 1:7] and
Col. 1.14 in order to bring out the contemporary significance of Christ's *person*
for all generations instead of only asserting Christ's work in the past. (Cf. my

demn? Is it Christ Jesus, who died, yes, who was raised from the dead, who is at the right hand of God, who indeed intercedes for us?' (Rom. 8:34). 'We have an advocate with the Father, Jesus Christ the righteous' (I John 2:1). 'For we have not a high priest who is unable to sympathize with our weaknesses, but one who in every respect has been tempted as we are, yet without sinning' (Heb. 4:15). We need, we have, and we believe in the living Christ. We believe in him because we know him; we have him as we know him; we know him because he dwelt among us, full of grace and truth, and chose for himself witnesses through whose word we are to believe in him (John 1:13, 14; cf. I John 1:1f.; John 15:27; 17:20).

Therefore, the reason we commune with the Jesus of our Gospels is because it is through them that we learn to know that same Jesus whom, with the eyes of faith and in our prayers, we meet at the right hand of God, because we know, with Luther, that God cannot be found except in his beloved Son,[20] because he is God's revelation to us, or, more accurately and specifically, because he who once walked on earth and now is exalted is the incarnate Word of God, the image of the invisible God—because he is for us God revealed.

That is what the believer seeks. That is what the church celebrates.

How important, therefore, the least little feature becomes! How indispensable the removal of every optical illusion created by the prism of tradition, the removal of every obscurity in the interpretation of his first witnesses! How inexpressibly important the reality of Jesus, down to the minutest detail! It would be serious if this were really the case. Just suppose that the art of modern historiography were able to carry out a spectral analysis on the Sun of our salvation. Suppose that we today were able to remove those obscurities in the tradition. What would that im-

Wissenschaft der christlichen Lehre, op. cit., pp.397, 411f., 432f.) We are speaking here—as will surely be recognized—not of conversion to Christianity but of the ongoing life of the Christian.

[20] Theodosius Harnack, *Luthers Theologie* (Erlangen, 1862-86), II, 81f.; cf. also *ibid.*, I, 111f., Gottfried Thomasius, *Christi Person*, II (2 ed., Erlangen 1857), 210f.; Julius Kostlin, *Luthers Theologie* (Stuttgart, 1863), II, 155, 300f., 383.

ply with respect to our fellow Christians in the early period? If
their contemplation and worship of the Jesus of the Gospels
were distorted and deflected by those obscurities which the
critic professes to find in their writings and feels bound to remove, then indeed they would not have known their Savior.
And the same would be true of all subsequent Christians, including ourselves. Yes, gentlemen and brethren, what about
ourselves? What would our situation be? Where do we come to
know this Jesus? Only a very few can carry on the work of historical science, and only a few are sufficiently trained to evaluate
such work. To be sure, such work would relieve us of the
authority of the Bible, but it would in turn subject us to the
authority, not of an empirical science, but of the alleged results
produced by this science. Meanwhile there is no one who can
answer our question, Where is that fifth evangelist[21] capable of
providing us with the picture of the exalted Christ, the picture
of God revealed? Which of the biographers can do this? We
have our choice in a series from Hess and Zündel, through
David Strauss, right up to Renan and Noack, to say nothing of
the Social-Democratic pamphlets.

If someone should object at this point, 'Our situation with
respect to dogmatics is the same as that with respect to historical
science, for in relation to dogmatics we are dependent upon
theologians', the comparison would be erroneous. Dogmatics is
a matter of judging data that are accessible to every Christian, so
long as it does not deal with detailed theological propositions
that are not really essential in understanding the Christian faith.
Historical research, on the other hand, requires the mastery of a
sophisticated technique and a massive erudition. In this field no
lay judgment is possible, except perhaps the kind made by in-
flated dilettantes.

Therefore, either we must do without the revealed God, or
the reality of Christ as our Savior must be something quite different from the scarcely accessible, or even inaccessible, reality of
those clear and transparent details of his personal life and development which are generally deemed essential in the writing of a
modern biography. There must be another way to reach the

---

[21] Assuming, that is, that one cannot be satisfied with Renan's fifth gospel
namely, with a geography and ethnography of modern Palestine.

historic Christ than that of scientific reconstructions which employ source criticism and historical analogy.

Consider for a moment. What is a truly 'historic figure', that is, a person who has been influential in molding posterity, as measured by his contribution to history? Is it not the person who originates and bequeaths a permanent influence? He is one of those dynamic individuals who intervene in the course of events. What they are in themselves produces effects, and through these effects their influence persists. In the case of thousands of people whose traces in the history of their contemporaries and of posterity are obliterated slowly or not at all, their earlier development remains for scholarship just so many roots hidden underground, and the particulars of their activity are forever forgotten. The person whom history remembers lives on through his work, to which, in unforgettable words and personal characteristics, a direct impression of his dynamic essence often attaches itself. And the effect left by that impression is necessarily conditioned by the material on which it leaves its mark and by the environment upon which it had to and was able to work.[22] Thus, from a purely historical point of view the truly historic element in any great figure is the discernible personal influence which he exercises upon later generations. But what is the decisive influence that Jesus had upon posterity? According to the Bible and church history it consisted in nothing else but the faith of his disciples, their conviction that in Jesus they had found the conqueror of guilt, sin, temptation, and death. From this one influence all others emanate; it is the criterion by which all the others stand or fall. This conviction of the disciples is summed up in the single affirmation, 'Christ is Lord'.

Contemporary history contributed nothing to this affirmation, and Jewish theology still less. The contemporary historical accounts in Josephus mention John, the son of Zechariah, but not a word about Jesus of Nazareth. Indeed, contemporary his-

---

[22] The solitary figures who left only a written legacy, but left no mark on their contemporary world, are not historic figures. Jesus, however, the ministering friend of men, is as different as is conceivable from this sort of 'eyeing' of posterity that reckons on being counted among 'the class of people that are still to come'.

tory counted him among the dead. After he died as a sacrifice for the sake of the nation (John 11:49f.), the Jews went raving and racing to their political destruction, without taking any notice of him. The small band of Nazarenes was of no importance to them. The rest of the world would have ignored him, had not Saul of Tarsus gathered a community in his name, the giant tree growing out of the mustard seed, under whose leaves the birds of the heaven build their nests. So much for contemporary history.

But what about Jewish theology and eschatology? We surely know how vigorously the unpretentious Rabbi had to contend with the terrestrial hopes for a splendiferous Son of David who was to lay the kingdoms of this world, in all their glory, at the feet of his people. Those images and metaphors from Jewish eschatology which Christians drew upon in painting their vivid pictures of the Christian hope still constitute the stumbling block which is apt to betray the hope of faith into denial of itself.

'Christ is Lord'—this certainty neither flesh nor blood can attain, sustain, or impart. Jesus himself said as much to Peter after his confession (Matt. 16:17), and he said it also in reproach of the unbelieving Jews (John 6:43f); it was confirmed by Peter's denial in the outer court of the High Priest and later by Paul, who could say it to his congregations in full expectation of their assent (I Cor. 12:3). Yet, wherever this certainty has arisen and exerted an influence, it has been bound up demonstrably with another conviction—that Jesus is the crucified, risen, and living Lord. And when we ask at what point in their discussions the historians deal with this certainty, we find that they begin not with the much disputed and disconnected final narratives of the evangelists but with the experience of Paul. They ascertain the unwavering faith of the early church as far as they can determine the testimonies and the traces left by those early witnesses. The risen Lord is not the historical Jesus *behind* the Gospels, but the Christ of the apostolic preaching, of the *whole* New Testament. To designate this Lord as 'Christ' (Messiah) is to confess his historical mission, or as we say today, his vocation, or as our forefathers said, meaning essentially the same thing, his 'threefold office'. That is to say, to confess him as Christ is to confess his unique, supra-historical significance for the whole of humanity.

Christians became certain that Jesus was the Messiah, the Christ, in total opposition to public opinion, not only with regard to the idea of the Messiah (that is, the way one conceived of the Messiah and what one expected of him), but also with regard to the person of this Jesus of Nazareth. This was as true then as it is today. When Christians tried to make the Messiahship of Jesus credible in their sermons and then in epistles and gospels, they always made use of two kinds of evidence: personal testimony to his resurrection, based on experience, and the witness of the Scriptures. As the living Lord he was for them the Messiah of the Old Covenant.

Therefore we, too, speak of the *historic Christ of the Bible*. It is clear that the historical Jesus, as we see him in his earthly ministry, did not win from his disciples a faith with power to witness to him, but only a very shaky loyalty susceptible to panic and betrayal.[23] It is clear that they were all reborn, with Peter, unto a living hope only through the resurrection of Jesus from the dead (I Pet. 1:3) and that they needed the gift of the Spirit to 'bring to their remembrance' what Jesus had said, before they were able to understand what he had already given them and to grasp what they had been unable to bear (John 14:26; 16:12, 13). It is clear that they did not later go forth into the world to make Jesus the head of a 'school' by propagating his teachings, but to witness to his person and his imperishable significance for every man. If all this is clear and certain, it is equally certain that Jesus' followers were capable of understanding his person and mission, his deeds and his word as the offer of God's grace and faithfulness only after he appeared to them in his state of fulfilment—in which he was himself the fruit and the eternal bearer of his own work of universal and lasting significance, a work (to be exact) whose most difficult and decisive part was the *end* of the histori-

---

[23] Jesus' statement in Matthew 16:15f does not mean that his person and ministry have produced this confession. Rather, he ascribes this confession to God's revelation. He is not speaking about faith at all; hence, faith is not the 'rock'. The faith in question had so little power to endure of itself that it needed an explicit prayer to God, whose revelation evoked the confession in the first place (Luke 22:32). The *biblical* Jesus expected that the disciples' witness to him would be with power only after the Spirit had been sent (Luke 24:48f.; John 15:26; Acts 1:4, 8).

cal Jesus. Even though we once knew the Messiah according to
the flesh, now we regard him thus no longer (II Cor. 5:16).

This is the first characteristic of Christ's enduring influence,
that he evoked faith from his disciples. And the second is that
this faith was *confessed*. His promise depends upon such confession (Rom. 10:9-10), as does also the history of Christianity and
our own decision of faith. The real Christ, that is, the Christ
who has exercised an influence in history, with whom millions
have communed in childlike faith, and with whom the great
witnesses of faith have been in communion—while striving, ap-
prehending, triumphing, and proclaiming—*this real Christ is the
Christ who is preached*. The Christ who is preached, however, is
precisely the Christ of faith. He is the Jesus whom the eyes of
faith behold at every step he takes and through every syllable he
utters—the Jesus whose image we impress upon our minds because we both would and do commune with, our risen, living,
Lord. The person of our living Savior, the person of the Word
incarnate, of God revealed, gazes upon us from the features of
that image which has deeply impressed itself on the memory of
his followers—here in bold outlines, there in single strokes—and
which was finally disclosed and perfected through the illumination of his Spirit.

This is no reassuring sermon. It is the result of a painstaking
consideration of the data at hand. It is the result achieved by a
dogmatics[24] which sorts and sifts the evidence and states the conclusions in biblical language only because they happen to agree
with the word of Scripture. Ought such a conformity to Scripture really provide a reason for looking with suspicion on this

---

[24] It is surely plain that I am here contrasting dogmatics with preaching,
and scientific statement with untested interpretations. In the context the far-
thest thing from my mind is the arrogant assertion of the superiority of dogmatics to historical study, or a 'tutelage' of historical study by dogmatics. Nevertheless this is the way Dr. Beyschlag interprets my sentence (see his *Leben
Jesu*, p.xx); and by putting a colon before the words 'This is', rather than indicating that they begin a new paragraph, he leaves readers with the impression
that such an assertion was made by me. He also omits everything which makes
clear that I am here referring to the portrayal of Jesus in the Gospels, interpreted of course from the viewpoint of the faith one encounters there as well
as in the rest of the New Testament.

kind of dogmatics, especially among those who base their criticisms on Reformation (!) theology?

In popular usage the word 'dogmatics' has come to connote arbitrary assertions, whereas 'historical study' of a subject is regarded as always laying hold of reality. The latter is unfortunately not always the case, since historical science does not always observe its limitations or fulfill its obligations, nor is it always in a position to do so. It is equally true that the popular assumption about dogmatics is basically unfounded, though understandable in view of the dogmaticians' aberrations. Dogmatics also has a 'given' with which it works, although this is not merely a past reality. Dogmatics is in a very real sense the mediator between past and present; it puts what is genuine and indispensable in the past at the service of the present. This task of mediation, then, belongs to dogmatics, after it has made a thorough and serious study of what historical study can accomplish and has learned from history what is important enough to warrant consideration by dogmatics. The task of dogmatics is to provide an inventory of our assets.

The 'data at hand' to which we referred above are not the individual events reported in the Gospels about the life of Jesus. In this whole discussion we are trying to explain how inadvisable and indeed impossible it is to reach a Christian understanding of Jesus when one deviates from the *total* biblical proclamation about him—his life as well as its significance. The factual data which have led me to this judgment have to do with the nature of the tradition at our disposal. I have in mind especially two far-reaching facts: first, the impossibility of extracting from the sources a 'genesis' of Jesus the Messiah and, second, the knowledge of what Christ has always meant to his church and still means to every believer today. These facts are, of course, a distillation of a series of other facts, as I have tried to indicate and as I intend to elaborate more fully. As far as the second is concerned, it is quite unwarranted to demand that the significance of Christ for Christianity be measured by what he means to those whose devotion to Christ has all but ceased. We must remind ourselves again and again that in trying to arrive at an understanding of man we must of course take into account the stages of his development, his existence as a fetus and as an adolescent, as well as his possible degeneration to the level of a cripple or an imbecile; nevertheless our conception of man will, in the last analysis, have to rest on a mature and healthy specimen of noble attributes. We may, if we wish, keep our christological formulae to the barest possible minimum; yet for Christians Christ must always be the object of faith in the 'strictly religious sense of the word', to use an expression in vogue today. Otherwise we fall outside the bounds of his church. For this reason Christian language about Christ must always take the form of a confession or a dogma.

Those are the limits of the circle within which I would expect the validity of these arguments to be acknowledged or at least to receive sympathetic consideration.

I can appreciate fully how a person will necessarily reach a totally different position if he denies or depreciates what we have called the second fact. If revelation is only an erroneous name for religious consciousness in its historically conditioned development, and if Jesus is merely a religious genius surpassing the rest of us only in degree, then doubtless the New Testament confession of faith, which also inspired the evangelists in their portrayal of Jesus, can only result in an obscuring of the facts. Then we must look with suspicion on everything, or almost everything, in that portrayal. Then we can only resort to the attempt to explain, at all costs, the mystery of this man in terms of the thought and life of his day, a man who not only wanted to be called the Messiah, but also was confessed and proclaimed as such by an astonishing number of people. Given these presuppositions, I do not look for widespread support of the affirmative side of my criticism. On the other hand, I expect the negative side of my criticism to be generally conceded, so far as it concerns the evaluation of the sources. At any rate, my arguments deal only with those theologians who wish to write a 'Life of Jesus' in the service of the confession of Christ, and who think (at least some of them) that their work can do more to strengthen this confession than can dogmatics. I am concerned with a correct evaluation of what the constructive historical method can accomplish, particularly what it can contribute toward the right attitude to Christ within the church, the bearer of the gospel.

The rest of this essay will emphasize why we have the right to be sensitive to, and on guard against, all later embellishments of the biblical picture of Christ. Such imaginative reconstructions cannot stand without criticism, not even as specialized theological research. I think I can explain its popularity and influence in wide circles, especially in the younger generation. Often we do not sufficiently appreciate to what extent the moods regarding the criterion and aim of knowledge change with the times. I say 'moods' advisedly. I believe I can observe such a mood at the present time. Historical detail is very much in vogue today, despite widespread skepticism. Historical novels have contributed much to the blurring of the boundaries. Even Christian readers have been spoiled. Instead of approaching the early witnesses sympathetically, searching for the truth in their writings, they prefer to be stimulated and excited by the curiosity of one who was a contemporary, of one who was enflamed into passionate involvement, of one who delighted in the victory of the controversial orator. Although the psychological novel presented in the form of letters may have declined in popularity, we have in its place biographies consisting almost wholly of diaries and fragments of letters. People like to view the remote past in a modern refraction. *Homo sum*—man in every time and place is one and the same, today as always, as is illustrated by the sensation which a short story can create. In spite of these objections one might be able to put up with such attempts in the area of theology if they held themselves in check and heeded admonition. To accommodate a current mood one might conceal his displeasure at such bold manipulations of the noble elements of Jesus' picture.

However, it is another matter when—pardon my bluntness—the Christ-novels ascend to the pulpit. Lengthy discourses about first century history, seemingly profound insights into Jesus' inner life (supported by observations on the differences in outlook between then and now), poetic descriptions of the countryside, all this keeps the listener preoccupied with things which, after all, are merely the vehicles of the events in the Gospels and keeps him from the real thing, or better, from the Person who alone is worthy of our attention, from the one Person in his incomparable uniqueness. Certainly no age should be prevented from speaking its own language and from remaining true to its own character. However, the restraint and sobriety of the first witnesses should remain the criterion for the message which the evangelical preacher has to deliver. We should attempt to do only one thing in our pulpits, namely, to present to our hearers these old, often heard, 'outdated' stories—just as they stand, yet freshly and as if heard for the first time. Each listener should receive an indelible impression of what these accounts mean for him. If we immerse ourselves in our Gospels and consider them from every angle without a slavish and lazy adherence to the appointed lessons of the church year, there will be no danger of monotony—unless by monotony one means the repetition of the one keynote, which indeed is unavoidable. This, after all, is the obligation and final aim of every evangelical preacher (Phil. 1:18).

It is a mistaken notion to think that it is enough simply to draw the attention of people to Jesus. The 'interest' that is aroused here might easily become an obstacle to genuine attentiveness. That is to say, an interest in antiquity or in a modern psychological interpretation of some well-known event may become an obstacle to a true estimate of Christ's worth for our day. It is as noxious for outsiders as it is for 'Christian' circles when Christ and the gospel become mere topics of conversation. A preacher must always be scrutinizing his sermons to see whether he is entertaining his congregation instead of witnessing to the gospel, whether he is engaging their intellect and judgment instead of reinforcing (with appropriate means) their inner stirrings in the direction of radical decision and providing their spiritual life with lasting nourishment. Even under the pretence of promoting biblical knowledge it is possible to do nothing more than 'beat the air'.

7

The Dialectical Theology

Rudolf Bultmann and Karl Barth

Martin Kähler's protest against the historical Jesus quest was taken up in a more developed form by two twentieth-century theologians, Rudolf Bultmann and Karl Barth. It is unfortunate that students of our own time are inclined to think of Bultmann (if they think of him at all) as a theological 'liberal', while Barth is regarded as a theological 'conservative'. For a closer study of both writers demonstrates the inadequacy of such labels. While these two great theologians would eventually part company, in the earliest stages of their careers they represented a common protest against the idea that historical research could provide a foundation for faith. Both were convinced that, while historical research could offer an understanding of Christianity as a religion, the proper subject of theology was not 'religion' but God himself. Before the revelation and the judgement of God, all human knowledge is reduced to silence.

Rudolf Bultmann (1884-1976)

Rudolf Bultmann was born in Wiefelstede in Northern Germany, and received his earliest education in the neighbouring town of Rastede before moving on to the *Gymnasium* (academic high school) in the city of Oldenburg. Having completed his schooling, he studied theology in Tübingen, Berlin and Marburg, where he also attended lectures in philosophy and the history of philosophy. During these years he had the good fortune to study under such leading figures as the Old Testament scholar Hermann Gunkel (1862-1932), the historian of dogma Aldolf Harnack (1851-1930), the New Testament scholar Johannes Weiss (see above) and the systematic theologian Wilhelm Herrmann (1846-1922). It was Weiss who encouraged Bultmann to prepare for a doctorate in New Testament studies. He gained his first theological qualification in 1910 with a dissertation on a theme which Weiss had proposed: a comparison of the style of the apostle Paul's argumentation with that of the Cynic and Stoic 'diatribe'. After a further dissertation on the exegesis of Theodore of Mopsuestia, Bultmann began his teaching career at Marburg in 1912. In 1916 he received a call to Breslau as an Assistant Professor and worked there until 1920; it was during this time that he published his *History of the Synoptic Tradition*. After a short period as Professor at Giessen, Bultmann returned to Marburg in 1921, where he remained for the rest of his life. It was at Marburg that he came into contact with the philosopher Martin Heidegger (1889-1976), who himself taught at Marburg from 1922-28, and whose analysis of human existence would offer Bultmann a set of categories within which to articulate his specifically theological insights.

Bultmann's approach to the Jesus question is marked by a strong contrast between 'the Jesus of history' and the 'Christ of faith'. The Jesus of history is both historically inaccessible and—in any case—a figure of little interest for Christian existence. (For Bultmann the historical Jesus is merely the 'Christ after the flesh' of 2 Cor 5:16.) The Christ of faith, on the other hand, is the figure who comes to us in the proclamation of the Gospel. When Bultmann writes a book on Jesus (as he did in 1926), he claims to be doing no more than uncovering the earliest level of the synoptic tradition, with a view to understanding the demands of Christian faith. He is most emphatically not attempting to create a historical portrait of Jesus on which Christians might base their faith. From this point of view Bultmann's perspective is thoroughly and unashamedly theological. Indeed no biblical scholar of modern times has been more aware of the need for a critical and self-conscious dialogue between the work of the theologian and that of the exegete.

The following extract is taken from an essay written in 1924, which Bultmann presents as an attempt to enter into discussion with the 'dialectical theology' which was being developed by Karl Barth (see below), Friedrich Gogarten (1887-1967) and Eduard Thurneysen (1888-1974). Bultmann acknowledges the contribution of nineteenth-century liberal theology, which he (unlike Barth) never wished to repudiate in its entirety. Yet the rest of the essay is devoted to a criticism of theological liberalism. Bultmann argues that, insofar as scholars hoped that historical research would free Jesus from the chains of dogma and offer a new foundation for Christian faith, it was doomed to disappointment. For historical research can only produce results which are at best approximations, and (at worst) hotly contested approximations, and thus historical reconstructions are a most unsatisfactory basis for faith. (Here Bultmann echoes some of Martin Kähler's concerns.) By regarding Christianity as product of human history, the liberal theologians were denying from the outset its claim to be a response to divine revelation and were replacing the proper subject of theology—God himself—with the study of (at best) the human religious consciousness. Liberal theologians—Bultmann continues—believed that they could do this, as theologians, because of what he calls a 'pantheism of history', namely, the conviction that the course of human history could be viewed as a revelation of the divine purpose. (We have already noted such a view in the work of Ernst Troeltsch.) The problem here is the reduction of God to that of an entity which can be grasped as part of our knowledge of the world.

However for Bultmann the problem with liberal theology goes deeper than that, for liberal theology overlooks the fact that the Word of God comes to us only as God's judgement upon our presumed knowledge. Here Bultmann recapitulates in modern terms the great Reformation theme of salvation by grace, not by works. Before the revelation of the holiness of God in Christ, our best human works no less than our worst are shown to be the works of sinful human beings. The

Christian ethical ideal is not a human ideal, which we can appropriate by our own efforts; it is an impossible ideal, which can be made possible only by way of the destruction and the re-creation of human nature by God's grace. It is in this way that Bultmann interprets the apocalyptic language of the Gospels, so strongly emphasised by Weiss and Schweitzer. What this language means is that no kind of approximation to the Kingdom of God can be achieved by human efforts within this world: the Kingdom of God comes only as God's work, and it comes first as judgement upon our attempts to create such a Kingdom.

Liberal Theology and the Latest Theological Movement[1]

Reprinted from *Faith and Understanding* Rudolf Bultmann, copyright ©1969 SCM. Used by permission of SCM.

In the polemic of the latest theological movement—a movement which is particularly associated with the names of Barth and Gogarten—the attack against the so-called liberal theology is not to be understood as a repudiation of its own past, but as a discussion with that past. The new movement is not a revival of orthodoxy, but rather a carefully reasoned consideration of the consequences which have resulted from the situation brought about by liberal theology.

It is no accident that the latest movement originated not from within orthodoxy but out of liberal theology. Barth was a student at Marburg, Gogarten at Heidelberg, Thurneysen at both.[2]

---

[1] *TB [Theologische Blätter]* (1921), pp.73-86.

[2] In this article (based on a previous lecture), I have confined myself to a discussion of the movement as represented by Barth and Gogarten only. My reason for so limiting myself in a treatment of the 'latest theological movement' is that I find that both the recognition of our present theological situation and the efforts to overcome the difficulties it presents have been most fruitful in their work. I do not overlook the fact that similar incentives are operative elsewhere and that important statements are being made by others.

It is essential to understand also that the issue raised by the new movement is not a debate with individual theologians but a protest against a specific theological trend. That trend is, of course, supported by individual theologians, but it is not to be identified with all their incidental pronouncements. Liberal theology therefore cannot evade criticism by showing that this or that liberal theologian has now and then said something quite different and is not responsible for what some other theologian has said. Moreover, it can be readily granted that themes can be seen in the work of some liberal theologians which would lead to the defeat of their own position. As examples, I would mention W. Herrmann and the great proponent of liberal theology, E. Troeltsch.

The subject of theology is *God,* and the chief charge to be brought against liberal theology is that it has dealt not with God but with man. God represents the radical negation and sublimation of man. Theology whose subject is God can therefore have as its content only the 'word of the cross' (λόγος τοῦ σταυροῦ). But that word is a 'stumbling-block' (σκάνδαλον) to men. Hence the charge against liberal theology is that it has sought to remove this stumbling-block or to minimize it.

I shall try to make clear how criticism of liberal theology develops out of this charge by a discussion of the liberal idea of history and of the actual situation of men in this world. I have chosen these two aspects because in them the position of liberal theology reveals itself most clearly. I cannot, of course, give an exhaustive presentation. We are still only at the beginning of our work of analysis and discussion. I should also emphasize that I am not presenting a criticism formulated on the basis of a fully-developed system of theology. We are in the midst of the process of self-examination. For this reason I have not dealt specifically with the question of christology, although the direction in which such inquiry should proceed will soon become clear. Nor have I specifically considered the matter of Scripture and Canon. I hope to deal with these questions elsewhere.

Here I shall seek to demonstrate conclusively what kind of conception of God and man serves as the basis of liberal theology and to make clear the objections raised against it.

I

Liberal theology owed its distinctive character chiefly to the primacy of *historical interest,* and in that field it made its greatest contributions. These contributions were not limited to the clarification of the historical picture. They were especially important for the development *of the critical sense,* that is, for freedom and veracity. We who have come from a background of liberal theology could never have become theologians nor remained such had we not encountered in that liberal theology the earnest search for radical truth. We felt in the work of orthodox university theology of all shades an urge towards compromise within which our intellectual and spiritual life would necessarily be fragmented. We can never forget our debt of gratitude to G. Krüger for that often cited article of his on 'unchurchly theology'. For he saw the task of theology to be to imperil souls, to lead men into doubt, to shatter all naïve credulity.[3] Here, we felt, was the atmosphere of truth in which alone we could breathe.

But to what result has the course of historical criticism actually led? If it was at first directed by a confidence that such critical research would free men from the burden of dogmatics and lead to a comprehension of the real figure of Jesus on which faith could be based, this confidence soon proved to be delusion. Historical research can never lead to any result which could serve as a basis for faith, for *all its results have only relative validity.* How widely the pictures of Jesus presented by liberal theologians differ from one another! How uncertain is all knowledge of 'the historical Jesus'! Is he really within the scope of our knowledge? Here research ends with a large question mark—and here it *ought* to end.

The error is not that men did this historical work and obtained results which are more or less radical; rather, it is that they did not understand the significance of such work nor the meaning of the inquiry. The real question was evaded even when it was put as precisely as Troeltsch stated it in his work, *Die Bedeutung der Geschichtlichkeit Jesu für den Glauben,* ['The Significance of the Historical Existence of Jesus for Faith'] (1911). No

---

[3] *CW* [*Die christliche Welt*], 14 (1900), pp.804-7.

matter in what sense, for Troeltsch a picture of the historical Jesus is necessary for the faith of the church, and, 'Accordingly there remains an actual dependence (if one likes to put it that way) on scholars and professors, or—better expressed—on the general sense of historical reliability which results from the impact of scientific research' (pp.34f.). Nicely put—but 'better'?

The very character which is the special 'gift' (χάρισμα) of liberal theology is denied if at the end of the road stands a sign: The situation is not yet really very bad; the results of historico-critical theology are still usable for faith. The position of liberal theology becomes frighteningly clear in the fourteenth question which von Harnack addressed to Barth. 'If the *person of Jesus Christ* stands at the centre of the Gospel, how can the foundation for a reliable and generally accepted knowledge of that person be gained except through *historico-critical research?* Is not such research essential to prevent the substitution of an *imagined* Christ for the real Christ? And who can carry on this research unless he pursues it as scientific theology?'[4] Barth answers rightly: 'Historico-critical research represents the deserved and necessary end of *the* "foundations" of this understanding (i.e. the understanding of *faith*). Such foundations do not exist except when they are laid by God himself. Anyone who does not yet know (and in truth all of us do not know *yet*) that we *cannot* any longer know Christ after the flesh should let himself be taught by critico-biblical research that the more radically he is horrified, the better it is for him and for the cause. This may well be the service which "historical science" can perform in the real task of theology.'[5]

Thus there can be no question of discarding historical criticism. But we must understand its true significance. It is needed to train us for freedom and veracity—not only by freeing us from a specific traditional conception of history, but because it frees us from bondage to every historical construction which is within the scope of historical science, and brings us to the realization that the world which faith wills to grasp is absolutely unattainable by means of scientific research.

---

[4] *CW* [*Die christliche Welt*], 37 (1923), p.8.
[5] *Ibid.*, p.91.

This truth becomes even clearer when a second error in the historical understanding of liberal theology is recognized. It forgets not only that all the results it presents within its overall picture of reality have merely a relative validity, but also that all historical phenomena which are subject to this kind of historical investigation are only relative entities, *entities which exist only within an immense inter-related complex.* Nothing which stands within this inter-relationship can claim absolute value. Even the historical Jesus is a phenomenon among other phenomena, not an absolute entity. Liberal theology has indeed recognized this conclusion up to a certain point. It speaks of the historical Jesus with great assurance, but in terms which do not ascribe an absolute value to him. Again it is Troeltsch who speaks most unambiguously. On page 14 of the work already cited, we read the plain statement that there cannot be a *necessary* binding of the Christian faith to the person of Jesus. Faith in God leads to acknowledgment of the person of Jesus, not vice versa.

But here again the final result is compromise. We are told that, almost as by a law of social psychology, the Christian church, like every religious organization, requires a cult with a concrete centre. The figure of Christ is such a centre. 'The linking of the Christian *idea* to the central position of Jesus in cult and teaching is not a conceptual necessity derived logically from the idea of salvation. But in terms of social psychology it is indispensable for the cult, for action, for proselytizing. That indispensability is sufficient justification for the assertion of the link' (p.30).

A statement of that kind makes it entirely clear that *Christianity* is understood as *a phenomenon of this world, subject to the laws of social psychology.* It is equally clear that such a conception runs exactly counter to the Christian view. Although Troeltsch's view may to some extent be justified—only orthodoxy would dispute that—certainly it is not *theology,* not if *God* is the subject of theology and the theologian is speaking as a *Christian.*

That such a conception could be offered and accepted as theology was possible partly because no objection was made to the inclusion of the person of Jesus in the complex of general historical inter-relations. Indeed, it was acceptable as theology because of the belief that *the revelation of God in history could be perceived precisely within this nexus of relations.* Therefore it is possible to speak of a 'pantheism of *history*' in liberal theology, analogous to a pantheism of nature. This pantheism depends on the assumption of a similarity between nature and history; that is, the concepts which are valid for nature are accepted as equally valid for history. And man, in so far as he acts in this history, is similarly regarded, as it were from outside, as an object, rather than under the categories which are drawn from man himself.

I shall try to make the nature of this pantheism of history clear by a comparison. In the religion of primitive peoples, deity is perceived in single objects, in a particular phenomenon of nature, in stone or tree, river or cloud, sky or constellation, storm or the burgeoning life of spring. This particularizing view of nature gradually yields to the tendency to conceive the objects and phenomena of nature as inter-related. The connectives, the cosmic powers, the laws of nature become divine for men. The farther the view of inter-relation develops towards the concept of nature as a whole, of the whole cosmos as a unity, the more completely is the naïve polydemonistic or polytheistic worship of the powers of nature transformed into a pantheism of *nature*. Such pantheism has of course lost most, if not all, truly religious motivation, as its attitude towards miracle shows. For in such pantheism the naïve view of a miraculous act of God, an act in which there is nothing natural at all, has been discarded in favour of the assertion that God acts within natural laws, that these laws are themselves forms of his activity, that they are 'miracles'.

There is actually no reason to ascribe divinity to the laws of nature; such pantheism of nature really merges into a deification of man. For it divinizes the concept of conformity to law and precisely that concept is the human element in the picture of the cosmos. Furthermore, it disregards precisely what is the basis of religion in the naïve conception of nature—the natural event which leaves man at a loss, bewilders him, reveals him to himself as nothing, 'calls him in question'.

Obviously, the idea of nature's conformity to law also *can* result in men's being at a loss. Consider, for example, Strindberg or Spitteler. But in that case pantheism is abandoned; and nature, the cosmos, is seen as a riddle which overwhelms man with terror and horror. By the kind of reaction which such modern figures as Strindberg and Spitteler exemplify, it becomes clear that no *direct* knowledge of God can be derived from nature and that the error of pantheism of nature lies really in its will to win direct knowledge of God. In other words, it tries to view God as a given entity, as an object of the kind to which the relationship of direct knowledge is possible for us.

W. Herrmann was always pointing out that 'the laws of nature hide God as much as they reveal him'. And although different terms are used, that statement is the equivalent of the constantly repeated assertion of Barth and Gogarten: 'There is no direct knowledge of God. God is not a given entity.'

The same objection holds against *the view of history held in liberal theology*. Indubitably, in primitive or ancient religions man saw the act of deity in historical events; but he saw it in particular events: in the misery or the prosperity of a people, in a battle, in a war, in servitude or liberation (for example, the Exodus from Egypt!), or in individual historical persons: Moses, the prophets, men of God of every kind. But here also occurs the shift to a recognition of inter-connection, to the concept of historical forces and laws, to the understanding of history as a unity. The views of individual adherents of liberal theology differ in detail, but on the whole a vague, idealistic, psychological concept of history prevails. Historical forces are viewed as spiritual powers which are none the less conceived entirely on the analogy of the forces of nature. Through the action of such forces, it appears, mankind develops from a state of nature to civilization and culture. History is a struggle in which the powers of the true, the good and the beautiful are victorious, and it is a struggle in which man participates, in that he is supported by these powers and thus emerges from his bondage to nature to become a free personality with all its riches.

In these powers of truth, goodness and beauty lies the meaning of history, its divine character. God reveals himself in human personalities who are the bearers of these powers. And Jesus, so far as he is also in this sense a personality, is the bearer of revelation. Such a doctrine is certainly a pantheism of history. The old 'history of salvation' is wholly divested of its character. By the demonstration of the inter-relatedness of historical phenomena, man thinks he has attained to the comprehension of divine powers. Proof of the historical necessity of the phenomenon of Christendom serves as its best apologetic.[6]

The same concept serves for the interpretation of the 'fullness of the time' (Gal. 4.4) and replaces the recognition of the truth that history has come to a dead end, that its meaninglessness has become plain. At the very least, the liberal view of history is assumed to serve Christian faith by demonstrating that such powers as are manifested in Christianity, the powers of love, of self-sacrifice and the like, are the forces actually operative in history. The essence of Christianity seems so easily understood when it is viewed in its place along with other forces and ideas which appear in principle in other spiritual movements.[7]

Along with such statements often appears—with a certain inconsistency of viewpoint—the attempt to prove that some ideas or impulses entered history for the first time in Christianity. Apart from the doubtful nature of the proof in specific instances, *newness* is not a category which is determinative for the divine. That category is eternity. Newness can be claimed equally for this or that imbecility. Newness is never a guarantee of the *value* of what claims to be new.

Neither by one road nor by the other can a way be found out of the *unending inter-relatedness* in which no single epoch and no single person can claim absolute significance. It is no more possible to see divine forces or the revelation of the divine in the inter-related complex of history and in historical forces than it is in the inter-relatedness of nature and natural forces. Truly, here, too, it is only man that is deified; for the human powers are alleged to be divine. Here again is to be seen merely the attempt to win direct knowledge of God. Here, too, is the concept of God as a given object.

---

[6] Cf. O. Pfleiderer, *Das Urchristentum*, 2nd ed., I, Berlin, 1902, p.vii; ET, *Primitive Christianity* I, London, 1906, pp.vii-viii.

[7] This idea finds naïve expression on page 398 of *Morgenandachten*, published in 1909 by the Friends of the Christian World. After a polemic against the idea of 'the splendid sins' (*splendida vitia*) of the heathen, we read, 'It cannot be denied that the spirit of the noblest nations of antiquity, which also is a spirit given by God, built the road for the ideas of the Christian world and helped the progress upward towards freedom.'

And here, too, appears the reaction—especially among the young. There is the realization that such inter-relatedness connotes fatalism, that the 'riches' which the personality wins are a curse, because the distinctively human characteristic, the creative in man, has been destroyed or imprisoned. They feel that history so understood 'puts man in question', leaves him at a loss and makes him a ghost. At every point—against both pantheism of nature and pantheism of history—the polemic of Barth and Gogarten is valid. For that polemic is aimed directly against the temptation to deify man; it is a protest against every kind of direct knowledge of God.

In so far as the Word of God is judgment upon the whole nature and condition of man, it is the 'stumbling block' for every kind of pantheism of history. But *only* in so far! It is not so easy to deal with the stumbling block as it seemed to be in the view of history commonly accepted by orthodox theology; that is, by asserting the occurrence of supernatural phenomena and powers within history. We are not required to make *that* sacrifice of reason *(sacrificium intellectus)*, which would involve the repudiation of all effort to gain a rational view of history. The meaning of history can be found only by relating visible history to an invisible origin—not by setting up a second, alien history alongside the other (Barth, *Der Römerbrief,* 3rd ed., München, 1923, p.90; ET, *The Epistle to the Romans,* London and New York, 1933, p.140). 'The judgment of God is the *end* of history, not the beginning of a new, a second, epoch' *(ibid.,* p.51; *ibid.,* p.77).

I am convinced that any one must be appalled if he really perceives the *specific consequences* which follow from the conception of history accepted by liberal theology. (The true nature of these consequences, of course, remains unrecognized by most of its adherents.) I will try to justify this verdict by illustration from the *problem of the Christ.* Ritschlian theology is persuaded of its ability to prove that history as known through scientific research has a positive value for faith. But it mistakenly places the origin of faith in God in man, in man's sense of value. Man has not only a yearning for God; he has also a vision of God as the supreme power and the moral will. And precisely this concept is accepted as 'value'. 'But value itself cannot prove reality to us. An external object is required, a bearer of this value, confronting our sense of value in such a way that out of the sense of value develops inevitably the conviction of the existence of a reality corresponding to that value.'[8] Such an object can only be a personality, which we encounter in Jesus. This statement can be interpreted to mean that the individual becomes conscious of the powers working in himself as real and meaningful powers because he sees them effective in history—or rather, since these are the powers of the spiritual life, in historical personalities. The reality to which I am referred in my search for the meaning of my existence is an historical reality.

How this idea works in the concrete is shown in Reischle's article entitled 'Do We Know the Depths of God?'[9] I shall quote an excerpt from it in full since it gives a characteristic exposition of the significance of the historical person, Jesus. The passage should make clear how wholly impossible that whole way of thinking has become for us today.

> In the first place, through Jesus Christ, the more unreservedly we submit ourselves to the influence of his person, the more our conscience is awakened. As the first disciples were made ashamed, sometimes by the word of Jesus, sometimes by his act, sometimes by his silent look, so also our hearts smite us if we open our hearts to Jesus' words, actions, and suffering. Furthermore, anyone who supposes that he has already attained to a religious and ethical character will, through the person Jesus, first come to understand what personality is and how incomplete and inwardly divided we really are in contrast to him. We know ourselves to be double-minded in our assurance of faith, vacillating also in our pursuit of our highest moral ideals, fettered by a grosser or a more refined sensuality, influenced even in noble deeds or heroic suffering by many secondary motives, never free from that self-dramatization (ὑπόκρισις) which enjoys playing a role for the applause of the gallery.
>
> In no other way can the confusion of our ethical concepts be more plainly revealed nor our moral self-deceit be more radically destroyed than by the inexorable clarity with which Jesus Christ displays before us in word and act the will of his heavenly Father. But if we let these harsh truths speak directly to us in the person

---

[8] R. Paulus, *Das Christusproblem der Gegenwart,* Tübingen, 1922, p.67.
[9] *ZThK* [*Zeitschrift für Theologie und Kirche*], I (1891) pp.287-366.

Jesus, provision has been made that no hatred of moral truth will arise out of the experience. For in him the supreme good meets us directly as true value. Only by this impression is self-judgment awakened in the conscience.

Opposition to that incorruptible moral judge is still less possible for us, since the person Jesus shows not the slightest trace of the pride in virtue which fears association with the pollution of sinners. The worst charge his enemies could bring against him was 'Behold, a glutton and a drunkard, a friend of tax collectors and sinners' (Matt. 11.19). The reproach of the Pharisees (Luke 15.2), 'He receives sinners', has become in all Christendom a ringing, jubilant witness to the second great influence which emanates from him—his love for sinners. That love breaks down for us all shrinking mistrust of him who is better than ourselves; it awakes in us courage for the joyful certainty that we exist for him and therefore for the kingdom of righteousness in which he himself lives and towards which all his work is directed. The conviction that we, in spite of everything, still belong to Christ and to the pure world in which he lives and moves is the conscience's comfort in face of the guilt by which we feel ourselves separated from the kingdom of the good—and this is the forgiveness of sin.

Anyone who clings to Jesus with all his heart in trust and conjoins his life to the person and the purpose of Jesus, already *has* forgiveness of sins. Jesus, in his dealing with the sinful woman who clung to him, the Saviour of sinners, bore witness to the forgiveness of her sins as a completed fact. From her actions it was manifest that her sins were forgiven. This is the mightiest influence which the person Jesus exerts on men's hearts. Sinners, in spite of their sins, feel themselves taken into fellowship with him and called to eternal life—that is, they find forgiveness.

Obviously, a figure of Jesus which modern criticism long ago made dubious is here accepted as historical. But quite apart from that difficulty, are there any of the experiences described which could not equally well result from intimate contact with other personalities of the past and present? The experience of the awakening and sharpening of conscience and the second experience of overcoming the shrinking distrust of someone who is better than I and the realization that even I myself am called to the kingdom of righteousness—these are experiences which have continually occurred in the past and will continue to recur in human society in the future. However, the most cogent objection to Reischle's statement is the fact that in every such experience, the final criterion of validity is man's own moral consciousness. Therefore it is wholly unjustifiable to equate that second experience with the forgiveness of sin, for that forgiveness could then be obtained by contemplating an historical person.

Actually, the forgiveness of sin can never be won through the contemplation of history. Only a *belief* in forgiveness, *acts* of love and forgiveness, *consciousness* of love and forgiveness can be demonstrated in knowable history. I cannot prove from history that more is present than phenomena of this world; I cannot prove that love and forgiveness are here revealed objectively as acts of God and as acts which affect me. The man who is seeking love and forgiveness for himself is not helped by evidence that someone else is confident of having received love and forgiveness. That confidence could be illusion. Jesus' love of sinners may destroy my shrinking distrust of one who is better than I. But my sins are not forgiven by that experience; in my sins I stand immediately before God. The evidence of the actuality of such phenomena in history can certainly disturb and upset us; but no immediate knowledge of God's love and forgiveness can be derived from them. Furthermore, with what right could we assume that consciousness of the forgiveness of sins is not equally reliable when it is based on asceticism or on sacrifice? In history I certainly cannot find love and forgiveness as a force directed towards me, as the Word of God.[10]

The same objection holds against similar formulations, for example, that found in Heitmüller's *Jesus* (Tübingen, 1913).[11] He affirms (p.158) that we have religious experiences even without Jesus. But those experiences 'acquire content and con-

---

[10] Cf. Barth, *Der Römerbrief,* 3rd ed. p.61 (cf. ET, *The Epistle to the Romans,* p.86): 'The fear of God as such is neither visible nor tangible nor in any immediate sense "real" in the world. It is not demonstrable historically or intellectually.'

[11] I am concerned—especially because of the voices raised in certain circles since Heitmüller's call to Tübingen—to emphasize once more that this whole discussion is directed against a theological trend and not against individual theologians. The statements I cite are characteristic of that position, not of Heitmüller individually. It would be very unfair to label his work as a whole 'liberal theology'.

vincing force and certainty, they become revelation, *only* and
first when they are conjoined with a powerful experience of the
divine *outside ourselves*, only through contact with the streams of
religious life which flow around us and encompass us'. Further
(pp.174f.), 'For the individual, the road to the Father does not
necessarily lead by way of Jesus Christ. But the more sure and
independent we wish to become in our faith, so much the less
can we refuse to go by that way ... No faith escapes periods of
uncertainty, of wavering, of trepidation—chiefly as consequence
of our own sins. In such times we find a basis and support for
our faith in the historical fact, Jesus of Nazareth, in whom we
encounter a faith full of power and strength, independent of our
desires, as a sure victorious reality.' A reality? What if Jesus' faith
were also illusion? Are not illusions which were characterized by
convictions of power and victory found elsewhere in history?
What is the criterion by which we can determine that we are
not allowing our illusions to be strengthened by the stream of
life which encompasses us?

The pantheism of history which marks such statements appears
especially clear in this excerpt (p.162): 'The consideration of this
figure, bringing him vividly before us, provides us with a means
of edification, exaltation and inspiration. All of the religious
forces, experiences, moods, impulses, and demands which are
active in Christianity are visible, embodied in the figure of Jesus.
His figure is the symbol and the bearer of all religious and ethical
goods and verities. It becomes ever richer, ever fuller of content.
For into this figure are woven all that later Christians have experienced...' But what if all that were illusion? Also, could the
statement not apply equally to the Roman Catholic cult of the
Virgin Mary?

Similarly, according to J. Weiss:[12] 'On the whole, for the
majority of Christians today, the figure of the "Lord" has only
this significance. It accompanies us on our way through life as a
reverently honoured travelling companion, warning us and
rousing our conscience, comforting us and encouraging us, a
living, personal, contemporary manifestation of the holy and

[12] *ZNW* [*Zeitschrift für die neutestamentliche Wissenschaft*], XIX (1919/20),
p.139.

gracious will of God.' In similar fashion, the credal confession 'Jesus lives' is understood solely in an earthly sense. 'The figure of Jesus and his kind of life with God and for God is felt as a moral power over our life—a power from which we cannot draw ourselves away.' Likewise the Christmas meditations which come from this circle have nothing higher to celebrate than the belief that Jesus was a 'personality'. 'I no longer see only the Christ-child. I see Christ; I gaze at him avidly, the man, the strong, noble man ... a person with a living pulse-beat, tempted like us but victorious. ... Before us we see his form, his personality.'[13] And in an Easter meditation we may read: 'Because the Lord gained the victory morally, even though outwardly he succumbed, therefore his cause cannot fail.'[14]

In all these varied formulations the 'stumbling block' (σκάν-δαλον) has been removed from Christianity. All of them totally lack the insight that God is other than the world, he is beyond the world, and that this means the complete abrogation of the whole man, of his whole history. Their common aim is to give faith the kind of basis which destroys the very essence of faith because what they seek is a basis here in this world.

II

Deeply rooted in modern Protestantism, including Protestant liberal theology, is the view based on Luther that our *secular daily work* in the place assigned to us in history is service to God. A man is not required to do some specific kind of work in order to serve God. Whatever work the labourer and artisan, the farmer and the merchant, the scholar and the official, perform in their own calling can be and ought to be performed as service to God. So far the view really is Luther's. But it becomes un-Lutheran when it is assumed that labour in every kind of occupation is in itself direct service to God; when it is forgotten that my activity in my own occupation can separate me from God and can become service to idols. My secular work, since it serves the purposes and forces which determine and promote

---

[13] *Morgenandachten* (see above, note 7), pp.404, 405, 406.
[14] *Ibid.*, p.119.

human cultural life, can be the service of God only indirectly—never directly. Only when I recognize that the work *in itself* does not serve God, only if I undertake it in *obedience* and maintain an inner detachment from it, only if I do it as if I did not, can it be the service of God.

Here, also, God's Word can act only as a 'stumbling block'. 'My kingdom is not of this world' holds true here, too. However conscientiously we do the work of our calling, that work as such can never make it possible for us to know ourselves as co-workers in the service of God. God is wholly 'Beyond'. He calls in question both ourselves and our faithfulness in our calling. The idea that our regular work is a service of God can, if it is carried consistently to its conclusion, confront us again with the precariousness of our whole self. We are forced to admit honestly that if we *are seeking* God we do not find him in our daily occupation, that we cannot of ourselves prove a right to call our work the service of God.

Here again youth's criticism is indicative of the true situation. The young are searching for some cult in which the meaning of the service of God finds its expression, distinct from all service to the objectively given, distinct from all career-work motivated by the goals of this world. Here again Barth's answer to Harnack's question 13 is valid. 'What kind of theological tradition is it which, having started from the deification of "feeling", now seems to have made a successful landing in the slough of the psychology of the unconscious? ... What kind of theology is it, if it notoriously stands in constant danger of losing its most gifted adherents to Dr Steiner ?'[15]

Such a theology is clearly a theology which has not yet become aware that no activity *within the world* can be service to God, that worldly activity means that man has surrendered to the arbitrary rule of the forces of practical life in this world. The one essential is to understand the question, to listen to the 'stumbling block' of God's Word, the Word which declares that the world exists in sin and that man in the world can do nothing which can sustain the character of service to God.

---

[15] *CW* [*Die christliche Welt*] 37 (1923), p.91.

But the identification of daily labour with the service of God is perhaps not an especially significant facet of liberal theology. Its attitude towards practical life may be more revealing in another aspect. Liberal theology betrays its true character in so far as it commits itself to the view that specific ideals for the activity of life in the world are to be derived from faith. That is to say, that Christian concepts of the kingdom of God, of love, *et al.*, can determine man's life within the world, that they can provide the norm, setting the goal and showing the road to it. The consequences of this view are clear in such slogans as 'the work of God's kingdom', 'the vineyard of God on earth',[16] 'Christian Socialism', 'Christianity and Pacifism'.

If anyone supposes that social work—i.e. work concerned with the creation of proper social conditions which are suitable for human beings, whether the work is officially 'welfare work' or not—is as such the work of God's kingdom, that it is 'Christian action', then he is unaware of the 'stumbling block' of the Word of God. The 'stumbling block' is very much bigger, very much more obvious when that Word speaks the stern judgment, 'That is not a Christian act', against actions which in themselves are a duty, worthy of honour, and terribly necessary.

No act exists which can relate itself directly to God and his kingdom. All forms of community life, the worst and the most ideal alike, stand equally under the judgment of God. We except ourselves from that judgment, we refuse to take it seriously, when we suppose that in social work or in total abstinence from alcohol or the like (just because the duty to perform such acts is recognized) it is possible to produce in this world some sort of situation which is more pleasing to God. Therefore, for example, the *general* question of whether a *Christian* must be a pacifist is to be rejected. *Each man* must answer the question for himself in his specific historical situation. If pacifism is an ideal of human society, then even if its realization lies in the infinite future, in which lie the realizations of all ideals, pacifism would be a *human* possibility. But God's Word demands the impossible from man, impossible in every sense. It demands that man live a sinless life. And we fail to recognize the 'stumbling block' when we ignore

---

[16] A. von Harnack, *Das Wesen des Christentums,* Leipzig, 1900, p.78; ET, *What is Christianity?*, New York and London, 1901, p.132.

the sinfulness of our whole life and activity, when we think we can fulfil God's demands in the historical course of human life.

Harnack fails to recognize this 'stumbling block' when he asks (in question 5); 'If God and the world (life in God and life in the world) are in absolute contradiction, how are we to understand the close conjunction, in fact the equation on one level of *the love of God and love of one's neighbour*, which forms the core of the Gospel? And how is this equation possible without giving *supreme* value to ethics?'[17] Barth answers: 'Precisely the Gospel's combination of love of God and love of neighbour is the strongest proof that the relation between our "life in the world" and our "life in God" is a relation of "absolute contradiction" which can be overcome only by a miracle of the eternal God himself. For what fact in the world is more alien, more incomprehensible than just a "neighbour"? Is there any fact on which we are more in need of God's revelation? The "supreme value of ethics"—yes! But in accepting that value, do we *love* our neighbour? Can we love him? And if we do *not love him*, what about our love of God? Could anything show more clearly than this "core"—not of the Gospel but of the Law—that God does not make alive until he has first put to death?'[18]

The problem of Christianity and Government finds a characteristic answer in Harnack's *Wesen des Christentums* (*What is Christianity?*).[19] When Jesus says: 'Give to Caesar what is Caesar's and to God what is God's'; when he says: 'You know that those who are supposed to rule over the Gentiles lord it over them and their great men exercise authority over them. But it shall not be so among you ...' one ought not to think at once of our contemporary governments. 'Law and legal requirements which depend only [!] on force, on actual force and its use, have no moral worth.' 'It is a mockery of the Gospel to say that it defends and sanctifies every authority which presents itself as law and government at a given moment.' Of course! But it is an absurdity to suppose that there can ever be any law and government which is apart from a given historical moment, that is apart from force, apart from sin. There can be *no legal authority* which

---

[17] *CW* [*Die christliche Welt*], 37 (1923), p.7.
[18] *Ibid.*, pp.89ff.
[19] Pp.67f.; ET, pp.113-116.

as such is sanctioned by the Gospel. All authority stands always under the judgment of God.

The Sermon on the Mount demands the impossible; therefore to make it the norm of activity within the world is not only entirely futile but also involves the refusal to recognize its character as a 'stumbling block'. This character is ignored when Harnack asks: 'And is the demand which they [the words of Jesus] impose really so out-of-this-world, so impossible?' And he ignores it equally when he speaks of 'the ideal which should hover before our historical development as goal and guiding star'. And what is our reaction today when we read: 'In contrast to two or three hundred years ago, we today already feel a moral obligation to move in this direction. The more sensitive and therefore more prophetic among us no longer view the kingdom of love and peace as a mere Utopia'?[20]

All attempts to derive ideals of possible human conduct from the Christian faith deny the 'stumbling block'. *In Christian faith* man is without sin and the fellowship of Christian believers is a fellowship without sin. Both, therefore, are impossibilities on earth. On earth there is no direct service of God. 'We cannot be blind to the warning which is raised against the whole, to the final all-encompassing provision which applies not only to forbidden actions, but with especial force to all permitted, even to all commanded actions.'[21]

There is service of God only when man surrenders himself to God's judgment and then obediently under God takes up the work in the world to which God has set him, when he never averts his eyes from the sin of the world—especially not from his own sins—and never dreams that any sort of approximation to God's world can be realized in this world. 'A system of ethics for this world, based on the Gospel, would have this singular character: its action would be without any immediate relation to God and the Eternal.'[22] Certainly the behaviour of the man of

---

[20] *Ibid.*, pp.70, 72; ET, pp.120, 122f. Cf. also *Morgenandachten* (see above, note 7), p.395: 'Now you are not obligated to do the impossible—only the possible.'

[21] Barth, *Der Römerbrief,* 3rd ed., p.276 (cf. ET, *The Epistle to the Romans*, p.293.

[22] Gogarten, *ZZ* [*Zwischen den Zeiten*] 2, (1923), p.21.

faith (if the existence of men of faith may be assumed) will appear different from that of the unbeliever. But in what respects it will differ cannot be deduced from his faith. He will learn the difference through his obedience when he takes upon himself service in this world with the responsibilities and the duties which are realities in this world and for this world.

The Word of God is a 'stumbling block' for this world and primarily a 'stumbling block' for an earnest mind, for the moral consciousness. Here again Barth and Gogarten state the conclusions which are actually inherent in liberal theology. For who has emphasized more forcibly than W. Herrmann that there is no specifically Christian ethic? And who has shown more convincingly than Troeltsch[23] the problematic character of the relation of the Christian to the world?

III

What conception of *God and man* forms the basis for this criticism of liberal theology? *God is not a given entity.* The question with which Reischle was concerned, the question of the adequacy of our knowledge of God, must be rejected completely. For that question conceives of God as a given entity of which direct knowledge is possible, as an object which we can recognize in more or less the same way as other objects. Such knowledge could be a possession and could produce effects within our life. It could progress and grow like other segments of knowledge. But it could still not take us to God, who can never be something given, something which is, so to speak, crystallized in knowledge. God, on the contrary, is known only when he reveals himself. His revelation comes only contingently; it is *act*, act directed towards *men*. God's revelation does not make him something known in the sense of intellectual knowledge.

God is not a given entity. This truth is equally valid against a religion of experience, which supposes it possible to achieve contact with the divine object by substituting spiritual states for intellectual knowledge. God becomes equally a directly accessi-

[23] *Die Soziallehren der christlichen Kirchen und Gruppen,* Tübingen, 1912; ET, *The Social Teaching of the Christian Churches,* London and New York, 1931.

ble object, whether he is conceived as creative life forces, or as the irrational, or as anything else of the sort.

Nor, however, is God 'self-actualizing' or 'unactualized' in the sense of idealistic philosophy, so that God may actualize himself to man's intellect by the process of revelation or may be actualized in the Logos, which lies at the roots of rational human life. That would involve the deification of man. *God represents the total annulment of man, his negation, calling him in question, indeed judging him.* Whether God is known adequately or inadequately, whether or not God is to be spoken of in anthropomorphic terms is irrelevant.[24] The one essential question is: What does God represent for men? And wherever the idea of God is really grasped, the result is the radical calling of man in question.

Now this result—this 'minus sign before the bracket'—does not mean *scepticism*. No doubt of man's intellectual capacity is involved, no degradation of his reason, no passive resignation. On the contrary, it becomes impossible to speak of God so cheaply as to call him 'the irrational'. Indeed it is impossible to think highly enough of reason. Precisely when reason has followed its road to the end, the point of crisis is reached and man is brought to the great question mark over his own existence.

'Calling in question' is *not pessimism*; it is not despair of the world under the impact of its evil or its suffering. All pessimism makes man its criterion—man's moral judgment or his claim to happiness. And for exactly that reason, such pessimism is sin before God, because it implies both man's claim to happiness and his claim to his own righteousness.

Man as such, the whole man, is called in question by God. Man stands under that question mark, whether he knows it or not. His moral transgressions are not his fundamental sin. 'It is not a matter of a few steps more or less on this road.'[25] *Man's fundamental sin is his will to justify himself as man*, for thereby he makes himself God. When man becomes aware of this, the whole world is taken off its hinges; for man then puts himself under the judgment of God. The whole world—which was

[24] Cf. Luther, *Genesisvorlesungen* 1535-45 on Gen. 1.2, Weimar ed., vol. 42, p.12; for English edition see J. Pelikan, ed., *Luther's Works*, vol. I: *Lectures on Genesis*, St Louis, 1958.

[25] Eduard Thurneysen, *Dostojewski*, München, 1921, p.53.

man's world—is annihilated; nothing in it any longer has meaning and value, for everything had received this from man. But to know this judgment is also to know it as grace, since it is really liberation. Man becomes free from himself. And for man to become free from himself is redemption. Man then knows that the question is also the answer; for it is only God who can *so* question him. And he knows that the answer is primary. A question so radical cannot originate from man, from the world. But if the question is asked by God, then it originates from the claim of *God* on man. Man is called.

The knowledge of this truth is called faith. *Faith* cannot generate itself in man; it can only arise as man's answer to the Word of God in which God's judgment and God's grace are preached to him. Indeed, faith can be in man only as God's creation. So far as faith is real in man, it manifests itself in him as obedience to God's Word. The man who has faith is therefore the man whom God has transformed, the man whom God has put to death and made alive again; he is never the natural man. Faith is never self-evident, natural; it is always miraculous. The belief that God is the Father and man is the child of God is not an insight which can be gained directly—it is not an insight at all. On the contrary, it must be believed, ever and again, as the miraculous act of God. But it must be *believed*, truly, in faith.

Evidence of the extent to which liberal theology has bypassed this 'stumbling block' is all too plentiful. For example, we are told that man's sonship to God 'appears in Paul as a definite, specific act of adoption of men who before were not sons of God. But *our* sonship *we* feel in Jesus' sense, like the sunshine which always surrounds us, which we thank for life and happiness, which is always there so that our task is only to make use of it.'[26]

The Word of the cross is often distorted. In orthodox theology it was reduced to the sacrifice of reason (*sacrificium intellectus*). In liberal theology it appears as the demand for sacrifice in a moral sense, as the demand for a self-denial which will serve the growth of personality. In the meditation for the Wednesday before Easter there is a section describing the school of suffering in

[26] J. Weiss, *ZNW* [*Zeitschrift für die neutestamentliche Wissenschaft*], XIX (1919/1920), p.131.

which the disciples of Jesus were trained. 'First under the impact of the suffering and death of Jesus and then through their own experience as disciples, the process of separation between the human and the divine continued spontaneously (!). They learned to understand the law of sacrifice, without which the kingdom of God cannot come, and the law of self-denial, without which personality cannot be fully shaped—all in the light of the cross of Christ.'[27]

The meditation for Good Friday reads: 'But how can I believe in the love of God if I do not feel it in my heart? How can I accept as blessing that which is clothed in the trappings of ill (namely, suffering)? There is only one way. You must make something good out of it for yourself. You must lift the stones, lay hold of them and fit them into your building. You may bruise your fingers on them; yet if you consider how the hidden man within your heart grows thereby and becomes strong, then in the apparent evil you will discover the eternal love, the hidden blessing.' Christ is the prototype for this experience. 'He knows the truth: I hold my life in my hands and make out of it what I will, not what they will. Thus he bore patiently the external conditions of his life; but he made something out of it. He moulded his life into something, into the great blessing by which we live and with, which we nourish ourselves unto this hour.'[28]

The Easter message reads: 'My work, my struggle, my life is not in vain. The whole has a future. ... Beyond humanity, yes far beyond and above humanity, grow the men of God. He who sanctifies and purifies himself for a higher life, begins to grow here among men, begins to grow into that "other world", the world of eternity. The meaning of the Easter message is this: there has been One who purified and sanctified his life for a higher life; and when he had fully matured into the complete, divine man, then he discarded this human existence and entered the fullness of the world of spirit, the eternal world of God. Jesus Christ is the first who grew into this world of eternity. He was the first, but he will not be the only one.'[29]

---

[27] *Morgenandachten* (see above, note 7), p.115.
[28] *Ibid.*, pp.117f.
[29] *Ibid.*, p.120.

In a meditation for New Year's Eve we find: 'Man is a creation of intelligence; and as he is the latest and newest such creation, his duty is to follow along the trail of that creativity. He must inquire into and ponder over the wonderful designs which are under his feet and visible to his eyes, from the tiny worm in the ground to the idea which like a star at midnight is fixed in the infinite. ... Keep in mind, you creation of Intelligence, how you have followed the trail of creation and by your observation and wonderment have glimpsed a whole behind the multiplicity as behind a veil. ... Yes, there is plan and meaning and order and intelligence in all and over all; it is called light.'[30]

It is hard to know whether to be more astonished at the absence of any trace of the message of the New Testament or at the ignorance which does not dream that all the ideas here expressed are a part of the homiletics of the Cynics and Stoics. Anyone acquainted with Epictetus, for example, will at once notice the similarity, which extends to partial verbal identity. The evaluation of Jesus accords with this view of the world and man. He is accepted as the pattern, as was Heracles or Diogenes among the Cynics and Stoics, as one who bore the burden of his labours and 'made something' out of his life. Of course, the passages I have quoted are extreme examples, but they are not exceptional. In their crassness they are symptomatic and they give proof that something significant has been forgotten in liberal theology.

It is not surprising that such disregard of what is essentially Christian has not remained unopposed within liberal theology. It is not only research into the history of religion with its attention focused on what is characteristic in historical phenomena which has registered opposition to the unrestrained rationalization and moralization of Christian ideas. Rudolf Otto's book, *The Idea of the Holy*, in particular, resulted from the theological situation very much as did the protest of Barth, Gogarten and their circle. Otto's designation of God as the 'Wholly Other' and his emphasis on 'creature feeling' as the essential element of religious piety are characteristic of that protest. Just as the purpose under-

---

[30] *Ibid.*, p.410.

lying his concept of 'the Holy' was to define the nature of the divine as beyond the sphere of the rational and ethical, so equally his emphasis on the inner relatedness of the moments of dread (*tremendum*) and fascination (*fascinans*) in the numinous has an analogy, which is more basic than the obvious parallelism, to the assertion of the inner conjunction of the knowledge of judgment and of grace. But certainly the theological solution which Otto proposed for this paradoxical situation leads in the opposite direction.

Barth's divergence is shown most plainly in his consistent emphasis on the truth *that faith is not a state of consciousness*. No doubt, along with faith there is also a state of consciousness—at least there can be. But as long as it is a state of consciousness it cannot be faith. To speak of the faith of men is to accept the full paradox of asserting something which cannot be affirmed of any visible man, something which is completely unverifiable as a spiritual situation and which must never be identified with any such situation. From this concept of faith arises the polemic against all 'religion of experience', against piety, sense of sin, and inspiration. Hence comes the utter scepticism of religion as such, since religion claims to be a particular area of human spiritual life in which inheres the relation of man to God. On the contrary, the real truth is that what is confessed in faith is the calling in question of the *whole* man by God. The justified man, the new man, is believed in faith.

Whatever belongs to religion is something present with man and in man. It can be, indeed it must be, doubted time and again. I can never so relate myself to my experience that I can put my trust in it. I can trust only the promises of God. Even if the revelation of God is understood as the revelation of judgment and grace, the meaning is not that the two are successive experiences. The despair is not conceived as a sort of overwhelming preliminary stage which must be surmounted so that it may be followed by the consciousness of redemption. The despair, radically conceived, is the realization that the natural man is trying to flee from before God and that he cannot flee because he was trying to flee before *God*. That despair, therefore, comes only when there is awareness of God. But when there is awareness of God as God, flight has ended and a turning to God has begun. There are not two acts. *Faith is not an act which can be performed once for all*, an act by which justification is achieved. Nor is it an act which is repeatable, so that judgment and grace, sin and forgiveness alternate in human life. Only the man who knows *himself* to be a sinner can know what grace is. He knows himself as a sinner only in so far as he stands before *God*; therefore he can only know of sin when he also knows of grace. The sight of God's judgment and God's grace *together* belongs to the nature of faith. There is no grace except grace for sinners, no grace except grace in judgment. And as man can only speak of sin with real meaning if he sees himself before God, so also he can speak of grace only as grace for sinners. There is no possible standing ground on some achieved insight; there is no position which can be permanently won. For man *always* remains a sinner and he is always under condemnation and justified. Here it is truly necessary to speak of 'walking on a knife edge'. Even that metaphor is a very inadequate expression of the paradoxical character of faith. The grace of God is never a general truth; it is always real only in the act of God directed to a specific man. The judgment of God is never universal. Anyone who thinks it can be so conceived does not yet stand under that judgment.

Justification is not a qualitative change in men of this world; it is never present except in the 'Beyond', in God's judgment. The 'new man' is always the man of the 'Beyond', whose identity with the man of this world can only be believed in faith. So Barth can repeat Luther's paradoxical dictum: 'We only believe that we believe.'

Faith so comprehended is distinct from every kind of *mysticism*. Mysticism, too, wills to seek God beyond the given, not only beyond the natural world but also beyond intellectual and spiritual life. Mysticism follows its path methodically, calling upon us to silence everything in us, even all intellectual and spiritual activity. In pure passivity, in the emptying of the self, the mystic is prepared for the revelation of God. God enters the soul so prepared and fills it with joy unutterable.

The first objection to such mysticism is the necessity of rejecting the possibility of any method of reaching God. Even silence as a method is human activity. In this falsity (ψεῦδος) is revealed the primary falsity (πρῶτον ψεῦδος), the delusion that an escape from the given is possible—as if man could escape from himself, as if he were not obliged to put up with himself just as he is.[31] We cannot suppose that the annulment of men and world is an act within the power of man to perform by abstraction, by averting his eyes or closing them—while all the time it is I myself who am practising the annulment.

No! The annulment can come from God alone and it is always dialectical—that is, this world is always sublimated by a 'Beyond' and never replaced by it. In the latter case, the Beyond would always itself become this world, just as it does become a very real this world in that 'joy unutterable'. Since the Beyond can never become this world, just as my justification can always be only justification in the Beyond in which I have faith, clearly this justification is not any kind of supernatural quality in me. Yet *I* am the justified person. This means that man does not need to escape from himself, as the mystic assumes. Only the *sinner is* justified. Hence the justified person is an individual man who accepts the whole burden of his past, present and future. With that burden he stands under God's judgment. To desire to escape that burden means to desire to flee from God's judgment and to know nothing of grace.

In view of the whole situation presented here, we can understand why Barth refuses to assume a definite theological position.[32] Naturally when he is engaged in a theological argument, he cannot avoid adopting a position. Yet there are good grounds for his refusal. One reason is that the refusal is an expression of the truth that faith, the exposition of which is theology, is not an actual position which a man, even if he is a theologian, *can* take. In practice faith always happens as an act of God; and seen from the human point of view it is the abandonment of every position. Faith is the supremely paradoxical cry: 'I believe, Lord help my unbelief.' But then it follows that because theology can

---

[31] Cf. W. Herrmann, *Realencyc.*, I.[3], p.498, lines 29ff. 'Where we ourselves are, there is the world. The man who seeks to reach God beyond this world is therefore attempting the impossible. When he thinks he has found God, he has got hold of nothing more than a fragment of the world or a world conceived as abstractly as possible, divested of its perceptual concreteness.'

[32] *ZZ* [*Zwischen den Zeiten*], I (1923), pp.3f.

be nothing other than the exposition of faith, no concepts of knowledge which have meaning can be gained from it apart from the miraculous actualization of faith. The subject of theology is God. Theology speaks of God because it speaks of man as he stands before God. That is, theology speaks out of faith.

Karl Barth (1886-1968)

No discussion of the early twentieth-century protest against the historical Jesus quest would be complete without some reference (however brief) to the work of Karl Barth. Barth was born in Basel in Switzerland, the son of a pastor in the Swiss Reformed Church, himself a capable theologian. In 1904 he began his theological education at the University of Bern, where his intellectual interests were awakened by the reading of Immanuel Kant. In 1906 Barth went to the University of Berlin, where he prepared a paper on the Acts of the Apostles for a seminar presided over by the great Adolf von Harnack (1851-1930) and first read the work of Friedrich Schleiermacher (1768-1834). It was here, too, that Barth fell under the influence of the Marburg theologian Wilhelm Herrmann (1846-1922), whose influence on Bultmann we have already noted. In 1907 the young Barth returned to Bern, where he took an enthusiastic role in the social life of the student society, before spending a short time at Tübingen. It was during this year that Barth also had his first experience of preaching and catechetical instruction, as an assistant pastor in a nearby parish. In 1908 he travelled to Marburg, to study under Herrmann and in 1909 he took up a post as assistant pastor in Geneva. In 1911 Barth became pastor of the Reformed Church in the village of Safenwil in canton Aargau, a post which he was to hold for the next ten years. It was during his time that Barth's defence of the rights of workers earned him the title of the 'red pastor'. Shocked by the readiness of so many of his former teachers to support the German war policy in 1914, Barth made a sharp break with the liberal theology in which he had been brought up. The year 1919 saw the publication of the first edition of his commentary on Romans, with its insistence on 'the infinite qualitative distinction between time and eternity' and the corresponding insistence that God's 'yes' is pronounced only after a decisive 'no' to all human claims to be able to know God or do his work. In 1921 Barth received and accepted a call to become Professor of Reformed Theology at the University of Göttingen, where he found himself beginning to draft the outlines of a systematic theology (or 'dogmatics'), before taking up a post in 1925 at the University of Münster in Westphalia. In 1930 Barth took up the chair of systematic theology at the University of Bonn, a position which had hitherto been occupied by the son of Albrecht Ritschl. At the end of 1934 his refusal to pledge an unconditional allegiance to the Nazi state led to his dismissal from the University, and Barth left Germany the following year to take up his final academic post at the University of Basel.

While Barth's status as a theologian is scarcely open to question, it may seem odd to include his work in the present anthology, for he devotes little attention to the question of the historical Jesus. However Barth's apparent indifference to this question is itself significant, for it says much about his attitude to the Bible and to revelation. For this reason the following short extract has been taken from volume one of Barth's monumental *Church Dogmatics*, published in 1939 and dedicated to 'The Doctrine of the Word of God'. Barth begins by describing the Bible as 'a witness to divine revelation'. This formula has a twofold purpose. On the one hand it avoids any simple identification of the Bible with revelation and, on the other, it runs counter to any suggestion that we can have revelation without the Bible. He argues that because of this second factor, namely, the inseparability of Bible and revelation, the Bible can be rightly described as 'the Word of God'.

This brings us to the core of Barth's argument. As the Word of God, the Bible not only conveys divine revelation, but it also tells us how that revelation occurs. It does so by speaking of the function of divinely-appointed prophets and apostles. Since the Bible may be regarded as the written expression of the prophetic and apostolic witness, in testifying to the role of the apostles and prophets the Bible also testifies to its own role. The prophetic and apostolic witness, embodied in the Scriptures, is the form in which the divine revelation reaches us, and—insofar as the prophets and apostles are God's chosen instruments—that form and that content cannot be separated. Alongside this theological argument, Barth calls to mind a more general interpretative principle, that of reading a text in the light of the purpose for which it was written. The interpreter's task is to pay attention above all to the subject-matter of the text. Since the biblical text speaks to us of God and of God's revelation, it is this greatest of all possible subject matters which ought to be the focus of exegesis. Historical critics are only avoiding the difficult task of grappling with these issues when they focus on the merely 'curious' question of the circumstances in which the biblical text was produced.

What significance, then, has history, and (by implication) the question of the historical Jesus? While Bultmann's essay (above) reflects many of Barth's concerns, the following reading focuses on the idea of revelation. Barth argues that historical criticism was theologically misguided when it sought to reach 'behind' the text, in the belief that the facts it discovered would be of religious significance. For insofar as the Bible is a witness to divine revelation, that revelation is to be found, not in the facts as reconstructed by the historian, but in the facts as presented by the biblical writers. The historical criticism of the Bible has a valuable role to play in helping us to understand the biblical proclamation of the action of God, but it loses all theological significance when it attempts to reach behind that witness in an attempt to discern the hand of God at work in human history.

In line with Barth's usual practice in the *Church Dogmatics*, the detailed discussion of the topic is set off from the main text by being printed in smaller type.

Church Dogmatics I/2

Reprinted from *Church Dogmatics, vol. 1:2: The Doctrine of the Word of God* Karl Barth, copyright ©1956 T. & T. Clark. Used by permission of T. & T. Clark.

Section 19. The Word of God for the Church

4. As the witness of divine revelation the Bible also attests the institution and function of prophets and apostles. And in so doing it attests itself as Holy Scripture, as the indispensable form of that content. But because this is the case, in this question of divine revelation the Church, and in and with it theology, has to hold fast to this unity of content and form. The distinction of form and content must not involve any separation. Even on the basis of the biblical witness we cannot have revelation except through this witness. We cannot have revelation 'in itself'. The purpose of the biblical witness is not to help us achieve this, so that its usefulness is outlived when it is achieved. Revelation is, of course, the theme of the biblical witness. And we have already seen that the perception of it is absolutely decisive for the reading and understanding and expounding of this biblical witness. But it always is the theme of this, the biblical witness. We have no witness to it but this. There are, therefore, no points of comparison to make it possible for us even in part to free ourselves from this witness, to put ourselves into direct relationship to the theme of it. And it is in keeping with the nature of this theme that (in the form of the calling and enlightening and empowering of these specific men) it has been indissolubly linked with its witness, i.e., their witness. In this question of revelation we cannot, therefore, free ourselves from the texts in which its expectation and recollection is attested to us. We are tied to these texts. And we can only ask about revelation when we surrender to the expectation and recollection attested in these texts.

'It holdeth God's word', is what Luther once said about the Bible (*Pred. üb. Rom.* 15:4f, 1522, *W.A.* 10:1,2. 75, 6). It only 'holds', encloses, limits and surrounds it: that is the indirectness of the identity of revelation and the Bible. But it and it alone does really 'hold' it: it comprehends and encloses it in itself, so that we cannot have the one without the other; that is why we have to speak about an indirect *identity*. The idea against which we have to safeguard ourselves at this point is one which has tacitly developed in connexion with modern theological historicism. It is to the effect that in the reading and understanding and expounding of the Bible the main concern can and must be to penetrate past the biblical texts to the facts which lie behind the texts. Revelation is then found in these facts as such (which in their factuality are independent of the texts). Thus a history of Israel and of Old Testament religion is found behind the canonical Old Testament, a history of the life of Jesus, and later of course a Christ-myth, behind the canonical Gospels a history of the apostolic age, i.e., of primitive Christianity behind the canonical Acts and epistles. The intention is to subject the biblical Canon to the question of truth as formulated in the sense of modern historicism. The Bible is to be read as a collection of sources. In the first instance this was all done in all good faith even from the ecclesiastical and theological standpoint. There was such confidence in the rightness and utility of the question of truth formulated in the sense of modern historicism that it could be thought the highest honour for the Bible and the greatest benefit for oneself, i.e., for Christendom, to proceed from a study of the texts to the formation, with the help of observations gained from them, of a conception or conceptions of what is true and proper in them, of a form of the spirit apart from the letter. Now we must not overlook the human significance not only of the genuine scientific concern but also of the religious earnestness which went to the making of these pictures, or of the enthusiasm with which it was thought they should be presented to the Church: 'These be thy gods, O Israel'. But at the same time we cannot ignore the fact that in substance it was a mistake from the very first. From the very first: not therefore from the moment when the Canon was approached critically as a collection of sources; not from the moment when it was read with caution, with actual doubt whether things did take place exactly as we read, with an assessment of the varying so-called 'values' of the different sources, with the disqualification of this or that constituent part, with conjectures on the true connexions of what actually took place instead of those given or omitted in the texts, with a more or less comprehensive correction of the biblical in favour of an 'historical' truth, and finally with a partial or total reconstruction of reality as it is thought to be better seen over the heads and shoulders of the biblical authors. It was a long way from Zacharias to Gunkel and Reimarus to Wrede. But once the way was entered we need not be surprised if the eventual results were so radical that they caused pain in the Church. And they could not be prescribed or suppressed. But it is not because of the results, which were, of course, opposed by other more harmless, i.e., conservative ones, that this road must be called the wrong one. It is so, because at bottom it means succumbing to the temptation to read the Canon differently from what it is intended to be and can be read—which is the same thing. The universal rule of interpretation is that a text can be read and understood and expounded only with reference to and in the light of its theme. But if this is the case, then in the light of the theme—not *a priori*, but from the text itself—the relationship between theme and text must be accepted as essential and indissoluble. The form cannot therefore be separated from the content, and there can be no question of a consideration of the content apart from the form. We cannot therefore put the question of truth in the direct way that it was arbitrarily thought it should be put. It is not that, when we have consulted Genesis and the Synoptics as unfortunately our only sources, the real question concerning the early history of Israel or the life of Jesus is a question of history, i.e., the history of the world of culture, of religion, somewhere behind Genesis and the Synoptics. Except in historical terms—in terms of the history of literature—these writings cannot be read merely as sources. If we have a particular interest in antiquities, we can read them in this way at our own risk, at the risk of failing to serve even our own interest and missing the real nature and character of the writings. Why should there not be occasional items of this kind in the Bible? But by obstinately putting this question of truth, by acting as though the interest in antiquities is the only legitimate interest, the true nature and character of the writings has been missed for over a hundred years. And that this should be so—even if there were more agreement than there actually is on the validity of this hermeneutic principle—we can only describe as a scandal even from the celebrated standpoint of 'pure scholarship'. At any rate it was a scandal in the Church; not, of course, that D.F. Strauss and Wellhausen came to all sorts of extreme results, but that theology allowed itself to be decoyed into this trap (without even being able to advance in excuse the pretext of being nominally a non-theological discipline). Theology at least, even and especially historical theology, which applies itself particularly to the biblical texts, ought to have (let us say it at once) the tact and taste, in face of the linking of form and content in those texts of which it must still be aware, to resist this temptation, to leave the curious question of what is perhaps behind the texts, and to turn with all the more attentiveness, accuracy and love to the texts as such. In its arbitrary attempt to sketch and create those pictures, it largely failed to do the work really laid upon it. It is only today that we can see how little we have really gained from that intensive and extensive ploughing of the field of New Testament literature to help us to explain even the simplest individual concepts not to speak of commenting on the texts both as they stand and in relation one to another. It is no accident that, when about 1920 Protestant theology made a kind of rediscovery of the objectivity of the New Testament and of the biblical witness generally, at almost the same time—with the emergence of the so-called '*formgeschichtlich*' ['form-critical'] method introduced by M. Dibelius, R. Bultmann and K. L. Schmidt (F. Overbeck was, of course, a forerunner)—in the case of the New Testament at least it came to a consciousness of the form of the witness corresponding to that objectivity. And it is also no accident that in our days it is to the preparation of a biblico-theological dictionary that the most powerful forces of biblical research are applied, although unfortunately we cannot say that the advance which we must now make is equally clear to all those who are co-operating in this enterprise. The real decision whether in this field we are going to make a move for the better will depend on two things. The first is whether there will be the rekindling of a similar interest in Old Testament scholarship. But the second is whether in both fields the time has not passed when we can select arbitrary themes, whether the exegesis of canonical Scripture as such, the coherent exposition of Genesis, Isaiah, the Gospel of Matthew, etc., according to their present status and compass is again recognised and undertaken as in the last resort the only possible goal of biblical scholarship. As material for the carrying out of this true and long neglected task, we must not and cannot ignore the insights won under the perverted sign of the earlier source-investigation of the Bible. There cannot, therefore, be any question of sealing off or abandoning so-called 'criticism', as it has been so significant for this investigation. All relevant, historical questions must be put to the biblical texts, considered as witnesses in accordance with their literary form. And the differences in exposition which result when we answer them can only be to the good, so long as criticism is clearly made to serve this task, so long as it no longer has to serve the foolish end of mediating an historical truth lying behind the texts. The historical truth which in its own way biblical scholarship does have to mediate is the true meaning and context of the biblical texts as such. Therefore it is not different from the biblical truth which has to be mediated. When that is seen and understood, when the foolish pursuit of an historical truth *supra scripturam* ['above the Scripture'] is on all sides abandoned in favour of a circumscribed investigation of the *veritas scripturae ipsius* ['truth of Scripture itself'], then we can and must give the freest possible course to critical questions and answers as demanded by the character of the biblical witness as a human document, and therefore an historical quantity. For in these circumstances the questions and answers can and will indicate only that Scripture is taken seriously as it actually is before us. And the questions and answers can and will help to safeguard our reading and understanding and expounding of Scripture from the arbitrary desire, by which it was continually threatened in the earlier days of the Church, which knew nothing of these questions and answers, to express its concrete form plastically, and in that way to direct and hold in definite lines the question of its objective content, the question of God's revelation. As I see it, this does not mean an annulling of the results of biblical scholarship in the last centuries, nor does it mean a breaking off and neglect of efforts in this direction. What it does mean is a radical re-orientation concerning the goal to be pursued, on the basis of the recognition that the biblical texts must be investigated for their own sake to the extent that the revelation which they attest does not stand or occur, and is not to be sought, behind or above them but in them. If in reply it is asked whether Christianity is really a book-religion, the answer is that strangely enough Christianity has always been and only been a living religion when it is not ashamed to be actually and seriously a book-religion. Expounding the saying in 2 Cor. 5:7 ('We walk by faith, not by sight') and linking it up with 1 Cor. 13:12, Calvin coined the statement, *videmus enim, sed in speculo et aenigmate; hoc est loco rei in verbo acquiescimus* ['for we see only in a mirror and in darkness; that is to say, we are satisfied with the word rather than the reality'] (*C.R.* 50, 63). Biblical theology can be as critical as it will and must—but if it carries out the programme outlined in this statement, it will always do good work as ecclesiastical scholarship: better than that done in recent centuries in spite of all the seriousness and industry applied to it. And it will have an honourable place as scholarship in the general sense.

8

Re-opening the Quest

Ernst Käsemann (1906-98)

If Bultmann consigned the historical Jesus to a position of theological insignificance, it was one of his own disciples, Ernst Käsemann, who was responsible for re-opening the question. The turning-point was a lecture delivered by Käsemann in 1953 to a conference of former theological students from Bultmann's university of Marburg. It is a translation of that speech which is reproduced below. Yet while Käsemann may be said to have re-opened the historical Jesus question, he did so in a way which clearly distanced this 'new quest' from its nineteenth-century predecessor.

Ernst Käsemann was born in Bochum-Dalhausen in Westphalia. He began his theological studies in 1925, firstly in Bonn and then at the Universities of Tübingen and Marburg, where he prepared a dissertation under the direction of Rudolf Bultmann on the Pauline concept of the 'body of Christ'. Käsemann then worked for some time as a pastor of the Lutheran congregation at Gelsenkirchen in the Ruhr. In 1937 he was arrested by the Gestapo and briefly imprisoned for a sermon based on Isa 26:13, in which he had resisted what he saw as the idolatrous claims of National-Socialism. During his imprisonment he drafted an initial version of his study of Hebrews, later published as *The Wandering People of God*. In 1942 Käsemann was drafted into the German army, and served first of all in occupied France and then in Greece. Along with many other conscript troops, he surrendered to the Americans in 1945 and was for a time detained in an internment camp. In 1946 he was invited to take up a position at the University of Mainz, and in 1947 received a doctorate from the University of Marburg. In 1951 Käsemann received a call to take up a chair at Göttingen, and in 1959 he was granted at post at Tübingen, where he remained until his retirement in 1971. Until his death Käsemann remained an active supporter of various causes characteristic of the political left, which he saw as an important expression of his theological reflection.

The following essay, delivered as a speech in 1953, needs to be read against the background of Rudolf Bultmann's rejection of the historical Jesus quest, which (as we have seen) was motivated by factors which were both historical and theological. Käsemann is quick to endorse the criticisms made of the nineteenth-century quest by his erstwhile teacher. On the side of theology, both Barth and Bultmann had rightly emphasized that Christianity was founded on an act of divine revelation, a revelation mediated by the New Testament witness. From the point of view of historical research, form criticism had made it clear that the Gospels are records of the proclamation of the earliest Christians rather than materials for a biography of Jesus. Therefore, even if one were to succeed in stripping away from the Gospels the multiple layers of Christian interpretation, the results would not only be highly speculative, but they would also be of little theological interest. Indeed Käsemann argues that it is not accident that the earliest Christian records of Jesus are already overlaid with interpretation. For the early Church realized, instinctively (as it were), that the facts of history are significant only when they are retold in a way which addresses the situation of a later audience. It is this which the Gospels writers were attempting to do, and it would be foolish to simply discard their insights. Nonetheless, the question of the historical foundation of the Christian *kerygma* (or 'proclamation') remains an important one. No matter how deeply the earliest Christians buried the historical Jesus under layers of reinterpretation, they clearly understood their proclamation of the Gospel to be grounded in the events of his life, death and resurrection. Indeed so deeply convinced were the early Christians of this historical grounding of the *kerygma* that they were prepared to invent a history in the light of the *kerygma*. In the infancy narrative of Matthew's Gospel (for example) we have the 'historification' of Old Testament legends: Matthew assumes that early life of Jesus must have taken the same form as that of Moses, and 'records' the stories of his birth accordingly.

Yet Käsemann immediately qualifies his conclusion. It is not entirely accurate to describe what (for instance) Matthew is doing as the invention of 'history', for Matthew's claims are rooted in an eschatological interpretation of Jesus' life. Indeed, the general pattern of the early Christian proclamation is to see the life of Jesus, not so much an event *within* history (comparable to other, similar events), but as the *end* of history. (Luke's two-volume work constitutes, for Käsemann, an unfortunate exception to this trend.) For the Gospel writers, the figure of Jesus cannot 'be comprehended within the category of the historical': there is no comparison between his life and any other human life (in accordance, we might say, with Troeltsch's principle of analogy), nor can the life of Jesus be understood as the product of a complex of historical causes (Troeltsch's principle of correlation). At this point Käsemann moves into theological mode; no longer merely describing the attitude of the Gospel writers, he endorses it (in a way which displays his closeness to Bultmann and—before him—to Kähler). What Käsemann seems to be suggesting is that divine revelation can only be understood as something which breaks into human history, an act of God which cannot be characterized as a product of human culture. Moreover, in that revelation I am confronted, not with certain facts about the past, but with a divine claim which I must accept or reject. Nonetheless, the life of Jesus remains of theological significance insofar as it is the moment when this eschatological claim of God intersects with human history. Over against all forms of Docetism, the early Church continued to insist on this intersection. By so doing, the Gospel writers remind us that salvation is (in Lutheran terms) *extra nos*: it comes from God, not from ourselves.

After reminding us once again of the difficulties of identifying the historical basis of the *kerygma*, Käsemann sketches what he sees as a starting-point for further research. He insists that we must look for 'the distinctive element in the earthly Jesus' in his preaching, and outlines the principle which has become known as that of 'double dissimilarity'. (We can be really confident of the authenticity of a saying only when it differs from both contemporary Judaism and the early Christian proclamation.) Käsemann focuses first of all on the extraordinary claims to authority implicit in the antitheses of the 'Sermon on the Mount' (Matthew 5-7). Jesus' claims to authority go beyond those of a rabbi or a prophet, who could never exceed the authority of Moses. His claims make sense only in the light of his proclamation of the Kingdom of God, a Kingdom which was future and yet in some sense inaugurated by Jesus' proclamation. These observations form an outline, which later research would need to fill in. Yet Käsemann insists that they are not an outline of a 'life of Jesus', since that would include an account of his inner development and the outer course of his life, of which the Gospels give us practically no indication. The best we can hope to achieve is a sense of the connection between the *kerygma* of the early Church and the preaching of Jesus himself. As the Gospel writers realized, the figure of Jesus himself escapes the categories of psychology, comparative religion or general history; it can be grasped only by those who allow the proclamation of Jesus to be today, as it was then, a challenge to faith.

The Problem of the Historical Jesus

1. The Present Position [1]

It is one of the marks of the upheaval in German work on the New Testament in this last generation that the old question

---

[1] A lecture given at the reunion of Marburg old students on 20 October 1953 in Jugenheim. First published in *ZTK* [*Zeitschrift für Theologie und Kirche*] 51, 1954, pp.125-53.

about the Jesus of history has receded rather noticeably into the background. And yet, for about two hundred years before that, the advance of our discipline had been set in motion, impelled on its way and determined in its very essence by this same question. Basically, two factors were responsible when, after the First World War, the problem, if not completely solved, seemed at least to have come to a kind of full-stop. The break made with Liberalism by the Dialectical Theology and the parallel renewal of interest in the message of the Reformation combined to reveal the impoverishment and distortion of the Gospel which takes place wherever the question of the Jesus of history is treated as decisive for theology and preaching. At the same time, the work of the Form Critics was designed to show that the message of Jesus as given to us by the Synoptists is, for the most part, not authentic but was minted by the faith of the primitive Christian community in its various stages. Thus, from the fact that the genuine tradition about Jesus has only been transmitted to us embedded in the preaching of primitive Christianity and overlaid by it, the conclusion was drawn that the true bearer and moulder of the Gospel had been the Easter faith. For Bultmann, this judgment involved radical consequences. As early as his book *Jesus*[2] he was no longer relying exclusively on the material the authenticity of which his *History of the Synoptic Tradition*[3] had left unimpeached. He was simply concerned to uncover the earliest stratum of primitive Christian proclamation, in which the preaching of Jesus himself and its reflection in the kerygma of the community had in historical fact been interwoven; no doubt his own failure to draw a clear line between them was conscious and deliberate. Then, in his *Primitive Christianity in its Contemporary Setting*,[4] he included his portrayal of Jesus within his account of late Judaism and, correspondingly, sketched New Testament Theology as a development of the primitive Christian message, thus making the preaching of Jesus appear the mere precondition

[2] Berlin, 1926; ET, *Jesus and the Word*, London, 1935.
[3] ET of 3rd ed., Oxford, 1963. Originally in FRLANT [Forschungen zur Religion und Literatur des Alten und Neuen Testaments] 29, 1st ed., 1921; 2nd ed., 1931; 3rd ed., 1957 with 1958 supplement.
[4] London, 1956; ET of *Das Urchristentum im Rahmen der antiken Religionen*, Zürich, 1949.

of the latter. But this in turn means that Christian faith is here being understood as faith in the exalted Lord for which the Jesus of history as such is no longer considered of decisive importance.

There has not yet been any final and definite parting of the ways on this point. That this is so is in no small measure connected with the fact that any criticism would have to reckon with M. Kähler's book *Der sogenannte historische Jesus und der geschichtliche, biblische Christus* ['The So-Called Historical Jesus and the Historic, Biblical Christ'],[5] which still, after sixty years, is hardly dated and, in spite of many attacks and many possible reservations, has never really been refuted. In essence, Bultmann has merely, in his own way, underpinned and rendered more precise the thesis of this book. But the unmistakable embarrassment of apologetics, exposed to criticism both from the side of exegesis and from the side of systematic theology, has had a paralysing effect throughout a whole generation. This state of affairs is obviously approaching its end today. The old conflict is flaring up again and will probably result in the formation of distinct fronts such as we have hardly known since the War, in spite of all the tensions and differences of opinion which have existed among German New Testament scholars. Knowledge proceeds by antitheses and Bultmann's radicalism is provoking a reaction. But over and above this, we are all without exception concerned at present with the question of a proper understanding of history and historicity which is bound to find concrete, necessary and, indeed, archetypal expression for the theologian in the problem of the historical Jesus and of his significance for faith. Developing this in more detail, we find that present-day criticism hinges on three points. First, efforts are being made to show that the Synoptists contain much more authentic tradition than the other side is prepared to allow. Secondly, a case is being made out with particular vigour for the reliability, if not of the whole of the Passion and Easter tradition of the Gospels, at least of the most primitive elements in it. In both cases, the concern is to counteract any drastic separation, or even antithesis, of kerygma and tradition. Those who take this line are, fundamentally, trying to maintain that the kerygma includes the recital of

[5] Leipzig, 1896; new ed. by E. Wolf, Munich, 1956.

facts as mediated by the tradition. And thus they arrive, thirdly, at the systematic conception of a 'salvation history' running parallel to universal history, embedded in it but yet separable from it, having its own laws and continuity and finding its vehicle in the history of faith and of the Church as the new divine creation.

The characteristic feature of our situation, then, is that the classic liberal question about the Jesus of history is increasingly regaining its theological importance; and that, paradoxically, this is happening at a time when liberalism is discredited over wide areas of Church life, and happening as a counter-blast to an historical and theological criticism which itself sprang from the soil of liberalism. This change of fronts is certainly among the most fascinating and fruitful phenomena in recent theological history. For two hundred years, critical research has been trying to free the Jesus of history from the fetters of the Church's dogma, only to find at the end that such an attempt was predestined to failure, and that we can learn nothing at all about the historical Jesus except through the medium of primitive Christian preaching and of the Church's dogma which is bound up with it; we can no longer detach him neatly and satisfactorily from the Christ of preaching and of faith. But at precisely the same moment, the very people who have hitherto been the opponents of the liberal quest of the historical Jesus are obviously going in fear and trembling lest the doors should for the first time be really opened to radical scepticism and lest, with the abandoning of any direct attack on the historical question, the historical reality of revelation itself should be endangered. This reality they themselves seek to defend by showing that the tradition is historically trustworthy. They are thus following in the footsteps of critics whose original intention in taking up the theme of history was precisely the reverse—to set it in opposition to dogma.

It would certainly not be a good thing to accept the stark fact of the surprising change of fronts so readily that we failed at least to inquire into this development, to see whether it might not perhaps have an inner necessity of its own. It might well be that each of the protagonists in this struggle was concerned, on his part, to pursue some interest which in fact ought not to be surrendered, and to this extent the two might be more than mere opponents; they might be partners in a genuine theological conversation. Such an assumption does not prejudice the issue as to the right and wrong in detail of the position we have provisionally adopted; it simply postulates the dialectic of two distinct standpoints. An over-emphasis on the one aspect is then met by a like over-emphasis on the other, and the change of posture by the first partner leads, provided that the conversation is conducted on a reasonable basis, to a corresponding change on the part of the other. Whether such an hypothesis is tenable can only be discovered from an examination of the underlying facts. We shall therefore next attempt to evaluate the significance of observable historical fact within the framework of the history which lies before us.

2. The Problem of the Historical Element in Our Gospels

Even the history which is recounted in the pages of the New Testament has become to us, who live nearly two thousand years later, *mere* history. In other words, we have no longer any immediate access to it, even if we take the most accurate and circumstantial conspectus of it which is possible. Over against those who were contemporary with it, we speak in another language, we think in other categories, we face other situations and decisions. In relation to it, we experience with peculiar force the sense that all history is conditioned by the fact of dying, and, as generation succeeds to generation, this sense emerges as discontinuity. Thus, if we desire to obtain knowledge of past history, we have to fall back on what has been narrated. History is only accessible to us through tradition and only comprehensible to us through interpretation. To be acquainted merely with what actually happened is of little use to us by itself. Both Rationalism and Supernaturalism have certainly striven hard on all sides to establish, in part or in sum, the credibility of the facts reported in the New Testament. But what has been the result of all these efforts, if the truth be told? Did not the Jesus of the Gospels become, under the hand of the Rationalists, a figure just like ourselves, thus showing how the wealth of portraits of Jesus assembled by A. Schweitzer corresponds to the multitude of possible viewpoints and beholders? And has not Supernaturalism succeeded only in depicting the miraculous aura of the θεῖος ἀνήρ ['divine man'], who can be accepted only by means of the *sacrificium intellectus* ['sacrifice of the intellect'], which enthusiasts in their self-induced delusions and transports so readily offer? In neither case is there any gain for faith. For if, on the one hand, it was established that certain happenings *did* take place which could be fitted into the same category as the long succession of similar happenings elsewhere, on the other hand prodigies were brought to light which may still arouse curiosity but which can give no certainty of revelation. We have at this stage no need whatever to labour either the point that the whole history of religion abounds in miracles and prodigies, or the point that historical criticism is bound to call in question a great deal of what is alleged to have happened or, finally, the point that the passion for objective facts can be shown to have led time and again to unrestrained and highly subjective flights of fancy. It ought also to be clear to us that the Gospel history has not come any nearer to us when we have resolved it into bare facts. To fail to grasp this is the peculiar self-deception of all those who want to extract a salvation history in an objectively convincing form from universal history and who can yet rest their case at best on an abundance of remarkable occurrences. No one has ever been compelled (in the true sense) to make his decision between faith and unbelief, simply because someone else has succeeded in representing Jesus convincingly as a worker of miracles. And nothing is settled about the significance of the Resurrection tidings for me personally, simply because the evidence for the empty tomb has been shown to be reliable. The handing on of relatively probable facts does not as such provide any basis for genuinely historical communication and continuity.

It is obvious that primitive Christianity was well aware of this. We cannot otherwise explain why its Gospels were not written primarily as reportage and why its own kerygma actually overlays and conceals the figure of the historical Jesus, thus facing us as historians with incalculable difficulties and very often making any reconstruction quite impossible. The community did not inadvertently and senselessly amalgamate its own message with that of its Lord, much less did it merely repeat the latter. If it was indeed concerned not with the reproduction of a notable happening, but with that decision between faith and unbelief which was demanded of it, then it had no alternative but to act as it did. By the very fact of acting thus, it shows that this concern cannot be preserved and defended historically, that is, by the enumeration of bare facts within a causal nexus. By acting as it did the community bore (and still bears) witness to history as being living and contemporary. It interprets out of its own experience what for it has already become mere history and employs for this purpose the medium of its preaching. It is precisely by this method that the community rescues the facts of the past from being regarded only as prodigies and wonders. And in so doing it demonstrates that in its eyes Jesus is no mere miracle-worker, but the *Kyrios* ['Lord'], from whom it knows itself to receive both grace and obligation. To state the paradox as sharply as possible: the community takes so much trouble to maintain historical continuity with him who once trod this earth that it allows the historical events of this earthly life to pass for the most part into oblivion and replaces them by its own message. It is not only at this point in its history that the community does this. The same process is always being repeated in the course of Church history. Time and again, continuity with the past is preserved by shattering the received terminology, the received imagery, the received theology—in short, by shattering the tradition. We can early see this happening in the differing forms of the Palestinian and Hellenistic kerygmas. The variation in the New Testament message, which finds its strongest and most problematic form of expression in the transition from the preaching of Jesus to the preaching about Jesus, is anything but accidental and arbitrary. It plunges us into great difficulties. For not only does it compel us to raise the question of the significance of individuality for Christian preaching, but at the same time it is also the outward sign of radical historical changes and of new developments. There is an ever-present temptation, into which many have fallen, to infer from this variation the complete discontinuity of Christian history. The truth is that it is this variation which makes continuity possible at all. For mere history becomes significant history not through tradition as such but through interpretation, not through the simple establishment of facts but through the understanding of the events of the past which have become objectified and frozen into facts. The variation in the New Testament kerygma demonstrates that primitive Christendom held fast the profession of its faith throughout all changes of time and place, although these changes forced upon it the modification of received tradition. Mere history, the existence of which can only be prolonged with difficulty by its presence to human consciousness has, as such, no genuine historical significance, even if it is full of curiosities and wonders. At any rate, it has no more historical significance than a lunar landscape which itself is not without curiosities and wonders. Mere history only takes on genuine historical significance in so far as it can address both a question and an answer to our contemporary situation; in other words, by finding interpreters who hear and utter this question and answer. For this purpose primitive Christianity allows mere history no vehicle of expression other than the kerygma.

This truth must be seen to be of fundamental significance for the whole New Testament message. But it must, further, not be overlooked that the relationship of the individual writings to the life history of Jesus varies very considerably. Above all, we cannot help being struck by the fact that the Gospels alone present the tidings of the Christ within the framework of the story of the earthly life of Jesus. It is true that the other writings indicate from time to time that they are not wholly without information about this life. But basically it is only the event of Cross and Resurrection which has any real importance for them. For this reason the historical element in the story of Jesus has, in these other writings, shrunk almost to vanishing point. We might even say that it is present only as a shadow. For Cross and Resurrection are no longer regarded from the standpoint of the historian, but are expounded in their saving significance. Seen from this angle it will appear strange that we encounter in the New Testament any writings like the Gospels, which concern themselves with the earthly life of Jesus.

Yet even the Gospels themselves are far from displaying agreement in the way in which they relate themselves to the historical life of Jesus. It can hardly be doubted that the Synoptists intended in all good faith to give their readers authentic tradition about Jesus. But it is impossible to ascribe the same intention to the fourth Evangelist, at least in the same sense. The real violence done by John to the narrative material, his striking neglect of the Synoptic tradition, the quite different arrangement of the whole and, above all, the peculiar way in which he has constructed the discourses; all these compel us to suppose that such a reflective writer could not have been simply deceiving himself about the discrepancy between his mode of presentation and that of all other existing Church tradition, but that he willed and intended it. For this reason, it is now widely acknowledged that for him the merely historical only has interest and value to the extent to which it mirrors symbolically the recurring experiences of Christian faith. It provides him with the opportunity and the framework of writing for his own day the history of the *Christus praesens* ['Christ (who is) present']. Mark, on the other hand, in Dibelius' excellent phrase, wrote the book of the secret epiphanies of Jesus. The words and deeds of the Christ, as W. Wrede has already established, appear here as an earnest of the glory of the Risen Lord, so that the life history of Jesus becomes almost the subject of a mystery play; the Son of God, who has come down to earth, lifts his incognito from time to time, until at Easter he allows it to drop away altogether. This earthly life is the battle which precedes the victory and can only be understood in the light of this victory. But if this is the case, then the historical life of Jesus is no longer the focus of Mark's attention. It merely provides the stage on which the God-man enters the lists against his enemies. The history of Jesus has become mythicized. Thus, when we inquire where in our Gospels a stronger emphasis is laid on the historical element, we are really left only with Matthew and Luke. What the situation in their case is, we shall have to discuss presently. But let us halt at this point to plot our series of findings.

We have been endeavouring to discover an answer to the problem of the position of the historical element in our Gospels. We owe the recognition of the existence of the problem to that radical criticism which, in the logic of its long and painful journey towards the ultimate datum of the Gospel tradition, arrived not, as it had hoped, at the historical Jesus but at the primitive Christian kerygma. In order to solve this problem, this criticism was finally compelled to give up the attempt to construct a life of Jesus out of the Synoptic Gospels. It did not take this step in order to throw itself anew into the arms of the Christological metaphysic of orthodoxy; but, by recognizing the necessity of re-formulating its original question, remained true to the impulse which gave it gave birth, and the historical method thus engendered. It does not deny the existence of the historical Jesus. But it recognizes that we can only gain access to this Jesus through the medium of the primitive Christian gospel and the primary effect of this gospel is not to open up the way for us but to bar it. The historical Jesus meets us in the New Testament, our only real and original documentation of him, *not* as he was in himself, *not* as an isolated individual, but as the Lord of the community which believes in him. Only in so far as, from the very outset, he was potentially and actually this Lord, does the story of his earthly life play any part in our Gospels. Anything else there was to him is completely overshadowed, so that we are no longer in a position to delineate with even approximate accuracy and completeness his portrait, his development, the actual course of his life: we are for the most part groping in absolute darkness so far as these are concerned. The significance of this Jesus for faith was so profound, that even in the very earliest days it almost entirely swallowed up his earthly history. The living experience of him which later generations enjoyed made the facts of his earthly life simply irrelevant, except in so far as they might serve to reflect the permanent experience. In such circumstances we must question whether the formula 'the historical Jesus' can be called at all appropriate or legitimate, because it is almost bound to awaken and nourish the illusion of a possible and satisfying reproduction of his 'life story'. The road of Liberalism had to be abandoned, because the hope of uncovering this 'life story' and of being able to correct the Church's dogma in the light of it proved a vain one. Anyone who tries to upset this verdict is seeking to rob us of the fruit and the meaning of all our research of the last two centuries and to conjure up once again the painful story of historical criticism, which would then have to be repeated in an even more drastic form. He is also failing to understand that the discovery of historical facts and their causal nexus is not necessarily of help to us in our own historical situation but that these must be interpreted before their relevance and their challenge can be made plain. Mere history is petrified history, whose historical significance cannot be brought to light simply by verifying the facts and handing them on. On the contrary, the passing on of the *bruta facta* ['bare facts'] can, as such, directly obstruct a proper understanding of it. Only that man is in genuine continuity with past history who allows it to place him in a new condition of responsibility; this is not yet true of the man who is concerned with its causality and teleology or who simply struggles on under the burden of tradition. In theological terms, this means that only in the decision between faith and unbelief can petrified history even of the life of Jesus become once again living history. This is why we only make contact with this life history of Jesus through the kerygma of the community. The community neither could nor would separate this life history from its own history. Therefore it neither could nor would abstract from its Easter faith and distinguish between the earthly and the exalted Lord. By maintaining the identity of the two, it demonstrated that any questioning directed only towards the historical Jesus seemed to it to be pure abstraction.

3. The Problem of Historification [*Historisierung*] in Our Gospels

What has hitherto been said has a converse, which must on no account be left out of our reckoning. For the decision taken by primitive Christianity obviously does not permit us to choke off the question about the Jesus of history, in spite of its dubious status when raised in isolation and in spite of the difficulty of finding an answer to it. No one may arbitrarily and with impunity exempt himself from tackling the problems which have come down to him from his fathers. The exponents of Liberal theology are, over a wide area, no longer acknowledged as fathers today; but this does not in any way alter the fact that they nevertheless do stand in that relationship to us. Secular historical science will also continue to confront us with this kind of question in some form or other; and every New Testament scholar has in fact dealt with it in his own particular way. But, most important of all, the New Testament itself justifies us to this extent in asking the question, inasmuch as it is to the earthly Jesus that the Gospels ascribe their kerygma, wherever it actually originated, and thus they invest him unmistakably with pre-eminent authority. However strongly their conceptions of the history of Jesus may differ, however much the real life history of Jesus may be buried under their own proclamation, it is interest in this history which we have to thank, both for their genesis and for their form, which stands out in such peculiar relief against both the rest of the New Testament and the other literature of the time. In no case may we allow the exaggeration of insights which may be correct in themselves to exempt us from the dialectic obtaining here or to drive us to one-sided solutions. That would equally happen if we were to absolutize the irrefragable proposition that the Christian message is founded on the Easter faith. Such a proposition has its proper place and validity primarily in antithesis to the Liberal *Leben-Jesu-Forschung* ['Life of Jesus research']. But it ought not to conceal a defeatist attitude which has already given up any attempt to penetrate the human individuality of Jesus, nor to appear to contest what the Evangelists would undoubtedly have maintained—namely, that the life history of Jesus has its relevance for faith. For if primitive Christianity identifies the humiliated with the exalted Lord, in so doing it is confessing that, in its presentation of his story, it is incapable of abstracting from its faith. At the same time, however, it is also making it clear that it is not minded to allow myth to take the place of history nor a heavenly being to take the place of the Man of Nazareth. In fact, the fight is already on against the docetism of the 'enthusiasts' and the *kenosis* ['self-emptying'] doctrine of the historicizers. Primitive Christianity is obviously of the opinion that the earthly Jesus cannot be understood otherwise than from the far side of Easter, that is, in his majesty as Lord of the community and that, conversely, the event of Easter cannot be adequately comprehended if it is looked at apart from the earthly Jesus. The Gospel is always involved in a war on two fronts.

Certainly we must now determine exactly what the reasons were which lay behind this attitude. They will be most easily discovered by taking for our new point of departure some part of the tradition which must necessarily be regarded as unauthentic. For there a procedure has been adopted which we may call the 'historification' of the unhistorical. The dominating interest, whatever it may be, will be found to determine the form in which the historical element is presented. Matthew's infancy narrative seems to me particularly instructive. Two motifs stand out clearly here. On the one side, constant allusion is made to the fulfilment of the Scriptures in what is being narrated; on the other, a parallel with the Moses *haggadah* ['story'] is being drawn, the sense of which is: as with the first Deliverer, so with the second. In both cases the birth of the child produces unrest on the part of the rulers, followed by consultation with wise men and the murder of children; in both cases there follows a wonderful deliverance in which Egypt becomes the land of refuge. From the study of the formation of tradition it can be established that the Moses legends have provided the tradition about Jesus with its characteristic features, while the comparative study of religion enables us to add that such a transfer of motifs is a frequent phenomenon and that we have before us a typical example of legendary overpainting and of mythologizing. However correct this analysis may be, we do not come up against the specifically theological problem until we ask ourselves what interest is being served by the combination of the already existing and originally mythical material with the story of Jesus. Here we can gain some help from the parallel of the proofs from prophecy in the very passages we have cited. Just as the Scriptures find their fulfilment in the events which are being portrayed, so the mythical scheme, taken up by Matthew, of the threat to the child and his miraculous deliverance marks him out as the future Saviour of the people of God—in concrete terms, the second and last Moses. Conversely, because Jesus is the future Saviour, the traditional and given scheme can be transferred to him and the events surrounding his birth and infancy must correspond to the stories already in existence concerning Moses. In this way an 'historification' of mythical material is arrived at. Its progress is rapid, in so far as Matthew has no longer any doubt that he is recapitulating genuine history. The process we have outlined takes on significance for us in that here we acknowledge unequivocally that the tradition concerning Jesus presupposes primitive Christian eschatology and has been shaped by it. It is not only here that this eschatology has conditioned the life story of Jesus as we have it in our Gospels. Matthew himself demonstrates this in a particularly impressive way, as some further examples may illustrate. The recital of the miracles takes place in his Gospel under the device of the compassion of God, which is revealing itself in the Last Days and at the same time visiting Israel in mercy. Matt. 9-10 offer us in more or less systematic fashion examples of what, in the answer to the Baptist's question in 11.5, are described as signs of the age of salvation. Our Evangelist is thus interested in the miracles of Jesus from the standpoint of his own particular eschatology. It emerges from the Sermon on the Mount that Matthew sees in Jesus the bringer of the Messianic Torah. We are to understand from this that Jesus is being consistently portrayed here as a rabbi and as founder of an eschatologically-orientated community life. This is by no means as self-evident a proposition as it may appear to us. Apart from the fact that an extraordinarily large number of logia ['sayings'] cannot be regarded as authentic and that any portrait of Jesus based on them is thus rendered problematical, it is also a question how this picture of the rabbi can be reconciled with the knowledge of Jesus' divine Sonship. The answer is, that the bringer of the Messianic Torah is not just any rabbi, nor is his righteousness that of the scribes and Pharisees. Once again the Evangelist's eschatology has determined the shape he has given to the life story of Jesus. At this point we may mention the different twist which Matthew gives to the theory of 'hardening' put forward in Mark 4.12. Like Mark, he emphasizes that the parables are so slanted as to veil the truth. Like Mark, he sees in this veiling a judgment of God on those who shut their ears to the voice of the divine emissary. But Matthew now applies this quite concretely to the Jews. For while the disciples are portrayed throughout as those who understand (and thus not as in Mark), the Jesus of Matthew, from ch. 13 until his last clash with his adversaries in Jerusalem, is consistently executing judgment on Jewry by the very fact of speaking to them in veiled language, i.e. in parables. The eschatological trend of the proof from prophecy in the Passion story is obvious; that of the Easter narratives is still more obvious. We may sum up thus: the whole life history of Jesus as Matthew presents it is not only seen from the standpoint of eschatology, but basically shaped by it. It is precisely here that the story of Jesus has been interwoven with traditional material which can only be described as being in itself unhistorical, legendary and mythical.

But once we are clear about this, we can easily see that the position is the same in the Second and Fourth Gospels. Even Mark is not concerned in the last resort to depict Jesus as a miracle-worker, however much some of his details may give this impression. Rather, he sees in the earthly life of Jesus the glory of the risen Son of God bursting victoriously into the demon-controlled world and revealing equally to the earth and to the principalities and powers their eternal Lord. Because in Mark— and this is characteristic of the Gentile Christian outlook—the overcoming of the demonic forces forms the core of the eschatological event, the history of Jesus as outlined by him looks quite different from that given to us by Matthew: and this accounts also for the pronounced shrinkage in the discourse material. In exactly the same way, there is a correspondence between the peculiarly Johannine eschatology, with its thoroughgoing elimination of the apocalyptic element, and the Johannine portrayal of the history of Jesus as the history of the *praesentia* ['presence'] of the Logos on earth; on this subject, I would at this point simply refer you to Bultmann's commentary on John.

The case of the Lucan corpus is more complicated. To begin with we have the unusually significant and equally problematical situation that the story of Jesus is given a kind of extension in that of the Apostles. Such an alteration could only be possible and meaningful for a writer at a time in which apocalyptic eschatology no longer controlled the whole of life, as it had done in primitive Christianity. You do not write the history of the Church, if you are expecting the end of the world to come any day. Acts thus shows clearly that, while the apocalyptic hope may still belong to the stock-in-trade of Christian doctrine, yet for Luke himself it no longer possesses any pivotal interest. If his Gospel creates at many points a quite different impression, this is to be placed to the account of the tradition which Luke has embraced and preserved. Primitive Christian eschatology is replaced by salvation history, which is characterised by an historically verifiable continuity and by a process of ever-extending devel-

opment, as H. Conzelmann has demonstrated to particularly
good effect in his *The Theology of St Luke*.[6] The preparation for
this development is God's consistent action throughout the Old
Testament and its culmination in the history of Jesus; the history
of the Church is its unfolding and the Last Day is its final conclusion. The same conception is reflected in the way in which
the various steps of Jesus' journey, and of the journey of the
Church, are distinctly marked and directly control the divisions
of the Lucan corpus. The outline of a chronological and geo-
graphical sequence determines this whole and gives it clarity of
arrangement. But, in this careful ordering of what is immediately
visible, we come to see the inward order created by the divine
plan of salvation. It is not an accident that the Areopagus discourse speaks of God as the great Orderer of the cosmos and of
the ages. Because Luke saw things in this light, he could and did
become the first Christian historian to try to sketch out the great
stages of the plan of salvation and to work consistently on that
basis. His gospel is indeed the first 'life of Jesus'. In it, consideration is given to the points of view of causality and teleology; and
psychological insight, the composition of the historian and the
particular slant of the writer who aims at edification are equally
discernible. It is true that the price Luke pays for all this is by no
means small. His Jesus is the founder of the Christian religion;
the Cross is a misunderstanding on the part of the Jews, who
have not properly understood the Old Testament prophecy, and
the Resurrection is the necessary correction of this human error
by the Great Disposer. The teaching of Jesus brings us a loftier
ethic, the miracles are heavenly powers bursting into the world,
wonders which provide evidence of divine majesty. The story of
Jesus becomes something absolutely in the past, namely, *initium
Christianismi* ['the beginning of Christianity']—mere history indeed. As such, therefore, it can properly be tied to the history of
the Apostles. To its own time—the era of the beginnings of
early Catholicism—it appears as the sacred past, the epoch of
great miracles, of right faith, and of first love, a model of all that
Church life should be and might be. This is the result of replacing primitive Christian eschatology by salvation history. There-

---

[6] *Die Mitte der Zeit* ['The Mid-Point of Time'], Tübingen, 1954; ET, London, 1960.

fore even Luke confirms for us in his own way—that is, *e contrario*—that the mode in which the life history of Jesus is presented depends on the eschatology prevailing at the time. To put this in the form of the epigram (but an epigram which expresses the eternal truth): if, in the other Gospels, the problem of history is a special form of the problem of eschatology, in Luke eschatology has become a special form of the problem of history.

4. The Significance of the Historical Element in Our Gospels

We have to ask at this point how this finding helps us to answer our particular questions. First, we have now come to see that our Gospels, with the necessary exception of Luke, are not in the least interested in the composition of a comprehensive biography of Jesus nor in investigating what has been reported about him to see how far it is reliable and how far it corresponds to historical reality. The story of his life is, for the Gospels, only a point where the eschatological events intersect and is only worthy of consideration as such; it receives its own peculiar life from these events and not from itself in isolation. This is supremely true of Jesus himself, in so far as he *is* the eschatological event. His historical existence is naturally presupposed and it enters the realm of the phenomenal to this extent, that his life on earth takes a human course. But as soon as he is portrayed as speaking and acting, this human course becomes an unbroken series of divine revelations and mighty acts, which has no common basis of comparison with any other human life and thus can no longer be comprehended within the category of the historical. All this finds its clearest expression in the fact that, while this human life runs, like any other, from birth to death, birth and death do not, however, appear as its beginning and its end; they do not appear as happenings within the ordinary course of nature but as events of salvation history. Because Luke has nevertheless attempted to contain this life within the category of historicity, he has ended up by making Jesus into a miracle-worker and the bringer of a new morality, the Cross into a misunderstanding on the part of the Jews and the Resurrection into the marvellous reanimation of a dead man.

But what meaning then has it for the other Evangelists, this life history which stands so deep within the shadow of the eschatological event, now almost swallowed up by it, now brought out again in strong relief; this life history which, in the first instance, prompted the very writing of the Gospels? It seems to me that it is not by accident that the New Testament's own answer is given in an eschatological key phrase, the ἐφ' παξ of which the two meanings—'once' and 'once for all'—merge in such a remarkable fashion. But this needs further explanation. A primary concern of the Gospels is unmistakably the particularity with which the eschatological event is bound to *this* man from Nazareth, to the arena of Palestine and to a concrete time with its special circumstances. For this eschatological event is not a new idea, nor is it the culminating point of a process of development, the significance of which can be explained by its causal connections and effects. Revelation ceases to be God's revelation once it has been brought within a causal nexus. It is what it is only when it is seen as an unconditioned happening. And it does not convey to me an idea or even a programme, it is an act which lays hold of me. In revelation, I do not primarily experience some *thing* or other, but my ultimate Lord, his word to me and his claim upon me. Because this is so, we can even reject revelation, while we may overlook facts but cannot meaningfully reject them. In the same way there is, in respect of revelation, a 'too late' of guilty procrastination which is not really the case in respect of an idea. Briefly, that particularity of revelation which is manifested in its unbreakable link with a concrete life history reflects the freedom of the God who acts and is the ground of our having a possibility of decision. In other words, revelation creates *kairos* ['a time of decision'] which is a situation of grace or guilt, as the case may be. Because primitive Christianity experienced the earthly history of Jesus in this way as *kairos*, it wrote Gospels and did not after Easter simply let the life story of Jesus go by the board. Easter did not render this experience superfluous; on the contrary, it confirmed it. So far as it is desirable or possible to speak of a variation in faith before and after Easter, we can only say that out of the 'once' came the 'once for all' and out of the isolated encounter with Jesus, limited as it had been by death, came the presence of the exalted Lord, as described in the Fourth Gospel.

But this brings us to a second motive for keeping faith firmly tied to the life history of Jesus. It is more than strange that the Gospel of John treats of the abiding presence of the exalted Lord precisely within the framework of a history of the earthly Jesus. Admittedly, the Synoptists also describe the life of Jesus from the standpoint of the post-Easter community and its faith. They portray their Lord from the beginning as the Son of God, whereas this insight was only given to the Church after Easter. Thus, even in the Synoptists, the story as presented by them is not 'once for all' in the sense that it excludes the experiences of those who come after. On the contrary, these people are expressly told that they can have the same experiences of Jesus. But this is not done with the same boldness which marks the procedure of the Fourth Evangelist. Indeed the Johannine symbolism, so often worked over, robs—there is no other word for it— what happened once upon a time of all intrinsic significance and only allows it any importance as a reflection of present experience. Even the events of Good Friday, Easter and Ascension Day are no longer clearly distinguished. We must admit that nowhere in the New Testament is the life story of Jesus so emptied of all real content as it already is here, where it seems to be almost a projection of the present back into the past. It is all the more astonishing that the Fourth Gospel can yet describe the story of the exalted Lord as one and the same with that of the earthly Lord. The explanation of this may well be summed up in the one key word 'condescension'. It is precisely the Fourth Gospel, originating in the age of the anti-docetic conflicts, which neither can nor will renounce the truth that revelation takes place on earth and in the flesh. Here it parts from Enthusiasm to which otherwise it approaches so suspiciously close. Whatever violence it may have done to biographical history, it found it neither possible nor desirable to abandon history altogether, because with history stands or falls not only the divine condescension of revelation but also earthly corporeality as the sphere of revelation. Revelation invades human history and takes its course within it. Thus it is possible for revelation to be overlooked, misunderstood, spurned, to be a cause of offence and tumult. The ambiguity of this particular history is preserved by the fact that it can and does become mere history, unless the *Christus praesens* is constantly re-entering the arena. But this ambiguity is the obverse of the divine condescension. The Evangelist expresses this last truth by writing the story of the exalted Lord and that of the humiliated Lord as one and the same story.

No concessions to John's kind of symbolism are as yet to be found in the Synoptists. They certainly bring out the relation of the Gospel story to the present experience of their readers, but see to it that what they narrate displays equally unmistakably the character of 'the past'. The contrast with the Fourth Gospel emerges most strongly with regard to the portrayal of the Passion and Resurrection. We must at least raise the question as to whether this is to be explained solely on the grounds of weaker powers of theological reflection. Rather, as it seems to me, a proper concern of faith is manifesting itself here also. For the more certainly history is determined by the possibilities and decisions of a given time, the less it can be resolved into a logical sequence of situations. Our possibilities and decisions are in historical reality always predestinated, and this through the events of the past, which bar certain possibilities and decisions to us, while opening up others. We are always finding ourselves in a *kairos* which overlaps the individual moment of decision. If the Synoptists differ from John in allowing considerable intrinsic importance to the past and are specially concerned to incapsulate the death and resurrection of Jesus within this past, this is surely because they want to draw attention to the *kairos* which began with Jesus, is determined by him and predestinates every subsequent situation and decision. They want, if I may so express it, to show that the *extra nos* ['outside of us'] of salvation is 'given' to faith. To cleave firmly to history is one way of giving expression to the *extra nos* of salvation. Yet Luke proves how dangerous this method is, by making the *kairos* into a mere epoch, predestination into the initial impulse of a development and the givenness of salvation to our faith into the accessibility of verifiable facts to our knowledge; and by making grace (which is our destiny, compelling every one of us to make the decision between faith and unbelief) into the validation of the Church as the organization of the *religio christiana* ['Christian religion'].

If these observations are in any way accurate, we conclude from them once again that it was in fact eschatological interests which led irresistibly to the setting out of the earthly history of Jesus in the Gospels. We conclude further that primitive Christianity was in any event not primarily interested in the *bruta facta* of the past as such, but was engaged in eliciting from the past the essence both of its faith and of its own history. And thirdly, it emerges that, as a result of this exercise, those concerned did not arrive at any monochrome outlook, but only at various partly interlocking, partly contradictory answers. They were agreed only in one judgment: namely, that the life history of Jesus was constitutive for faith, because the earthly and the exalted Lord are identical. The Easter faith was the foundation of the Christian kerygma but was not the first or only source of its content. Rather, it was the Easter faith which took cognizance of the fact that God acted before we became believers, and which testified to this fact by incapsulating the earthly history of Jesus in its proclamation. How far are we obliged, or even able, to appropriate to ourselves the decision which was then taken? The immediate answer to this question is that we also cannot do away with the identity between the exalted and the earthly Lord without falling into docetism and depriving ourselves of the possibility of drawing a line between the Easter faith of the community and myth. Conversely, neither our sources nor the insights we have gained from what has gone before permit us to substitute the historical Jesus for the exalted Lord. Thus we are faced afresh with the problem which our Gospels grasped and solved in their own fashion. And the fact that they did not arrive at a unanimous viewpoint makes this a radical problem for us and shows that the clash over the historical Jesus has as its object a genuine theological problem.

5. The Embarrassment of Historical Criticism in the Face of Our Problem

It will be useful to reflect for a brief moment on the extent to which this problem has become a radical one for us. For our

Gospels believed, in all good faith, that they possessed a tradition about the earthly Lord, which was reliable over wide stretches of its content. Historical criticism has shattered this good faith as far as we ourselves are concerned. We can no longer assume the general reliability of the Synoptic tradition about Jesus. Worse still, we cannot improve the situation merely by making corrections in the tradition in the light of historical criticism. With the work of the Form-Critics as a basis, our questioning has sharpened and widened until the obligation now laid upon us is to investigate and make credible not the possible unauthenticity of the individual unit of material but, on the contrary, its genuineness. The issue today is not whether criticism is right, but where it is to stop. If we usually prefer to discuss the former question, then this means that we are really closing our eyes to the fact that the Gospels offer us primarily the primitive Christian kerygma, and individual words and deeds of Jesus only as they are embedded in it; and also to the fact that this kind of criticism can only help us to arrive at corrections and modifications in the kerygma but never at a word or action of the earthly Jesus himself. The inevitable consequence is a bewildering confusion of allegedly trustworthy portraits of Jesus: now he appears as a rabbi, now as a teacher of wisdom, now as a prophet; or again, as the man who thought of himself as the Son of Man or the Suffering Servant, who stood for an apocalyptic or a realized eschatology: or finally, as some sort of a mixture of all these. As far as the narratives of the miracles, of the Passion and of the Resurrection are concerned, every conceivable possibility is open to us, from complete scepticism through a cautious, milk-and-water kind of criticism to the greatest possible confidence. In practice, all these are defensible, once you are prepared to give credence to the tradition, because they are all actually contained in the tradition. Only, it is very difficult to arrive by this method at anything better than a judgment which may satisfy you personally but will still leave chaos all around. Only radical criticism can therefore do justice to the situation with which we are faced whether we like it or not, to the questions of principle which it raises and to the tasks which it sets us. By 'radical' in this context I naturally do not mean an uncontrolled passion for

any and every extreme position, but a single-minded openness
to the problems posed by the facts.

But even this kind of criticism finds itself in very great methodological difficulties because, apart from the parables, we possess
absolutely no kind of formal criteria by which we can identify
the authentic Jesus material. We do have such criteria for Palestinian and Hellenistic tradition, for the saying from Wisdom literature, for the prophetic utterance, for rabbinic doctrine, for
prescriptions concerning the life of a community, for apocalyptic
predictions and for anything else we like to name. Indeed, it is
Form Criticism which has rendered us the best service here. But
even Form Criticism leaves us in the lurch when we come to
ask what are the formal characteristics of the authentic Jesus
material. It cannot be otherwise, for Form Criticism is concerned with the *Sitz-im-Leben* ['setting in life'] of narrative forms
and not with what we may call historical individuality. The only
help it can give us here is that it can eliminate as unauthentic
anything which must be ruled out of court because of its *Sitz-
im-Leben*.

The case is not markedly different if we take as criteria the
primitive Christian chronology of the actual content of what is
set forth. True, we can reach some more or less satisfying position concerning the supplanting of the post-Easter enthusiasm by
a Christian rabbinate and so on through the subsequent development up to and including early Catholicism, however obscure
some of the details may remain. But it is just the earliest phase of
all, upon the comparison of which with the Jesus tradition everything might well depend, which remains absolutely opaque to
us, particularly as regards its soteriology and ecclesiology. From
this there springs a never-ending conflict over such questions as
whether or not Jesus founded a Church and instituted sacra-
ments. The situation is made even more difficult by the fact that
we cannot draw an exact line between Palestinian and Hellenistic Jewish Christianity, nor, conversely, can we simply identify
the two. Correspondingly, we may adopt a highly sceptical attitude to Lohmeyer's attempted differentiation of Jerusalem and
Galilee without, however, regarding the question it raises as being already settled. For the polity of the community will in fact
have had a different look in the capital and in the province.

This state of affairs brings us up against a multitude of enigmas. How long had the rivalry between Hellenists and Palestinians (Acts 6) been going on? What part did Peter really play? How did he come to be supplanted by James? What is the significance of these things for the course of primitive Christian missionary history? As long as these problems are not even half solved, there is little prospect of arriving at a greater understanding of the principle on which the earliest sections of the Synoptic material were divided up and arranged; as might be illustrated from an analysis of Matt. 23, from the tradition about Peter, from the saying about the ransom, from the prayer at the end of Matt. 11, to say nothing of the Passion and Easter narrative. But I cannot go into too much detail, as we should then never finish. We can only sketch in a few bold strokes the embarrassment of critical research. It lies in this: while the historical credibility of the Synoptic tradition has become doubtful all along the line, yet at the same time we are still short of one essential requisite for the identification of the authentic Jesus material, namely, a conspectus of the very earliest stage of primitive Christian history; and also there is an almost complete lack of satisfactory and water-tight criteria for this material. In only one case do we have more or less safe ground under our feet; when there are no grounds either for deriving a tradition from Judaism or for ascribing it to primitive Christianity, and especially when Jewish Christianity has mitigated or modified the received tradition, as having found it too bold for its taste. We shall conclude by examining some material of this kind, although only in summary fashion. But in so doing we must realize beforehand that we shall not, from this angle of vision, gain any clear view of the connecting link between Jesus, his Palestinian environment and his later community. The frontiers here lie wide open to the most diverse hypotheses. However, it is even more important for us to gain some insight into what separated him from friends and foes alike.

6. The Distinctive Element in the Mission of Jesus

In what follows I must renounce any attempt at completeness or at a detailed statement of my reasons for disagreeing with opinions that differ from my own. I shall content myself with setting out in the dogmatic form of a thesis what seems to me essential. All exegesis is agreed that the authenticity of the first, second and fourth antitheses in the Sermon on the Mount cannot be doubted. In fact, these words are among the most astonishing to be found anywhere in the Gospels. In their form, they elaborate the wording of the Torah as a rabbi interpreting the sense of the Scripture might have done. The determining factor however, is that the words ἐγὼ δὲ λέγω ['but I say'] embody a claim to an authority which rivals and challenges that of Moses. But anyone who claims an authority rivalling and challenging Moses has *ipso facto* set himself above Moses; he has ceased to be a rabbi, for a rabbi's authority only comes to him as derived from Moses. Rabbis may oppose each other in debate by the use of the formula 'But *I* say'; but this is only a formal parallel, because, in the case we are discussing, it is not another rabbi but the Scriptures and Moses himself who constitute the other party. To this there are no Jewish parallels, nor indeed can there be. For the Jew who does what is done here has cut himself off from the community of Judaism—or else he brings the Messianic Torah and is therefore the Messiah. Even the prophet does not stand alongside Moses but under him. The unheard-of implication of the saying testifies to its genuineness. It proves, secondly, that while Jesus may have made his appearance in the first place in the character of a rabbi or a prophet, nevertheless his claim far surpasses that of any rabbi or prophet; and thirdly, that he cannot be integrated into the background of the Jewish piety of his time. Certainly he was a Jew and made the assumptions of Jewish piety, but at the same time he shatters this framework with his claim. The only category which does justice to his claim (quite independently of whether he used it himself and required it of others) is that in which his disciples themselves placed him—namely, that of the Messiah.

This passage is not an isolated one so far as the Synoptists are concerned. The same dialectical relationship to the law, seeking the will of God and, in pursuit of it, shattering the letter of the law, is reflected in the attitude to the Sabbath commandment and the prescriptions for ceremonial purity. We can hardly say here that Jesus has left the law as such untouched and merely

made its demands more radical. This is certainly Matthew's understanding of what happened. But the history of the Gospel is
always at the same time a history of misunderstandings, as the
Synoptists themselves frequently show us. And the majesty of
Jesus is most plainly revealed when we see his first disciples already feeling that they must soften or correct his words, because
otherwise they could not endure him. Most interesting in this
connection is the pericope concerning the rubbing of the ears of
corn in Mark 2. 23ff. Only Mark has the sentence: 'The sabbath
was made for man, not man for the sabbath.' All the Synoptists
then go on to say that the Son of Man is Lord also of the sabbath. It is obvious that these two sayings clash, and equally obvious that it is only the first which really fits into the pattern of the
exchanges, which have so far not been christologically orien-
tated. Perhaps we ought to take note here that it is very ques-
tionable whether Jesus in his lifetime claimed for himself the title
of 'Son of Man'. On this point Bultmann has made the admittedly very speculative suggestion that the predicate 'Son of Man'
should be regarded as a mistaken translation from the Aramaic.
He maintains that the original had 'child of man', that is, 'man',
without qualification. He, too, considers that it is the former of
the two sentences that has the correct bearing. We can clinch
the argument by pointing out that the second saying—that
about the freedom of the Son of Man—represents a distinct
limitation and weakening of the first. But by now we have come
very close to the hypothesis that the community embarked on
this process of watering-down the saying because, while it might
credit its Lord with the freedom he had assumed, it was not prepared to allow it to all men. Its members felt themselves more
tightly bound by the law than he had been and, as the subsequent pericope about the healing on the sabbath shows, they
exercised their freedom only in exceptional cases and not as a
matter of principle; and certainly not in that spirit of unforced
responsibility to God, which was Jesus' legacy to them. The
greatness of his gift caused the community to take fright.

The same process may also be observed in the conflict over
the law of purification. Again, Matthew obviously thought that
Jesus was only attacking the rabbinate and Pharisaism with their
heightening of the demands of the Torah. But the man who

denies that impurity from external sources can penetrate into man's essential being is striking at the presuppositions and the plain verbal sense of the Torah and at the authority of Moses himself. Over and above that, he is striking at the presuppositions of the whole classical conception of cultus with its sacrificial and expiatory system. To put this in another way, he is removing the distinction (which is fundamental to the whole of ancient thought) between the *temenos* ['sacred precinct'], the realm of the sacred, and the secular, and it is for this reason that he is able to consort with sinners. For Jesus, it is the heart of man which lets impurity loose upon the world. That the heart of man should become pure and free, this is the salvation of the world and the beginning of that sacrifice which is well-pleasing to God, the beginning of true worship, as the Pauline paraenesis in particular will expound. Finally, by this saying, Jesus destroys the basis of classical demonology which rests on the conception that man is threatened by the powers of the universe and thus at bottom fails to recognize the threat which is offered to the universe by man himself. It is true that throughout the Gospels there are reports of the healing of demoniacs by Jesus; and in the saying in Mark 3.27 (= Matt. 12.28), the authenticity of which can hardly be questioned, he claims for himself this kind of authority. It all depends in what sense he did this; whether as a magician, believing that the world is literally bedevilled (thus subscribing to a metaphysical dualism), or as one who knew the evil of the human heart and its demonic power and took possession of this heart for God. It is certain that Jesus did not put forward any metaphysical dualism—if he had done, how could he ever have been portrayed as a teacher of wisdom?—and was conscious of being sent, not to fight the devil but to minister to man. But the foregoing must suffice for the formulation of our first finding: Jesus felt himself in a position to override, with an unparalleled and sovereign freedom, the words of the Torah and the authority of Moses. This sovereign freedom not merely shakes the very foundations of Judaism and causes his death, but, further, it cuts the ground from under the feet of the ancient world-view with its antithesis of sacred and profane and its demonology.

In establishing this, it is impossible not to contract lively doubts
about the widely current picture of the pious Jew, perhaps from
the circle of the Anavim ['the poor' or 'the pious poor'], studying the Scriptures day and night and finding described in them
the pattern of his way as the Servant of God or the suffering
Messiah. We have no reason to doubt that Jesus had the same
familiarity with the Old Testament which we should assume in
every pious Jew. But it is quite another question whether we
should make this the decisive factor in his actions. There is
much to be said on the other side. If this was so, then what was
the cause of the highly credible break with his family and what
drove him to be baptized by John (for this element in the tradition is undoubtedly reliable)? In any event, his relationship to
the Torah and to Moses hardly seems to support this view. We
have already established that Matthew and the tradition he inherited had their own reasons for depicting Jesus as a rabbi. But
apart from the fact that it was not all that easy to become a rabbi
and that, in any case, the rabbinate would have nothing to do
with the Baptist's movement, there was never a rabbi who did
not derive his authority from that of Moses. Also, most of the
quotations from Scripture in the Gospels are undoubtedly out-
crops of the theology of the community. Finally, it is striking
that the Jesus of the Synoptists is noticeably different in at least
two respects both from the image of the rabbi and from that of
the model Jewish devotee. There is, first, the remarkable importance which the writers attach to representing him as a
teacher of wisdom. It must be admitted from the outset that the
authenticity of the material we have in mind here is particularly
difficult to maintain, because in so much of it we are concerned
with popular images and with proverbs. Nevertheless some of
the sayings involved are so paradoxically formulated or juxta-
posed that this very fact could be an argument for the genuineness. To name two examples: the logion Matt. 10.26f. and parallel, with its demand that what is heard in secret should be
shouted from the housetops, is traced back by Bultmann to a
proverb which enjoins caution because secrets can so seldom be
kept secret. If that is correct, the problem then arises as to why
the warning has here been converted into a demand. Now if the
sense of the saying were perhaps this, that in the Last Times

caution must be thrown overboard, then that would square very well with the saying about not being anxious in Matt. 6.25ff. Here also the tradition of the Jewish belief in Providence is modified in a very odd fashion. Because we are now being called to thirst for the reign of God, we can, may, and must live without anxiety and be assured of God's loving care. They who, according to Matt. 10, exist as dying men in the aeon which is passing away, may and must be the ones who trust in God. To leave all is the obverse of receiving all. However this may be, the portrayal of the teacher of wisdom accords but ill with that of the rabbi, because the former lives by immediacy of contemplation, such as is familiar to us from the parables of Jesus, while the latter's existence is determined by meditation and by the bond which keeps him tied to Scripture.

We may concede that the full significance of this observation only becomes visible in the light of a second one. According to the saying in Matt. 12.28, which we have already cited, Jesus ascribes his conquest of the demons to the Spirit of God which fills him. We need not try to decide here whether this saying in its present form comes from Jesus himself. But what is certain is that he regarded himself as being inspired. This we can gather above all from the remarkable use of the word 'Amen' at the beginning of important logia, which has been so faithfully preserved by the Evangelists. 'Amen' is, of course, primarily a response. Even if we do not feel able to go as far as Schlatter, who, in the light of this, interpreted the words of Jesus as the repetition of what the divine Voice was saying to him, this prefix expresses an assurance which is much akin to the confirmation of an oath; and it signifies an extreme and immediate certainty, such as is conveyed by inspiration. Out of this certainty the antitheses of the Sermon on the Mount are pronounced, the Sabbath commandment and the law of purification are assailed; out of it, that dialectical relationship to the Scriptures originates, which is ready to pass by their literal meaning in order to seek in them the will of God; and out of it, the demand for intelligent love is set up and placed in opposition to the demand of the rabbinate for blind obedience. It is by this immediate assurance of knowing and proclaiming the will of God, which in him is combined with the direct and unsophisticated outlook of the teacher of wisdom and perhaps lies behind it, that Jesus is distinguished from the rabbis. It does not matter whether he used the actual words or not; he must have regarded himself as the instrument of that living Spirit of God, which Judaism expected to be the gift of the End.

It is thus very tempting to call him a prophet. But this will not do at all. No prophet could remove himself from the jurisdiction of Moses without thereby becoming a false prophet. Above all, no prophet could be credited with the eschatological significance which Jesus obviously ascribed to his own actions. A most enlightening passage in this connection seems to me to be the much puzzled over logion in Matt. 11.25f., according to which the kingdom of God suffers violence from the days of the Baptist until now and is hindered by men of violence. (This is, in my opinion, the only interpretation which makes sense.) Such a conception is strange enough. For in what sense can it be said that this happens to the kingdom of God? Luke had already asked himself this question and, being unable to answer it, had altered the sense. With his eye on the mission to the world, he makes Jesus proclaim that each man will be brought into the kingdom by force. Neither is Matthew really able to make anything of the saying. This is why he puts the sentence 'The law and the prophets are in force until John' (which Luke has in its original position before our logion) as a connecting link with the excursus on the Baptist's role as Elijah *redivivus* ['come back to life']. The history of the saying shows that we are dealing with very primitive tradition, already unintelligible by the time of the Evangelists. Yet the content suggests quite unambiguously that the logion is authentic. For in it the Old Testament epoch of salvation history concludes with the Baptist, who himself already belongs to the new epoch and is not to be counted among the prophets. The situation in this epoch is that the kingdom of God has already dawned, but is still being obstructed. The Baptist has introduced it, and thus ushered in the turning-point of the aeons. Yet even he still stands in the shadow of him who now speaks and utters his 'until today'. Who but Jesus himself can look back in this way over the completed Old Testament epoch of salvation, not degrading the Baptist to the position of a mere forerunner as the whole Christian community and the whole

New Testament were to do, but drawing him to his side and—
an enormity to later Christian ears—presenting him as the initia-
tor of the new aeon? But who then is this, who thus does justice
to the Baptist and yet claims for himself a mission higher than
that entrusted to John? Evidently, he who brings with his Gospel the kingdom itself; a kingdom which can yet be obstructed
and snatched away, for the very reason that it appears in the de-
fenceless form of the Gospel.

It was the belief of Jesus that, in his word, the *basileia* ['kingdom'] was coming to his hearers. Does this mean that he understood himself to be the Messiah? The only way of dealing briefly
with this question is simply to express at this point one's own
personal opinion. I personally am convinced that there can be
no possible grounds for answering this question in the affirmative. I consider all passages in which any kind of Messianic pre-
diction occurs to be kerygma shaped by the community. I do
not feel able to admit as genuine even the saying in Mark 8.38,
that the Son of Man will in the future be ashamed of the man
who here and now is ashamed of him and his words. For this
saying has preserved the peculiar character of the speech of the
Palestinian Christian prophets, which utters maxims of holy law
for the guidance of the community and attaches heavenly promise or divine curse in the eschatological future to the fulfilment
or non-fulfilment here on earth of certain conditions. This
means, then, that Jesus was not reckoning on the coming of a
Son of Man other than himself, as Bultmann assumes. Indeed
what would be the position of such a figure if the Baptist has
already ushered in the turn of the aeons and yet, for his part, still
stands in the shadow of Jesus? The predication 'Son of Man'
must have reflected the Christology and the apocalyptic of post-
Easter Christianity and from there must have found its way into
the Jesus tradition which today includes so many pronouncements of Christian prophecy, originally uttered as the voice of
the exalted Lord. But if this really was the case and Jesus never
expressly laid claim to the Messiahship, it would be extraordinarily characteristic of him. He would have differentiated himself equally from late Jewish expectation and from the proclamation of his own community. He would not have produced a

picture of the future but done what needed doing in the present; he would have placed not his person but his work in the forefront of his preaching. But his community would have shown that they understood the distinctive nature of his mission precisely by responding to his proclamation with their own acknowledgment of him as Messiah and Son of God.

Our investigation has led us to the conclusion that we must look for the distinctive element in the earthly Jesus in his preaching and interpret both his other activities and his destiny in the light of this preaching. Here we can do no more than touch lightly on the difficult problem of how far the preaching itself was determined by apocalyptic expectation. This problem is doubly difficult because it is unsafe to predicate authenticity of any passage where there is agreement with contemporary Judaism and/or the post-Easter community. However, we shall have to concede, against the exaggerations of Dodd and his advocacy of realized eschatology, that Jesus did speak of the kingdom of God as future; the only question is, in what sense? But this follows from the manner of the kingdom's manifestation: the *basileia* breaks through on earth in the word of Jesus, setting men in its presence and facing them with the decision between obedience and disobedience. Its power drives away the demons and any sacrifice is worth while in order to establish its dominion. Its badge is the love of those who can forgive because God forgives his enemies and who indeed must forgive if forgiveness is to be their own portion. Jesus did not preach realized eschatology, but, to use E. Haenchen's terminology, inaugurated eschatology. Confirmation of this is to be found above all in the parables, the clarity and self-containedness of which stand out sharply from the rabbinic parallels and reach a standard from which the compositions of the later community represent a declension. We can, however, only use them in support of our case if we are prepared to criticize in one respect the indispensable work of Jülicher on the subject, to which we are all so indebted; we must not isolate, as he does, the parables from the rest of Jesus' preaching in such a way as to make their interpretation depend on the *tertium comparationis* and nothing else. Otherwise we cannot really escape the moralization so frequently castigated in

Jülicher; and ignorance of the situation to which they were directed will cause us very great embarrassment. But although we
may be for the most part ignorant of the original circumstances
in which the individual parables were spoken, we do know him
who uttered them well enough to be aware of the eschatological
orientation of his message and to realize that we may not abstract from it. For Jesus did not come to proclaim general religious or moral truths, but to tell of the *basileia* that had dawned
and of how God was come near to man in grace and demand.
He brought, and lived out, the liberty of the children of God,
who only remain the Father's children and only remain free so
long as they find in this Father their Lord.

7. Conclusion

What then is the general sense of this very superficial outline,
the filling in of which in any detailed or even approximately
complete manner would far exceed the limits of a single lecture?
Have I not arrived back on the road, the problematical nature of
which I originally set myself to show? Have not some central
points emerged, around which we might, if with the utmost
caution and reserve, reconstruct something like a life of Jesus? I
should reject such a view as being a misunderstanding. In writing a life of Jesus, we could not dispense with some account of
his exterior and interior development. But we know nothing at
all about the latter and next to nothing about the former, save
only the way which led from Galilee to Jerusalem, from the
preaching of the God who is near to us to the hatred of official
Judaism and execution by the Romans. Only an uncontrolled
imagination could have the self-confidence to weave out of
these pitiful threads the fabric of a history in which cause and
effect could be determined in detail.

But conversely, neither am I prepared to concede that, in the
face of these facts, defeatism and scepticism must have the last
word and lead us on to a complete disengagement of interest
from the earthly Jesus. If this were to happen, we should either
be failing to grasp the nature of the primitive Christian concern
with the identity between the exalted and the humiliated Lord;
or else we should be emptying that concern of any real content,

as did the docetists. We should also be overlooking the fact that there are still pieces of the Synoptic tradition which the historian has to acknowledge as authentic if he wishes to remain an historian at all. My own concern is to show that, out of the obscurity of the life story of Jesus, certain characteristic traits in his preaching stand out in relatively sharp relief and that primitive Christianity united its own message with these. The heart of our problem lies here: the exalted Lord has almost entirely swallowed up the image of the earthly Lord and yet the community maintains the identity of the exalted Lord with the earthly. The solution of this problem cannot, however, if our findings are right, be approached with any hope of success along the line of supposed historical *bruta facta* but only along the line of the connection and tension between the preaching of Jesus and that of his community. The question of the historical Jesus is, in its legitimate form, the question of the continuity of the Gospel within the discontinuity of the times and within the variation of the kerygma. We have to put this question to ourselves and to see within it the element of rightness in the liberal *Leben-Jesu-Forschung*, the presuppositions of whose questioning we no longer share. The preaching of the Church may be carried on anonymously; the important thing is not the person, but the message. But the Gospel itself cannot be anonymous, otherwise it leads to moralism and mysticism. The Gospel is tied to him who, both before and after Easter, revealed himself to his own as the Lord, by setting them before the God who is near to them and thus translating them into the freedom and responsibility of faith. This he did once without any demonstrable credentials, even without claiming to be the Messiah, and yet he did it as having the authority of him whom the Fourth Gospel calls the only-begotten Son. He cannot be classified according to the categories either of psychology or of the comparative study of religion or, finally of general history. If he can be placed at all, it must be in terms of historical particularity. To this extent the problem of the historical Jesus is not our invention, but the riddle which he himself sets us. The historian may establish the existence of this riddle, but he is unable to solve it. It is only solved by those who since the Cross and the Resurrection confess him as that which, in the days of his flesh, he never claimed to be and yet was—their Lord, and the bringer of the liberty of the children of God, which is the correlate of the kingdom of God. For to his particularity there corresponds the particularity of faith, for which the real history of Jesus is always happening afresh; it is now the history of the exalted Lord, but it does not cease to be the earthly history it once was, in which the call and the claim of the Gospel are encountered.

INDEX